NOAH WEBSTER'S
SPELLING BOOK METHOD
FOR TEACHING READING AND SPELLING

Teaching Students to Read from the **Sounds** of the Letters
Rather than Guess from the **Meaning** of the Words

An Adaptation of Noah Webster's
1908 *Elementary Spelling Book* to the
Needs of Twenty-First Century Students

*Bringing the Reading Standards of Today
Up to the High Standards of Yesterday*

NOAH WEBSTER'S SPELLING BOOK METHOD
FOR TEACHING READING AND SPELLING

Copyright © 2014 Donald L. Potter
ISBN-10: 1496153278
ISBN-13: 978-1496153272

www.donpotter.net

Dedicated to Miss Geraldine E. Rodgers, B.A., M. S.

Retired Primary Grades Teacher with
Twenty-Three Years of Experience

Author of

The Hidden Story: How America's Present-Day Reading Disabilities Grew Out of the Underhanded Meddling of America's First Experimental Psychologist, Young William James. ((1996, 1997, 1998)

Why Jacques, Johann and Jan CAN Read. 1977-1978 Research in oral reading accuracy. (2005) The rediscovery of "objective readers" and "subjective readers."

The History of Beginning Reading: From Teaching by "Sound" to Teaching by "Meaning." (1995, 2001) This is Mrs. Rodgers' three-volume magnum opus of library research into the history of instruction in beginning reading America. No college library should be without this in-depth study.

The Case for the Prosecution: In the Trial of Silent Reading "Comprehension" Tests, Charged with the Destruction of American Schools. (2007) This is a book of essays from 1981 to 1983.

"Why Noah Webster's Way Was the Right Way." (June 10, 2004) It was this essay that motivated me to start teaching Webster's spelling book method of teaching reading and spelling. The happy results further motivated me to retype Webster's method and re-publish it in the present format, which I use with my tutoring students of all ages.

"Historical Introduction to Leonard P. Ayres' *A Measuring Scale of Ability in Reading*." (1984) Explaining the cumulative high frequency word effect.

Born-Yesterday World of Reading "Experts" - A Critique on Recent Research on Reading and the Brain. (2003) This paper was prompted by a request from Dr. Patrick Groff.

PREFACE

Excerpts from the 1866 Edition with Comments

In Syllabication it has been thought best not to give the etymological division of the Quarto Dictionary, but to retain the old mode of Dr. Webster as best calculated to teach *young* scholars the true pronunciation of words. [*My experience proves that this is the best way to divide the words for purposes of teaching reading and spelling. This is basically the respelling division in the modern dictionaries.*]

The plan of classification here executed is extended so as to comprehend every important variety of English words, and the classes are so arranged, with suitable directions for the pronunciation, that any pupil, who has mastered the *Elementary Tables*, will find little difficulty in learning to form and pronounce any word properly belonging to our vernacular language. [*Webster's Speller is a "System" of English orthography in the true sense. It will enable students to develop the skills necessary to be proficient in English reading and spelling. It can be used on all levels: beginning, intermediate, and advanced.*]

The Tables intended for *Exercises* in Spelling and forming words, contain the original words, with the terminations only of their derivatives. The tables answer the important purpose of teaching the *manner* of forming the various derivatives, and the distinctions of the parts of speech, and thus anticipate in some degree, the knowledge of grammar; at the same time they bring into small compass a much greater number of words than could be otherwise comprised in so small a book. [*The Spelling book concentrates an enormous amount of practice in reading and spelling into an exceptionally small space, allowing students to attain high levels of reading ability in an amazingly short period of time.*]

The reading lessons are adapted, as far as possible, to the capacities of children, and to their gradual progress in knowledge. These lessons will serve to substitute variety for the dull monotony of spelling, show the practical use of words in significant sentences, and thus enable the learner to better understand them. The consideration of diversifying the studies of the pupil has also had its influence on the arrangement of the lessons for spelling. It is useful to teach the signification of words, as soon as they can comprehend them; but the understanding can hardly keep pace with the memory, and the minds of children may well be employed in learning to spell and pronounce words whose signification is not within their capacities; for what they do not clearly comprehend at first they will understand as their capacities are enlarged.

The objects of a work of this kind being chiefly to teach *orthography* and *pronunciation*, is judged most proper to adapt the various Tables to these specific objects, and omit extraneous matter. In short, this little book is so constructed as to condense into the smallest compass a complete SYSTEM of ELEMENTS for teaching the language; and however small such a book may appear, it may be considered as the most important class book, not of religious character, which the youth of our country are destined to use. [*I know of no other book that concentrates so much language power into such a small space.*]   New York, 1866. William G. Webster. (Comments: Odessa, TX, 2009. Donald L. Potter)

PREFACE TO THE 1908 EDITION

The modifications in this revision are not of a character to embarrass those teachers who used the previous editions in the same class. The principal changes are:

In many instances an improved form of type;

The substitution of living words in the place of those words that have become obsolete.

The omission of orthoëpical marks where they are clearly unnecessary, as explained below;

The correction of a few errors in pronunciation, etc. etc.;

The addition at the end of the book, of four new pages of common words difficult to spell.

The repetition of orthoëpical mark has been omitted as needless in a succession of two or more words having the same vowel letter and sound. In such cases only the first word is marked – the syllable of this leading word being the key to the corresponding unmarked syllables in the words, which follow. But whenever there is liability to mispronounce, the right way is indicated by marking the doubtful syllable.

PREFACE TO THE 2011 EDITION

The Tables have been converted from columns of words into rows in this edition to encourage good left to right word scanning. This allowed me to increase the type size for ease of reading while reducing the number pages.

Bold has been substituted for Webster's accent marks. Students find this an acceptable method for indicating stress. A key element in the book's uncommon success is the classification of polysyllables according to accent. No modern work that I am aware of makes use of this important feature. In the 1822 edition of his *American Spelling Book*, Webster informs us, "In nine-tenths of the words in our language, a correct pronunciation is better taught by a natural division of the syllables and a direction for placing the accent, than by a minute and endless repetition of characters."

A few words have been modernized in their pronunciation.

The Syllabary has been slightly expanded to make it more complete, and the Syllabary Tables are organized in a more logical manner.

Helpful resources for teaching Webster's method are available on the Internet at www.donpotter.net.

Students who complete *Webster's American Spelling Book Method of Teaching Reading and Spelling* will gain a command English reading, vocabulary, and spelling that is available in no other single book.

I consider it a privilege of a lifetime to make this edition available to educators whose minds are open to going to **the past** to improve **the future**.

Donald L. Potter, Odessa, Texas, 2009, 2011, 2013, 2014, 2016.

ANALYSIS OF SOUNDS
IN THE ENGLISH LANGUAGE

The Elementary Sounds of the English language are divided into two classes, ***vowels*** and ***consonants.***

A *vowel* is a clear sound made through an open position of the mouth-channel, which molds or shapes the voice without obstructing its utterance; as *a* (in *far*, or *fate*, etc.), *e, o.*

A *consonant* is a sound formed by a closer position of the articulating organs than any position by which a vowel is formed, as *b, d, t, g, sh.* In forming a consonant the voice is compressed or stopped.

A *diphthong* is the union of two simple vowel sounds, as *ou* (äŏŏ) in *out, oi* (a̤ĭ) in *noise.*

The English Alphabet consists of twenty-six letters, or single characters, which represent vowel, consonant, and diphthongal sounds – a, b, c, d, e, f, g, h, i, j, k, l, m, n, o, p, q, r, s, t, u, v, w, x, y, z. The combinations *ch, sh, th,* and *ng* are also used to represent elementary sounds; and another sound is expressed by *s,* or *z*; as in *measure, azure,* pronounced **mĕzh**-*yoor,* **ăzh**-*ur.*

Of the foregoing letters, *a, e, o,* are always simple vowels; *i* and *u* are vowels (as in *in, us*), or diphthongs (as in *time, tune*); and *y* is either a vowel (as in *any*), a diphthong (as in *my*), or a consonant (as in *ye*).

Each of the vowels has its regular long and short sounds which are most often used; and also certain *occasional* sounds, as that of *a* in *last, far, care, fall, what; e* in *term, there, prey, i* in *firm, marine*; *o* in *dove, for, wolf, prove;* and *u* in *furl, rude,* and *pull.* These will now be considered separately.

A. The regular long sound of *a* is denoted by a horizontal mark over it; as in **ān**-cient, pro-**fāne**; and the regular short sound by a curve over it; as, căt, **păr**-ry.

Occasional sounds. –The Italian sound is indicated by two dots over it; as bär, **fä**-ther; –the short sound of the Italian *a,* by a single dot over it; as, fȧst, lȧst (Modern English, as fȧst, lȧst); –the broad sound, by two dots below it; as, ba̤ll, sta̤ll; – the short sound of broad *a,* by a single dot under it; as, wha̤t, **qua̤d**-rant; – the sound of *a* before *r* in certain words like *care, fair,* etc., is represented by a sharp or pointed circumflex over the *a,* as, câre, hâir, fâir, etc.

E. The regular long sound of *e* is indicated by a horizontal mark over it; as, mēte, se-**rēne**; the regular short sound, by a curve over it; as, mĕt, re-**bĕl**.

Occasional sounds. –The sound of *e* like *a* in *care* is indicated by a pointed circumflex over the *e*, as in thêir, whêre; and of short *e* before *r* in cases where it verges toward short *u*, by a rounded circumflex, or wavy line, over it; as, hẽr, pre-**fẽr**.

I, O, U. The regular long and short sounds of *i, o,* and *u* are indicated like those of *a* and *e* by a horizontal mark and by a curve; as, bīnd, bĕnd; dōle, dŏll; tūne, tŭn.

Occasional sounds. –When *i* has the sound of long *e* it is marked by two dots over it; as, fa-**tïgue**, ma-**rïne**; –when *o* has the sound of short *u*, it is marked by a single dot over it; as, dȯve, sȯn; –when it has the sound of o͞o, it is marked with two dots under it; as, mọve, prọve. –when it has the sound of o͞o, it is marked with a single dot under it; as, wọlf, **wọ**-man; –when it has the sound of broad *a*, this is indicated by a pointed circumflex over the vowel; as, nôrth, sôrt; –the two letters *oo*, with a horizontal mark over them have the sound heard in the words bo͞om, lo͞om; –with the curve mark, they have a shorter form of the same sound; as, bo͝ok, go͝od; –when *u* is sounded like short *oo*, it has a single dot under it; as, fụll, pụll; while its lengthened sound, as when preceded by *r*, is indicated by two dots; as in rụde, **rụ**-al, **rụ**-by.

NOTE. –The long *u* in unaccented syllables has, to a great extent, the sound of *oo*, preceded by *y*, as in *educate*, pronounced ĕd-yoo-kāte; *nature*, pronounced **nāt**-yoor.

The long sound of *a* in *late* when shortened, coincides nearly with that of *e* in *let*; as *adequate, disconsolate, inveterate*.

The long *e*, when shortened, coincides nearly with the short *i* in *pit* (compare *feet* and *fit*). This short sound of *i* is that of *y* unaccented, at the end of words; as in *glory*. The short sound of broad *a* in *hall*, is that of the short *o* in *holly* and of *a* in *what*.

The short sound of long *oo* in *pool*, is that of *u* in *pull*, and *oo* in *wool*.

The short sound of long *o* in *not,* is somewhat lengthened before, *s, th,* and *ng*; as in *cross, broth, belong*.

The pronunciation of diphthongs *oi* and *oy* is the same and uniform; as, in *join, joy*.

The pronunciation of diphthongs *ou* and *ow* is the same and uniform; as, in *sound, now*. But in the terminations *ous, ou* is not a diphthong, and the pronunciation is *us*; as, in *pious, glorious*.

A combination of two letters used to express a single sound is called a digraph; as, *ea* in *head*, or *th* in *bath*.

The digraphs *ai* and *ay,* in words of one syllable, and in accented syllable, have the sound of *a* long. In unaccented syllables of a few words, the sound of *a* is nearly or quite lost; as, in *certain, curtain*. The digraphs *au* and *aw,* have the sound of broad *a* (*a* as in *fall*); *ew*, that of *u* long, as in *new;* and *ey* in unaccented syllables, that of *y* or *i* short, as *valley* (Modern English long e: ēy).

When one vowel of a digraph is marked, the other has no sound; as in cōurt, rōad, slōw.

The digraphs *ea, ee, ei, ie,* when not marked, have in his book, the sound of *e* long; as in *near, meet, seize, grieve*.

The digraph *oa,* when unmarked, has the sound of o long.

Vowels, in words of one syllable, following by a single consonant and *e* final, are long; as, in *fate, mete, mite, note, mute,* unless marked, as in dȯve, gĭve.

The articulation or sounds represented by the consonants are best apprehended by placing a vowel before them in pronunciation, and prolonging the second of the two elements; thus, eb, ed, ef, eg, ek, el, em, en, ep, er, es, et, ev, ez.

Those articulations, which wholly stop the passage of the breath from the mouth, are called, *close,* or *mute*, as b, d, g, k, p, t.

Those articulations which are formed either wholly or in part by the lips, are called *labials*; as, b, f, m, p, v.

Those articulations which are formed by the tip of the tongue and the teeth, or the gum covering the roots of the teeth, are called *dentals*; as, d, t, th, (as in *thin, this)*.

Those which are formed by the flat surface of the tongue and the palate, are called *palatals;* as, g, k, ng, sh, j, y.

The letters *s* and *z* are also called *sibilants,* or hissing letters.

W (as in *we*) and **y** (as in *ye*) are sometimes called *semi-vowels,* as being intermediate between vowels and consonants, or partaking of the nature of both.

B and **p** represent one and the same position of the articulating organs; but *p* differs from *b* in being an utterance of the breath instead of the voice.

D and **t** stand for one and the same articulation, which is a pressure of the tongue against the gum at the root of the upper front teeth; but *t* stands for a whispered, and *d* for a voiced sound.

F and **v** stand for one and the same articulation, the lower teeth placed on the upper lip; but *f* indicates an expulsion of voiceless breath; *v* of vocalized breath, or tone.

Th in **thin** and **th** in **this** represent one and the same articulation, the former with breath the latter with voice.

S and **z** stand for one and the same articulation, *s* being a hissing or whispered sound, and *z* a buzzing and vocal sound.

Sh and **zh** have the same distinction as *s* and *z*, whispered and vocal; but *zh* not occurring in English words, the sound is represented by *si* or by other letters; as in, *fusion, osier, azure*.

G and **k** are cognate letters, also **j** and **ch** the first of each couplet being vocal, the second aspirate or uttered with breath alone.

Ng represents a nasal sound.

B has one sound only, as in *bite*. After *m*, or, before *t*, it is generally mute; as in *dumb, doubt*.

C has the sound of *k* before *a, o, u, l* and *r*, as in *cat, cot, cup, clock,* and *crop* and of *s* before *e, i,* and *y,* as in *cell, cit, cycle*. It may be considered as mute before *k*; and in *sick, thick*. C, when followed by *e* or *i*, before another vowel, unites with *e* or *i* to form the sound of *sh*. Thus, *cetaceous, gracious, conscience,* are pronounced *ce-**ta**-shus, **gra**-shus, **con**-shense*.

D has its proper sound, as in *day, bid;* when preceded in the same syllable by a whispered or non-vocal consonant, it uniformly takes the sound of *t*, as in *hissed* (hist).

F has only one sound; as in *life, fever,* except *of*, in which it has the sound of *v*.

G before *a, o,* and *u*, is a close palatal articulation; as, in *gave, go, gun;* before *e, i,* and *y*, it sometimes represents the same articulation, but generally indicates a compound sound like that of *j*; as in *gem, gin, gyves*. Before *n* in the same syllable it is silent; as, in *gnaw*.

H is a mark of mere breathing or aspiration. After *r* it is silent; as, in *rhetoric*.

I in certain words has the use of *y* consonant; as, in *million*, pronounced *mill-yun*. Before *r* it has a sound nearly resembling that of short *u*, but more open; as in *bird, flirt*.

J represents a compound sound, pretty nearly equivalent to that represented by *dzh;* as, in *joy*.

K has one sound only; as, in *king*. It is silent before *n* in the same syllable; as, in *knave*.

L has one sound only; as in *lame, mill*. It is silent in many words, especially before a final consonant; as, in *walk, calm, calf, should*.

M has one sound only; as, in *man, flame*. It is silent before *n* in the same syllable; as, in *mnemonics*.

N has only one sound only; as, in *not, sun*. It is silent after *l* and *m;* as, in *kiln, hymn, solemn*.

P has one sound only; as, in *pit, lap*. At the beginning of words, it is silent before *n, s,* and *t;* as, in *pneumatics, psalm, pshaw, ptarmigan*.

Q has the sound of *k,* but it is always followed by a *u,* and these two letters are generally sounded like *kw;* as, in *question*.

R is sounded as in *rip, trip, form, carol, mire*.

S has its proper sound, as in *send, less;* or the sound of *z,* as in *rose*. Followed by *i* preceding a vowel, it unites with the vowel in forming the sound of *sh;* as in *mission,* pronounced **mish**-*un;* –or of its vocal correspondent *zh;* as in *osier* pronounced **o**-*zher.*

T has its proper sound, as in *turn,* at the beginning of words and at the end of syllables. Before *i,* followed by another vowel, it unites with *i* to form the sound of *sh,* as, in *nation, partial, patience,* pronounced **na**-*shun,* par-shal, pa-shense. But when *s* or *x* precedes *t,* this letter and the *i* following it preserve their own sounds; as in *bastion, Christian, mixtion,* pronounced **băst**-yun, **krist**-yan, **mikst**-yun. **T** is silent in the terminations *ten* and *tle* after *s;* as in *fasten, gristle;* also in the words *often, chestnut, Christmas,* etc.

V has one sound only; as, in *voice, live,* and is never silent.

W before *r* in the same syllable is silent, as in *wring, wrong*. In most words beginning with **wh** the *h* precedes the *w* in utterance, that is, *wh* is simply an aspirated *w;* thus *when* is pronounced *hwen*. But if *o* follows this combination, the *w* is silent, as in *whole,* pronounced *hole*.

X represents *ks,* as in *wax;* but it is sometimes pronounced like *gz;* as, in *exact*. At the beginning of words, it is pronounced like *z;* as, in *Xenophon*.

Z has its proper sound, which is that of a vocal *s;* as, in *maze*.

Ch has very nearly the sound of *tsh;* as, in *church:* or the sound of *k;* as, *character;* or of *sh* in *machine*.

Gh is mute in every English word, both in the middle and at the end of words, except in the following: *cough, chough, clough, enough, laugh, rough, slough, tough, trough,* in which it has the sound of *f;* and *hiccough,* in which it has the sound of *p*. At the beginning of a word, it is pronounced like *g* hard; as in *ghastly, ghost, gherkin,* etc.; hence this combination may be said not to have a proper or regular sound in any English word.

Ph has the sound of *f,* as in *philosophy;* except in Stephen, pronounced **Ste**-*vn.*

Sh has one sound only; as in *shall*.

Th has two sounds; whispered, as in *think, both;* and vocal, as in *thou, this.* When vocal, the th is marked thus, (th), as in thou.

C has the sound of *sk* before *a, o, u,* and *r;* as in *scale, scoff, sculpture, scroll;* and the sound of *s* alone before *e, i,* and *y;* as, *scene, scepter, science, Scythian.*

ACCENT.

Accent is the forcible stress or effort of voice on a syllable, distinguishing it from others sin the same word, by a greater distinctness of sound.

The accented syllable is designated by **bold** font.

The general principal by which accent is regulated, is, that the stress of voice falls on that syllable of a word, which renders the articulations most easy to the speaker, and most agreeable to the hearer. But this rule has the accent of most words been imperceptibly established by a long and universal consent.

When a word consists of three or more syllables, ease of speaking requires usually a secondary accent, of less forcible utterance than the primary; but clearly distinguishable from the pronunciation of unaccented syllables; as in **su**-per-**flu**-it-y, **lit**-er-**ar**-y. The strongest accent is on the underlined font.

KEY TO THE PRONUNCIATION
VOWELS

REGULAR LONG AND SHORT SOUNDS

LONG. –ā, as in *fame*; ē, as in *mete* (and y as in *lady*); ī as in *fine*; ō, as in *note;* ū as in *mute*; ȳ, as in *fly.*

SHORT. –ă, as in *fat*; ĕ, as in *met*; ĭ, as in *fin*; ŏ as in *not* ŭ, as in *but;* y̆, as in *nymph.*

VOWELS. –OCCASIONAL SOUNDS

EXAMPLES.

â, as in *care,*	âir, shâre, pâir, beâr.
ä *Italian,* as in	fäther, fär, bälm, päth.
à, as in *last* (ă in Modern American English)	àsk, gràss, dànce, brànch.
ạ *broad,* as in *all*	cạll, tạlk, hạul, swạrm.
ạ, as in *what* (like short o)	wạn, wạnton, wạllow
ê like â, as in	thêre, hêir, whêre, êre.
ẽ, as in *term,*	ẽrmine, vẽrge, prefẽr.
ẹ, like long *a,* as in	prẹy, thẹy, ẹight.
ï, like long *e* as in	pïque, machïne, mïem.
ĩ, as in *bird,*	fĩrm, vĩrgin, dĩrt.
ȯ like short *u,* as in	dȯve, sȯn, dȯne, wȯn.
ọ like long *oo,* as in	prọve, dọ, mọve, tọmb.
ọ like short *oo,* as in	bọsom, wọlf, wọman.
ô like broad *a,* as in	ôrder, fôrm, stôrk.
ōō (long *oo*), as in	mōōn, fōōd, bōōty.
o̅o̅ (short *oo*), as in	fŏŏt, bŏŏk, wŏŏl, gŏŏd.
ụ long, preceeded by *r,* as in	rụde, rụmor, rụral.
ụ like o̅o̅, as in	pụt, pụsh, pụll, fụll.
e, i, o (italic) are silent	tok*e*n, cous*i*n, mas*o*n.

REGULAR DIPHTHONGAL SOUNDS

EXAMPLES

oi, or oy (unmarked), as in	oil, join, toy
ou, or ow (unmarked), as in	out, owl, vowel

CONSONANTS

ç, *soft,* like *s sharp*, as in   çede, merçy

e, *hard* like *k*, as in   eall, eoneur.

ch (unmarked), as in   child, choose, much.

çh *soft*, like *sh* as in   maçhine, çhaise.

eh *hard*, like *k*, as in   ehorus, epoeh.

ḡ *hard,* as in   ḡet, beḡin, foḡḡy.

ġ *soft*, like *j*, as in   ġentle, ġinġer, eleġy.

s *sharp* (unmarked), as in   same, gas, dense.

s̲ *soft* or *vocal*, as in   ha̲s, amu̲se, pri̲son.

th *sharp* (unmarked) as in   thing, path, truth.

th *flat*, or *vocal*, as in   thine, their, wither.

ng (unmarked), as in   sing, single.

n̲ (much like *ng*), as in   lin̲ger, lin̲k, un̲cle.

x̲, like *gz*, as in   ex̲ist, aux̲iliary.

ph (unmarked), like *f:* as in sylph.   qu (unmarked), like *kw*, as in queen.
wh (unmarked), like *hw* as in what, when, awhile.

This "Key to Pronunciation" is from *Noah Webster's Elementary Spelling Book* (1908). This form of diacritical marks was first introduced in the 1829 edition. It is quite similar to the 1908. Interestingly, no major changes were introduced during those dates. Before 1829, Webster used "figures" or numbers over the vowels to indicate sounds.

An audio for the "Analysis of English Sounds" and the "Key" is available for free on the "Spelling Book Reference Page" of the www.donpotter.net web site.

THE ALPHABET.

Roman Letters.		Italic		Names of Letters
A	a	*A*	*a*	a
B	b	*B*	*b*	be
C	c	*C*	*c*	ce
D	d	*D*	*d*	de
E	e	*E*	*e*	e
F	f	*F*	*f*	ef
G	g	*G*	*g*	ge
H	h	*H*	*h*	aytch
I	i	*I*	*i*	i
J	j	*J*	*j*	ja
K	k	*K*	*k*	ka
L	l	*L*	*l*	el
M	m	*M*	*m*	em
N	n	*N*	*n*	en
O	o	*O*	*o*	o
P	p	*P*	*p*	pe
Q	q	*Q*	*q*	cu
R	r	*R*	*r*	ar
S	s	*S*	*s*	es
T	t	*T*	*t*	te
U	u	*U*	*u*	u
V	v	*V*	*v*	ve
W	w	*W*	*w*	double u
X	x	*X*	*x*	eks
Y	y	*Y*	*y*	wi
Z	z	*Z*	*z*	ze
	&*		*&* *	and

DOUBLE LETTERS
ff, ffl, fi, fl, ffi, æ, œ.
*This is not a letter, but a character standing for *and*.

SCRIPT (CURSIVE) ALPHABET.

A B C D E F G H

I J K L M N O

P Q R S T U V

W X Y Z

a b c d e f g h

i j k l m n o

p q r s t u v

w x y z

1 2 3 4 5 6 7 8 9 0

The Syllabary

No. 1

bā	bē	bī	bō	bū	bȳ
ca	çe	çi	co	cu	çy
da	de	di	do	du	dy
fa	fe	fi	fo	fu	fy
ga	ge	gi	go	gu	gy
	ġe	ġi			ġy

Most syllables ending in a vowel (open syllables) are long. They say their letter name. *ce, ci* and *cy* are pronounced *se, si, sy*.

No. 2.

hā	hē	hī	hō	hū	hȳ
ja	je	ji	jo	ju	jy
ka	ke	ki	ko	ku	ky
la	le	li	lo	lu	ly
ma	me	mi	mo	mu	my
na	ne	ni	no	nu	ny

No. 3

pā	pē	pī	pō	pū	pȳ
ra	re	ri	ro	rụ	ry
sa	se	si	so	su	sy
ta	te	ti	to	tu	ty
va	ve	vi	vo	vu	vy
wa	we	wi	wo	wu	wy

11

No. 4

ăb	ĕb	ĭb	ŏb	ŭb
ac	ec	ic	oc	uc
ad	ed	id	od	ud
af	ef	if	of	uf
ag	eg	ig	og	ug

Syllables ending in a consonant (closed syllables) are short (i.e., *cab*, *Jeb*, *fib*, *bob*, *cub*)

No. 5

ăj	ĕj	ĭj	ŏj	ŭj
ak	ek	ik	ok	uk
al	el	il	ol	ul
am	em	im	om	um
an	en	in	on	un
ap	ep	ip	op	up

No. 6

är	ẽr	îr	ôr	ûr
ăs	ĕs	ĭs	ŏs	ŭs
at	et	it	ot	ut
av	ev	iv	ov	uv
ax	ex	ix	ox	ux
az	ez	iz	oz	uz

The closed syllables with *r* are prounounced like: *car, her, first, corn* and *nurse*.

No. 7

blā	blē	blī	blō	blū	blȳ
cla	cle	cli	clo	clu	cly
fla	fle	fli	flo	flu	fly
gla	gle	gli	glo	glu	gly
pla	ple	pli	plo	plu	ply
sla	sle	sli	slo	slu	sly

No. 8

brā	brē	brī	brō	brụ	brȳ
cra	cre	cri	cro	crụ	cry
dra	dre	dri	dro	drụ	dry
fra	fre	fri	fro	frụ	fry
gra	gre	gri	gro	grụ	gry
pra	pre	pri	pro	prụ	prȳ
tra	tre	tri	tro	trụ	try
wra	wre	wri	wro	wrụ	wry

No. 9

thā	thē	thī	thō	thū	thȳ
tha	the	thi	tho	thu	thy
cha	che	chi	cho	chu	chy
sha	she	shi	sho	shu	shy
pha	phe	phi	pho	phu	phy

No. 10

quā	quē	quī	quō	qu-	quȳ
spa	spe	spi	spo	spū	spy
sta	ste	sti	sto	stu	sty
ska	ske	ski	sko	sku	sky
sca	sçe	sçi	sco	scu	sçy
swa	swe	swi	swo	swu	swy

sce, sci, scy are pronounced s*e, si, sy*.

No. 11

splā	splē	splī	splō	splū	splȳ
spra	spre	spri	spro	sprụ	spry
stra	stre	stri	stro	strụ	stry
shra	shre	shri	shro	shrụ	shry
scra	scre	scri	scro	scrụ	scry
scla	scle	scli	sclo	sclū	scly

No. 12. – 53 Words

căb, dab, nab, tab, nĕb, web, bĭb, fĭb, jib, nib, rib, bŏb, cob, fob, hob, job, lob, mob, rob, sob, dŭb, sub, hub, rub, tub, lăp, sap, rĭp, nip, sŏp, băd, gad, had, lad, mad, pad, sad, lĕd, red, wed, hĭd, did, lid, rid, kid, mid, ḡŏd, hod, sod, nod, odd, pod, rod.

No. 13. – 38 Words

lŏg, dog, bog, bŭd, mud, băg, cag, sag, fag, hag, jag, lag, nag, tag, rag, wag, lĕg, keg, pĭg, fĭg, rig, wig, bŭg, dug, hug, jug, tug, mug, pug, rug, dăm, ham, jam, kam, lam, ram, tam, yam.

No. 14. – 41 Words

hĕm, ġem, dĭm, him, rim, dŭm, ḡum, hum, mum, rum, sum, băn, dan, fan, man, pan, ran, tan, rĕn, pen, ten, wen, bĭn, fin, hin, kin, pin, sin, tin, win, cŏn, don, bŭn, dun, fun, gun, pun, run, sun, tun, nun.

No. 15. – 47 Words

hăp, rap, map, lap, pap, tap, gap, dĭp, hip, rip, tip, lip, pip, sip, kip, nip, fŏp, hop, top, pop, sop, lop, bär, far, tar, jar, mar, par, băt, fat, rat, hat, mat, sat, pat, vat, bĕt, jet, ḡet, let, met, net, wet, pet, set, yet, hăs.

No. 16. – 48 Words

pĭt, çit, fit, lit, mit, nit, pit, sit, wit, bŏt, cot, dot, jot, lot, not, pot, rot, sot, got, wot, bŭt, cut, hut, jut, nut, rut, lăx, tax, wax, sĕx, vex, fĭx, mix, pix, six, bŏx, fox, wạd, wạn, wạr, wạs, wạt, căn, cap, cat, sap, ġĭn, chit.

Ann can hem my cap. She has a fan. He hid in his den. The pig is in his pen. I see ten men. He had a gun. I can see him run. The map is wet. She will sit by me. He has cut my pen. I had a nut. Can he get my hat? It is in my lap. I will get a map. A bat can fly. A cat can catch a rat. I met the lad. He sat on my box. The sun is set. I met six men. Ten men sat by me. I set the pin on my tin box. Let him get the wax.

No. 17. – 56 Words

bābe, cade, fade, jade, lade, made, wade, bīde, hide, ride, side, tide, wide, ōde, bode, code, mode, lode, node, rode, lobe, robe, cūbe, tube, āçe, dace, face, lace, pace, race, mace, īce, bice, dice, lice, mice, nice, rice, vice, āġe, caġe, gaġe, paġe, raġe, saġe, dōġe, hūġe, bāke, lake, take, make, rake, sake, hake, wake, cake.

No. 18. – 47 Words

dīke, like, pike, tike, cōke, joke, poke, woke, yoke, dūke, Luke, fluke, āle, bale, cale, gale, dale, male, hale, pale, sale, tale, bīle, file, mile, pile, tile, vile, wile, bōle, cole, dole, hole, mole, pole, sole, tole, mūle, rule, cāme, dame, fame, game, lame, name, same, tame.

No. 19. – 36 Words

āpe, cape, tape, nape, rape, pīpe, ripe, wipe, tȳpe, cōpe, pope, lope, mope, hope, rope, mēre, here, sere, ōre, bore, core, fore, gore, lore, more, sore, tore, yore, cove, rove, wove, gāze, haze, maze, raze, craze.

No. 20. – 53 Words

cūre, lure, pure, dīne, fīne, line, mine, kine, nine, pine, sine, wine, vine, bāne, lane, mane, pane, sane, cane, wane, base, āte, date, gate, fate, hate, late, mate, bīte, çite, kite, mite, rite, site, dive, dōse, bone, cone, zone, hone, tone, Jūne, tīne, fāne, vane, vāse, case, rāte, pate, rīve, fūme, tune, sāne.

No. 21. – 47 Words

tōrn, worn, sworn, ûrn, burn, churn, spurn, turn, ălps, scalp, hĕlp, kelp, yelp, gŭlp, pulp, dămp, camp, lamp, clamp, ramp, cramp, stamp, vamp, hĕmp, ĭmp, ḡimp, limp, pimp, crimp, shrimp, pŏmp, romp, bŭmp, dump, chump, jump, lump, clump, plump, mump, rump, crump, trump, cärp, scarp, harp, sharp.

No. 22. – 42 Words

asp, gasp, hasp, clasp, rasp, grasp, lĭsp, crisp, wisp, drĕgs, tŏngs, lŭngs, lĕns, gŭlf, chŏps, ăct, fact, pact, tact, tract, sĕct, pĭct, strict, dŭct, ăft, baft, haft, shaft, raft, craft, draft, graft, waft, hĕft, left, weft, gĭft, shift, lift, rift, drift, sift.

No. 23. – 48 Words

ŏft, loft, soft, tŭft, bĕlt, felt, melt, smelt, pelt, welt, ḡĭlt, hilt, milt, spilt, tilt, bōlt, colt, dolt, jolt, hold, cănt, scant, plant, rant, ant, chant, grant, slant, pant, bĕnt, dent, lent, pent, çent, spent, rent, sent, tent, vent, went, dĭnt, lint, flint, splint, mint, print, tint, stint.

No. 24. – 48 Words

brŭnt, grunt, runt, wĕpt, swept, ärt, smart, part, tart, snôrt, sort, tort, lăst, blast, mast, zĕst, hest, chest, ăpt, chapt, kĕpt, slept, crept, cärt, dart, hart, chart, mart, start, pẽrt, vert, wert, shôrt, hûrt, shĩrt, flirt, căst, fast, past, vast, dĭdst, midst, bĕst, jest, lest, blest, nest, pest.

No. 25. – 30 Words

rĕst, crest, drest, test, vest, quest, west, zest, fĩst, list, mist, grist, wrist, wist, lŏst, cost, fĩrst, bûrst, curst, durst, thĩrst, bŭst, dust, gust, just, lust, must, rust, crust, trust.

Fire will burn wood and coal. Coal and wood will make a fire. The world turns round in a day. Will you help me pin my frock. Do not sit on the damp ground. We burn oil in tin and glass lamps. The lame man limps on his lame leg. We make ropes of hemp and flax. A rude girl will romp in the street. The good girl may jump the rope. A duck is a plump fowl. The horse drinks at the pump. A pin has a sharp point. We take up a brand of fire with the tongs. Good boys and girls will act well. How can you test the speed of your horse? He came in haste, and left his book. Men grind corn and sift the meal. We love just and wise men. The wind will drive the dust in our eyes. Bad boys love to rob the nests of birds. Let us rest on the bed, and sleep, if we can. Tin and brass will rust when the air is damp.

No. 26. – 82 Words

WORDS OF TWO SYLLABLES, ACCENTED ON THE FIRST.

bā-ker, **sha**-dy, **la**-dy, **tī**-dy, **hō**-ly, **li**-my, **sli**-my, **bo**-ny,
po-ny, **ti**-lẽr, **ca**-per, **pa**-per, **ta**-per, **vi**-per, **bi**-ter, **fē**-ver,
o-ver, **tro**-ver, **clo**-ver, **do**-ner, **va**-por, **fa**-vor, **sa**-vor,
ha-lo, **so**-lo, **he**-ro, **ne**-gro, **tȳ**-ro, **sa**-go, **tū**-lip, **çe**-dar,
bri-er, **fri**-ar, **so**-lar, **po**-lar, **so**-ber, **pa**-çer, **ra**-çer, **gro**-çer,
çi-der, **spi**-der, **wa**-fer, **ti**-ḡer, **ma**-ker, **ta**-ker,
ra-ker, **se**-ton, **ru**-in, **wo**-ful, **po**-em, **Sa**-tan, **fu**-el, **du**-el,
cru-el, **gru**-el, **pu**-pil, **la**-bel, **li**-bel, **lo**-cal, **fo**-cal, **vo**-cal,
le-gal, **re**-gal, **di**-al, **tri**-al, **pa**-pal, **co**-pal, **vi**-al, **pe**-nal,
fi-nal, **o**-ral, **ho**-ral, **mu**-ral, **na**-sal, **fa**-tal, **na**-tal, **ru**-ral,
vi-tal, **to**-tal, **o**-val, **pli**-ant, **ḡi**-ant.

Bakers bake bread and cakes. A pony is a little horse. The best paper is made of linen rags. Vipers are bad snakes, and they bite men. An ox likes to eat clover. A tulip is very pretty, growing in the garden. A sundial shows the hours of the day. Cedar trees grow in the woods. The blackberry grows on the brier. Cider is made from apples. A tiger will kill and eat a man. A raker can rake hay. A vial is a little bottle. A giant is a very stout, tall man. The Holy Bible is the book of God.

No. 27. – 48 Words

scăb, stab, blab, slab, crab, drab, glĭb, snib, crib, drib, squib, chŭb, club, snub, scrub, drub, grub, shrub, stub, shăd, clad, glad, grad, flĕd, bled, bred, sped, shred, shed, sled, shŏd, clod, plod, trod, scŭd, stud, slug, brăg, crag, shag, stag, scrag, snag, drag, swag, flag, shăm, cram.

No. 28. – 48 Words

clăm, dram, slam, swam, stĕm, skĭm, brim, grim, prim, trim, swim, frŏm, scŭm, plum, grum, drum, scăn, clan, plan, span, bran, glĕn, chĭn, skin, spin, grin, twin, chăp, clap, flap, slap, snap, trap, scrap, strap, chĭp, ship, skip, clip, flip, slip, grip, scrip, drip, trip, strip, frit, split.

No. 29. – 42 Words

chŏp, shop, sop, crop, stop, prop, scär, spar, star, stir, blûr, slur, spur, flăt, plat, spat, brat, frĕt, whet, tret, slĭt, smit, spit, split, grit, scŏt, shot, blot, clot, plot, spot, grot, trot, shŭt, slut, smut, smĭt, glut, strut, flăx, flŭx, flŏss.

Ann can spin flax. A shad can swim. He was glad to see me. The boy can ride on a sled. A plum will hang by a stem. The boy had a drum. He must not drink a dram. He set a trap for a rat. Ships go to sea. The boy can chop. The man shot a ball. I saw her skim the milk in a pan.

No. 30. – 60 Words

bŭlb, bärb, garb, *h*ĕrb, verb, cûrb, chīld, mild, wild, ōld, bold, cold, gold, fold, hold, mold, sold, told, scold, ănd, band, hand, land, rand, bland, grand, gland, sand, stand, strand, brand, ĕnd, bend, fend, lend, mend, rend, send, tend, vend, wend, blend, bīnd, find, hind, kind, mind, rind, wīnd, bŏnd, fond, pond, fŭnd, bärd, card, hard, lard, pard, scarf, bĭrd.

hẽrd, cûrd, surd, turf, surf, scurf, rĭch, mŭch, such, flĭch, milch, lànch, blănch, branch, stanch, bŭnch, hunch, lunch, punch, lătch, match, patch, snatch, ärch, march, starch, harsh, marsh, pouch, crouch, tôrch, chûrch, lurch, crŏtch, botch, blotch, ĭtch, bitch, ditch, hitch, pitch, stitch, witch, switch, twitch, skĕtch, stretch, clŭtch, crutch, Dutch, plush, flush, crush.

To filch is to steal. We must not filch. A bird sits on a branch to sing.

No. 32 – 89 Words

Words of Two Syllables, Accented on the Second.

a-**bāse**, de-**base**, in-**case**, de-**bate**, se-**date**, cre-**ate**, ob-**late**, re-**late**, in-**flate**, col-**late**, trans-**late**, mis-**state**, re-**plēte**, com-**plete**, se-**crete**, re-**çīte**, in-**çite**, po-**lite**, ig-**nite**, re-**deem**, es-**teem**, de-**claim**, re-**claim**, pro-**claim**, ex-**claim**, de-**mēan**, be-**mōan**, re-**tain**, re-**main**, en-**grōss**, dis-**crete**, al-**lay**, de-**lay**, re-**play**, in-**lay**, mis-**lay**, dis-**play**, de-**cay**, dis-**may**, de-**fray**, ar-**ray**, be-**tray**, por-**tray**, a-**stray**, un-**say**, as-**say**, a-**way**, o-**b<u>ey</u>**, con-**vey**, pur-**vey**, sur-**vey**, de-**fȳ**, af-**fy**, de-**ny**, de-**cry**, re-**boil**, de-**spoil**, em-**broil**, re-**coil**, sub-**join**, ad-**join**, re-**join**, en-**join**, con-**join**, mis-j**oin**, pur-**loin**, ben-**zoin**, a-**void**, a-**droit**, ex-**ploit**, de-**coy**, en-**joy**, al-**loy**, em-**ploy**, an-**noy**, de-**stroy**, con-**voy**, es-**pouse**, ca-**rouse**, de-**vour**, re-**dound**, de-**vout**, a-**mount**, sur-**mount**, dis-**mount**, re-**count**, re-**nown**, en-**dow**, a-**vow**.

Strong drink will debase a man. Hard shells incase clams and oysters. Men inflate balloons with gas, which is lighter than common air. Teachers like to see their students polite to each other. Idle men often delay till to-morrow things that should be done to-day. Good men obey the laws of God. I love to survey the starry heavens. Careless girls mislay their things. The fowler decoys the birds into his net. Cats devour rats and mice. The adroit ropedancer can leap and jump and perform as many exploits as any monkey. Wise men employ their time in doing good to all around them. In time of war, merchant vessels sometimes have a convoy of ships of war. Kings are men of high renown, Who fight and strive to wear a crown. God created the heavens and the earth in six days, and all that was made was very good. To purloin is to steal.

No. 33. – 47 Words

deed, feed, heed, bleed, meed, need, speed, breed, seed, weed, bee, fee, see, lee, flee, glee, free, tree, eel, feel, heel, peel, reel, steel, deem, seem, teem, sheen, keen, spleen, screen, green, seen, teen, steen, queen, ween, leek, cheek, sleek, meek, reek, creek, Greek, seek, week, beef.

No 34. – 42 Words

deep, sheep, keep, sleep, peep, creep, steep, weep, sweep, beer, deer, cheer, sheer, jeer, leer, fleer, sneer, peer, seer, steer, queer, lees, bees, beet, feet, sheet, fleet, sleet, meet, greet, street, sweet, food, mood, rood, brood, geese, fleeçe, sleeve, reeve, breeze, freeze.

No. 35. – 65 Words

bōōm, coom, doom, loom, bloom, gloom, room, broom, groom, boon, loon, moon, noon, spoon, soon, swoon, loo, coo, two̧, cōōp, scoop, loop, sloop, droop, troop, stoop, swoop, boor, moor, poor, loose, goose, boose, choose, noose, cŏŏk, hook, look, stook, nook, rook, brook, crook, took, wool, wood, good, stood.

fōōl, pool, tool, spool, roost, boot, coot, moot, root, roof, woof, proof, blȯȯd, flȯȯd, sȯn, wȯn, tȯn.

Plants grow in the ground from seeds. The man cuts down trees with his ax. Eels swim in the brook. Sharp tools are made of steel. The sun seems to rise and set each day. The ax has a keen edge and cuts well. In the spring the grass looks green and fresh. I have seen the full moon. A king and queen may wear crowns of gold. I will kiss the babe on his cheek. We go to church on the first day of the week. The man put a curb round our deep well. Wool makes the sheep warm. Men keep their pigs in pens. We lie down and sleep in beds. The new broom sweeps clean. The wild deer runs in the woods. The red beet is good to eat. If I meet him in the street, I will greet him with a kind look, and show him my new book.

No. 36. – 41 Words

băck, hack, jack, lack, black, slack, smack, pack, rack, crack, sack, tack, stack, quack, bĕck, deck, check, neck, peck, speck, quĭck, chick, click, kick, lick, nick, pick, rick, brick, crick, trick, sick, tick, stick, wick, clŏck, lock, block, hock, shock, flock.

No. 37. – 54 Words

pŏck, rock, brock, crock, frock, mock, sock, bŭck, duck, chuck, luck, cluck, pluck, muck, truck, struck, suck, tuck, stuck, ĕlk, welk, yelk, ĭlk, bilk, silk, milk, kilt, bŭlk, hulk, skulk, băṉk, dank, hank, shank, lank, blank, clank, flank, plank, slank, rank, crank, drank, frank, shrank, prank, tank, ĭnk, link, blink, clink, slink, sink, brink.

No. 38. – 54 Words

prĭṉk, shrink, mink, wink, drink, pink, spŭṉk, junk, skunk, drunk, trunk, sunk, slunk, ärk, lark, dark, hark, shark, mark, park, spark, stark, jĕrk, clerk, perk, smĩrk, shirk, irk, dirk, kirk, quirk, côrk, fork, stork, lûrk, Turk, ăsk, bask, cask, hask, flask, mask, task, dĕsk, whĭsk, disk, risk, brisk, frisk, bŭsk, dusk, husk, bŏss, tŭft,

The smell of the pink is sweet. I can play when my task is done.

No. 39. – 36 Words

bŭsk, musk, rusk, tusk, dusk, märl, snarl, twĩrl, whirl, cûrl, furl, hurl, churl, purl, ĕlm, helm, fĭlm, ärm, barm, farm, harm, charm, spĕrm, term, bärn, tarn, yarn, hẽrn, fern, stern, bôrn, corn, scorn, morn, lorn, horn.

No. 40. – 47 Words

ḡàff, staff, quaff, skĭff, cliff, tiff, stiff, off, scoff, doff, bŭff, cuff, huff, luff, bluff, muff, puff, ruff, stuff, ădd, ŏdd, egg, ạll, ball, call, fall, ḡall, hall, mall, pall, tall, stall, wall, thrall, small, squall, smĕll, spell, sell, tell, quell, well, dwell, swell, ĭll, quill, ĕbb.

No. 41. – 42 Words

ġĭll, ḡill, hill, mill, rill, drill, frill, kill, skill, shrill, spill, trill, sill, fill, still, quill, squill, will, swill, bōll, poll, roll, scroll, droll, troll, stroll, toll, cŭll, dull, gull, hull, skull, lull, mull, trull, ĭnn, bin, wrĕn, bûrr, purr, buṣh, puṣh.

No. 42. – 42 Words

ăss, bass, lass, glass, class, mass, pass, trass, brass, grass, çĕss, dress, press, stress, ḡuess, less, bless, mess, cress, chess, tress, kĭss, bliss, miss, Swiss, bŏss, loss gloss, moss, cross, dross, cost, bŭss, fuss, muss, truss, bust, bûr, buḷl, fuḷl, puṣs, hûrt.

No. 43. – 28 Words

Singular – Plural

stāve, staves; clĭff, cliffs; mill, mills; baḷl, balls; ĕgg, eggs; haḷl, halls; wall, walls, bĭll, bĭlls; sill, sills; quĭll, quĭlls; pōll, pōlls, skŭll, skulls; ĭnn, ĭnns, bĕll, bĕlls.

A skiff is a small rowboat. A cliff is a high steep rock. Leave off your bad tricks. A tarn is a small lake among the mountains. A ship has a tall mast. I like to see a good stonewall round a farm. A pear tree grows from the seed of a pear. A good boy will try to spell and read well. Do not lose or sell your books. A good son will help his father. I dwell in a new brick house. If you boil dry beans and peas they will swell. A duck has a wide flat bill. One quart of milk will fill two pint cups. One pint cup will hold four gills. I saw a rill run down a hill. A brook will turn a mill. A bull has a stiff neck. The frost will kill the leaves on the trees. When the cock crows, he makes a shrill loud noise. A cat will kill and eat rats and mice. Hogs feed on swill and corn. The skull is the bony case that encloses the brain. Puss likes to sit on your lap and purr. A gull is a large sea-fowl that feeds on fish. Some sea bass are a large as shad. Brass is made of zinc and copper. The rain will make the grass grow. You must keep your dress neat and clean. The moon is much smaller than the sun. I will try to get a mess of peas for dinner. Let me go and kiss that sweet young babe. Moss grows on trees in the woods. Fire will melt ores, and the metal will run off and leave the dross. God will bless those who do his will.

No. 44 – 150 Words

WORDS OF TWO SYLLABLES, ACCENTED ON THE FIRST.

ban-quet, gus-set, rus-set, cos-set, çiv-et, riv-et, vel-vet, hab-it, rab-bit, ôr-bit, còm-fit, prof-it, lim-it, sum-mit, vom-it, hẽr-mit, ärm-pit, mĕr-it, spĭr-it, cul-prit, vis-it, pot-ash, fil-lip, gos-sip, gal-lop, shal-lop, trol-lop, tûr-gid, beg-gar, vul-gar, çel-lar, pil-lar, col-lar, dol-lar, pop-lar, gram-mar, nec-tar, tär-tar, môr-tar, jab-ber, rob-ber, pitch-er, butch-er, ush-er, witch-cràft, tan-ġent, pun-ġent, co-ġent, ûr-ġent, tal-ent, frāg-ment, seg-ment, fĭg-ment, pig-ment, păr-rot, piv-ot, băl-lot, mär-mot, ram-pärt, mod-est, tem-pest, fŏr-est, bran-dy, can-dy han-dy, stûr-dy, stud-y, lack-ēy, jock-ey, mòn-key, tûrn-key, med-ley, al-ley, gal-ley, văl-ley, vol-ley, pul-ley, bär-ley, pars-ley, mot-ley, kid-ney, don-key, chim-ney, tran-sit, can-to, shiv-er, sil-ver, còv-er, sul-phur, mûr-mur, muf-fler, sam-pler, mel-on, sẽr-mon, drăg-on, cou-pon, grand-sòn, lack-er, **grot**-to, **kid**-nap, **lub**-ber, **blub**-ber, **am**-ber, **mem**-ber, **lim**-ber, **tim**-ber, **um**-ber, **cum**-ber, **lum**-ber, **num**-ber, **bär**-ber, **mẽr**-cer, **wȯn**-der, **yŏn**-der, **ġin**-ġer, **char**-ġer, **trench**-er, **in**-quest, **con**-quest, **här**-vest, **in**-mōst, **ut**-mōst, **im**-pōst, **ches***t*-nut, **con**-test, **jack**-daw, **mil**-dew, **cûr**-few, **ed**-dy, **ḡid**-dy, **mud**-dy, **rud**-dy, **ġen**-try, **sul**-try, **hȯn**-ēy, **mȯn**-ey, **joûr**-ney, **cum**-frey, **lam**-prey, **jẽr**-sey, **ker**-sey, **cler**-ġy, **tan**-sy, **ral**-ly, **sal**-ly, **tal**-ly, **jel**-ly, **sil**-ly, **fol**-ly, **jol**-ly, **ōn**-ly.

Cotton velvet is very soft to feel. Rabbits have large ears and eyes so that they may hear quickly, and see well in the dark. We like to have our friends visit us. Visitors should not make their visits too long. Silver spoons are not apt to rust. Beggars will beg rather than work. Cents are made of copper, and dollars, of silver. One hundred cents is worth a dollar. A dollar is worth one hundred cents. Dollars are our largest silver coins. Silver and copper ores are dug out of the ground, and melted in very hot fire. A mercer is one who deals in silks and woolen cloths. A grotto is a cavern or cave.

No. 45. – 42 Words

bădġe, fadġe, ĕdġe, hedġe, ledġe, pledġe, fledġe, sledġe, wedġe, mĭdġe, ridġe, bridġe, lŏdġe, podġe, bŭdġe, judġe, grudġe, hĭnġe, crinġe, frinġe, sinġe, swĭnġe, twinġe, lounġe, plŭnġe, sẽrġe, verġe, dĩrġe, gôrġe, ûrġe, ḡurġe, purġe, surġe, ġẽrm, cŏpse, pärse, ẽrse, terse, verse, côrse, gorse, morse.

No. 46. – 45 Words

house, louse, mouse, souse, cûrse, purse, pärese, pĕrch, scôrch, rĭch, bĕlch, bĭrch, bĕnch, blench, drench, French, tench, trench, quench, stench, wench, ĭnch, clinch, fĭnch, flinch, pinch, winch, mŭnch, gulch, bătch, hatch, catch, snatch, scratch, ĕtch, fetch, ketch, retch, flĭtch, nŏtch, potch, hŭtch, sȳlph, lymph, nymph.

The razor has a sharp edge. A ledge is a ridge of rocks. The farmer splits rails with a wedge. A judge must not be a bad man. Doors are hung on hinges. Birch wood will make a hot fire. If you go to near a hot fire it may singe or scorch your frock. The troops march to the sound of the drum. Six boys can sit on one long bench. The birds fly from branch to branch on the trees and clinch their claws fast to the limbs. The first joint of a man's thumb is one inch long. I wish I had a bunch of sweet grapes. A cat can catch rats and mice; and a trap will catch a fox. A hen will sit on a nest of eggs and hatch chickens. The latch holds the door shut. We can light the lamp with a match. Never snatch a book from anyone. A cross cat will scratch with her sharp nails.

No. 47. – 20 Words

rīse, wise, ḡuise, chōse, close, nose, rose, prose, ūse, fuse, muse, phrase, ḡuīde, ḡuile, quite, quote, thȳme, shrīne, sphēre, ḡrīme.

The sun will set at the close of the day. Good boys will use their books with care. A man can guide a horse with a bridle. The earth is not quite round. It is not so long from north to south as it is from east to west. A sphere is a round body or globe. In the nose are the organs of smell. We love to hear a chime of bells. A shrine is a case or box; a hallowed place. A great heat will fuse tin. His prose is written in good style. A phrase is a short form of speech, or a part of a sentence.

No. 48. – 36 Words

void, oil, boil, coil, foil, roil, spoil, broil, soil, toil, oint, joint, point, coin, loin, join, groin, quoin, noise, poise, coif, quoif, quoit, foist, hoist, joist, moist, bound, found, hound, pound, round, ground, sound, wound, mound.

No. 49. – 60 Words

loud, proud, cloud, shroud, ounce, bounce, flounce, pounce, grout, crout, trout, chouse, grouse, spouse, rouse, browse, touse, crown, frown, town, pouch, foul, owl, cowl, prowl, scowl, stout, brown, clown, gown, flour, sour, count, fount, fowl, howl, growl, rout, couch, slouch, mount, out, bout, scout, gout, shout, lout, our, scour, _h_our, clout, flout, snout, pout, spout, sprout, choiçe, voiçe, poi_se_, noi_se_.

We can burn fish oil in lamps. We boil beets with meat in a pot. Pears are choice fruit. When you can choose for yourself, try to make a good choice. The cat and mouse live in the house. The owl has large eyes and can see in the night. One hand of a watch goes round once in an hour. Wheat flour will make good bread. Limes are sour fruit. A hog has a long snout to root up the ground. A trout is a good fish to eat. An ox is a stout, tame beast. Fowls have wings to fly in the air. Wolves howl in the woods in the night. A dog will growl and bark. The cold frost turns the leaves of the trees brown, and makes them fall to the ground. Rain will make the ground moist. You can broil a beefsteak over the coals of fire. We move our limbs at the joints. Land that has a rich soil will bear large crops of grain and grass. A pin has a head and a point. A dime is a small coin worth ten cents. Men play on the bass vi-ol. A great gun makes a loud noise. Men hoist goods from the hold of a ship with ropes. The beams of a wooden house are held up by posts and joists, these are parts of the frame. God makes the ground bring forth fruit for man and beast. The globe is nearly round like a ball. The dark cloud will shed its rain on the ground and make the grass grow.

No. 50. – 36 Words

sēa, pea, flea, plea, bead, mead, read, gōad, load, road, toad, woad, āid, laid, maid, staid, bōard, hoard, gōurd, sourçe, course, crēase, grease, çease, peaçe, lease, prāiṣe, cōarse, hoarse, brēve, heave, weave, leave, blūe, flue, glue.

No. 51. – 42 Words

bȳe, lye, eye, ēaṣe, tease, sēize, cheeṣe, bāsize, raiṣe, maize, shēaf, leaf, neaf, ōak, loaf, fiēf, chief, lief, brief, grief, wāif, ēach, beach, bleach, peach, reach, breach, preach, teach, cōach, roach, broach, lēash, beak, leak, bleak, fleak, speak, peak, sneak, creak, freak.

Few men can afford to keep a coach.

No. 52. – 41 Words

breāk, steāk, strēak, screak, squeak, weak, shriēk, twēak, ōak, croak, soak, bēal, deal, heal, meal, neal, peal, seal, veal, weal, zeal, cōal, foal, goal, shoal, āil, bail, fail, rail, frail, grail, trail, sail, tail, vail, quail, wail, bōwl, sōul, bēam, dream.

No. 53. – 41 Words

flēam, gleam, ream, bream, cream, scream, team, steam, fōam, loam, roam, āim, claim, maim, bēan, dean, lean, clean, glean, mean, wean, miēn, mōan, loan, roan, groan, fāin, gain, grain, brain, strain, chain, lain, blain, plain, slain, main, pain, rain, drain, train.

When the wind blows hard the sea roars, and its waves run high. We have green peas in the month of June. No man can make a good plea for a dram. Girls are fond of fine beads to wear around their necks. Girls and boys must learn to read and spell. Men load hay with a pitchfork. A load of oak wood is worth more than a load of pinewood. A toad will jump like a frog. Sawmills will saw logs into boards. A gourd grows on a vine, like a squash. The man who drinks rum may soon want a loaf of bread. The waves of the sea beat upon the beach. Bleachers bleach linen and thus make it white. The miller grinds corn into meal. The flesh of calves is called veal. Apples are more plentiful than peaches. The preacher is to preach the gospel. A roach is a short, thick, flat fish. Men get their growth before they are thirty. The beak of a bird is its bill, or the end of its bill. Greenland is a bleak, cold place.

No. 54. – 77 Words

WORDS OF THREE SYLLABLES, ACCENTED ON THE FIRST.

bot-a-ny, **el**-e-ġy, **prod**-i-ġy, **ef**-fi-ġy, **eb**-ȯ-ny, **en**-er-ġy, **lit**-ur-ġy, **in**-fa-my, **biḡ**-a-my, **blas**-phe-my, **en**-e-my, **am**-i-ty, **vil**-lain-ny, **com**-pa-ny, **lit**-a-ny, **lar**-çe-ny, **des**-ti-ny, **cal**-um-ny, **tyr**-an-ny, **fel**-ȯ-ny, **col**-o-ny, **har**-mo-ny, **cot**-ton-y, **glut**-ton-y, **can**-o-py, **oc**-cu-pȳ, **quan**-ti-ty, **sal**-a-ry, **reġ**-is-try, **beg**-gar-y, **bur**-gla-ry, **gran**-a-ry, **gloss**-a-ry, **lac**-ta-ry, **hĕr**-ald-ry, **hus**-band-ry, **rob**-bĕr-y, **chan**-çe-ry, **sor**-çer-y, **im**-aġe-ry, **witch**-er-y, **butch**-er-y, **fish**-er-y, **quack**-er-y, **crock**-er-y, **mock**-er-y, **cook**-er-y, **cut**-ler-y, **gal**-ler-y, **rār**-i-ty, **em**-er-y, **nun**-ner-y, **flip**-per-y, **flop**-per-y, **or**-re-ry, **är**-ter-y, **mas**-ter-y, **mys**-ter-y, **bat**-ter-y, **flat**-ter-y, **rev**-el-ry, **lot**-ter-y, **but**-ter-y, **ev**-er-y, **rev**-er-y, **liv**-er-y, **cav**-al-ry, **bot**-tom-ry, **pil**-lo-ry, **mem**-o-ry, **ärm**-o-ry, **fac**-to-ry, **vic**-to-ry, **his**-to-ry, **black**-ber-ry, **bär**-ber-ry, **rib**-ald-ry.

Botany is the science of plants. An elegy is a funeral song. A prodigy is something very wonderful. An effigy is an image or likeness of a person. Blasphemy is contemptuous treatment of God. Litany is a solemn service of prayer to God. Larceny is theft, and liable to be punished. Felony is a crime that may be punished with death. Salary is a stated allowance for services. Husbandry is the tillage of the earth. We are delighted by the harmony of sounds. A glossary is used to explain words. History is the account of past events. A great part of history is an account of men's crimes and wickedness.

No. 55. – 67 Words

blāde, shade, glade, spade, grade, trade, braid, jade, chīde, glide, slide, bride, pride, stride, crụde, prude, glōbe, probe, glēbe, ġībe, bribe, scribe, tribe, plāçe, spaçe, braçe, graçe, traçe, slīçe, miçe, spiçe, priçe, twiçe, stāġe, shake, fake, stake, snake, spake, brake, drake, slake, quake, strīke, spike, chōke, poke, broke, spoke, smoke, stroke, smīle, stile, spile, frāme, shame, blame, clīme, chime, slime, prime, crime, plūme, spume, chīne, swine, twine.

A blade of grass is a single stalk. The leaves of corn are also called blades. The shade of the earth makes the darkness of night. A glade is an opening among trees. A grade is a degree in rank. An officer may enjoy the grade or rank of captain or lieutenant. Trade is the purchase and sale, or exchange of goods. Smoke rises, because it is lighter than air. A globe is a round body, like a ball. A bribe is giving to corrupt the judgment. A smile shows that we are pleased. We have heard the chime of church bells.

WORDS OF TWO SYLLABLES, ACCENTED ON THE FIRST.

ban-ter, **can**-ter, **çen**-ter, **en**-ter, **win**-ter, **fes**-ter, **pes**-ter, **tes**-ter, **sis**-ter, **fos**-ter, **bat**-ter, **hat**-ter, **mat**-ter, **tat**-ter, **let**-ter, **fet**-ter, **el**-der, **ne**-ver, **ev**-er, **sev**-er, **liv**-er, **riv**-er, **man**-or, **ten**-or, **lic**-tor, **vic**-tor, **doc**-tor, **tin**-der, **ped**-dler, **til**-ler, **sut**-ler, **ham**-mer, **ram**-mer, **sum**-mer, **lim**-ner, **ban**-ner, **tan**-ner, **in**-ner, **din**-ner, **tin**-ner, **sin**-ner, **côr**-ner, **ham**-per, **tam**-per, **tem**-per, **ten**-ter, **sim**-per, **clap**-per, **pep**-per, **dip**-per, **cop**-per, **hop**-per, **up**-per, **sup**-per, **ves**-per, **reb**-el, **can**-çel, **cam**-el, **pan**-nel, **ken**-nel, **fen**-nel, **tun**-nel, **kẽr**-nel, **ḡos**-pel, **băr**-rel, **sôr**-rel, **dôr**-sal, **môr**-sel, **ves**-sel, **tin**-sel, **grav**-el, **bev**-el, **lev**-el, **rev**-el, **hov**-el, **nov**-el, **mär**-vel, **pen**-çil, **man**-fụl, **sin**-fụl, **aw**-fụl, **pĕr**-il, **ton**-sil, **dos**-sil, **fos**-sil, **len**-til, **cav**-il, **çiv**-il, **an**-vil, **bez**-il, **cŏr**-al, **băr**-ter, **car**-ter, **màs**-ter, **cas**-tor, **pas**-tor, **pär**-lor, **ḡar**-ner, **far**-del, **art**-fụl, **dar**-nel, **har**-per.

We have snow and ice in the cold winter. The little sister can knit a pair of garters. Never pester the little boys. Hatters make hats of fur and lamb's wool. Peaches may be better than apples. The rivers run into the great sea. The doctor tries to cure the sick. The new table stands in the parlor. A tin peddler will sell tin vessels as he travels. The little boys can crack nuts with a hammer. The farmer eats his dinner at noon. I can dip the milk with a tin dipper. We eat bread and milk for supper. The farmer puts his cider into barrels. Vessels sail on the large rivers. My good little sister may have a slate and pencil; and she may make letters on her slate. That idle boy is a very lazy fellow. The farmer put his bridle and saddle upon his horse. Paper is made of linen and cotton rags. Spiders spin webs to catch flies.

No. 57. – 48 Words

mōurn, borne, shorn, ōwn, shown, blown, flown, sown, grown, vāin, wain, swain, twain, train, stain, lāne hēap, cheap, leap, neap, reap, sōap, ēar, dear, fear, year, hear, shear, blear, clear, smear, near, spear, rear, drear, sear, tēar weâr, sweâr, teâr, ōar, hoar, roar, soar, boar, piēr, tier, bier.

No. 58. – 54 Words

âir, fair, hair, chair, lair, pair, stair, *h*êir, fōur, your, tọur, ēave*s*, leave*s*, greave*s*, pāin*s*, shēar, ḡu̇ĕss, g*u*est, stĭlts, chintz, ēat, beat, feat, heat, bleat, meat, neat, peat, treat, seat, greāt, ōat, bloat, coat, goat, float, moat, grọat, ẹi*gh*t, frei*gh*t, wei*gh*t, bāit, gait, plait, trait, wait, br*u̇*it, fruit, sūit, mĭlt, b*u*ilt, ḡ*u*ilt, cōurt, sāint.

No. 59. – 58 Words

ēast, beast, least, feast, yeast, bōast, roast, toast, wāist, dew, few, hew, chew*, Jew, view, blew, flew, brew*, slew, mew, new, view*s*, pew, spew, crew*, screw*, drew*, grew*, shrew*, strew*, stew, yew, bōw, show, low, blow, glow, slow, mow, row, snow, crow, grow, strow, sōw, stow.

*ew, in the starred words, is pronounced like ō͞o; in other words, like **ū.**

We do not like to see our own sins. I like to see a full-blown rose. A vain girl is fond of fine things. The moon is in the wane from full to new moon. A dog can leap over a fence. Much grain will make bread cheap. I like to see men reap grain. God made the ear, and He can hear. Men shear the wool from sheep. Flint glass is white and clear. Fowls like to live near the house and barn. Can a boy cry and not shed a tear? Twelve months make one year. I love to eat a good ripe pear. The good boy will not tear his book. A wild boar lives in the woods. The lark will soar up in the sky to look at the sun. The rain runs from the eaves of the house. The sun heats the air and makes it hot. The old sheep bleats, and calls her lamb to her. I wish you to treat me with a new hat. A chair is a better seat than a stool. I will wear my greatcoat in a cold wet day. I have seen the ice float down the stream. Boys and girls are fond of fruit. The sun will rise in the east, and set in the west. A beast cannot talk and think, as we do. We roast a piece of beef or a goose. A girl can toast a piece of bread. We chew our meat with our teeth. Live coals of fire glow with heat. A moat is a deep trench round a castle or other fortified place.

daunt, haunt, flaunt, aunt, vaunt, grȧnt, slant, lärġe, charġe, bärġe, sä*l*ve, scarf.

No. 60. – 39 Words

frȧud, broad, sauçe, cause, ḡauze, clause, pause, paunch, squȧsh, wȧsh, swash, quash, gawk, hawk, haul, maul, ȧwl, bawl, sprawl, brawl, crawl, drawl, trawl, waul, yawl, dawn, fawn, lawn, pawn, spawn, brawn, yawn, dwarf, wȧtch, vȧult, fault, aught, naught, caught.

No. 61. – 44 Words

brīne, tine, shōne, crone, prone, stone, prṳne, drṳpe, scrāpe, drape, shape, crape, grape, snīpe, gripe, stripe, tripe, scōpe, trope, snore, slāte, state, grate, grave, brave, crave, shave, slave, plate, prate, quīte, smite, spite, sprite, trite, drīve, drōve, strove, grove, clove, gloze, froze, prīze, smōte.

Forks have two, three, or four tines. We keep salt meat in brine. Grapes grow on vines, in clusters. Smoke goes through the pipe of a stove. The boy loves ripe grapes. Bedcords are long ropes. Nut wood and coal will make a warm fire. Shut the gate and keep the hogs out of the yard. Slates are stone, and used to cover roofs of houses. We burn coal in a grate. I had some green corn in July, on a plate. Dig up the weeds and let the corn grow. Bees live in hives and collect honey. He was dull, and made trite remarks.

No. 62. – 76 Words

WORDS OF THREE SYLABLES, ACCENTED ON THE FIRST.

am-i-ty, **jŏl**-li-ty, **nul**-li-ty, **en**-mi-ty, **san**-i-ty, **van**-i-ty, **bal**-co-ny, **len**-i-ty, **dig**-ni-ty, **dep**-ū-ty, **trin**-i-ty, **păr**-i-ty, **com**-i-ty, **věr**-i-ty, **den**-si-ty, **en**-ti-ty, **cav**-i-ty, **lev**-i-ty, **lax**-i-ty, **pen**-al-ty, **nov**-el-ty, **fac**-ul-ty, **mod**-est-y, **prob**-i-ty, **am**-nes-ty, **bot**-a-ny, **ob**-lo-quy, **sin**-ew-y, **gal**-ax-y, **ped**-ant-ry, **in**-fant-ry, **gal**-lant-ry, **big**-ot-ry, **an**-çes-try, **tap**-es-try, **min**-is-try, **in**-dus-try, **çent**-ū-ry, **měr**-cu-ry, **in**-ju-ry, **pěr**-ju-ry, **pen**-ū-ry, **lŭx**-ū-ry **hěr**-e-sy, **em**-bas-sy, **dē**-i-ty, **fe**-al-ty, **pī**-e-ty, **pō**-e-sy, **cru̯**-el-ty, **pū**-ri-ty, **nu**-di-ty, **dȳ**-nas-ty, **gay**-e-ty, **loy**-al-ty, **roy**-al-ty, **ū**-s̱u-ry (*ū-zhoo-*), **rā**-pi-er, **nau̯**-ti-lus, **pau**-çi-ty, **moi**-e-ty, **prel**-a-çy, **ăl**-i-quot, **man**-i-fest, **up**-per-mōst, **con**-tra-ry, **çel**-e-ry, **plē**-na-ry, **sā**-li-ent, **lē**-ni-ent, **ve**-he-ment, **brī**-er-y, **boun**-te-oŭs, **coun**-ter-feĭt, **frau̯d**-ū-lent, **wa̱**-ter-y.

WORDS OF THREE SYLABLES, ACCENTED ON THE SECOND.

a-**bāse**-ment, al-**lūre**-ment, de-**bāse**-ment, in-**çīte**-ment, en-**slāve**-ment, a-**maze**-ment, in-**quī**-ry, un-**ēa**-sy, con-**vey**-ançe, pur-**vey**-or, sur-**vey**-or sur-**vey**-ing, dis-**bûrse**-ment, ärch-**bish**-op, ad-**vent**-ūre, dis-**fran**-chise, mis-**con**-strue, de-**pos**-it, re-**pos**-it, at-**trib**-ūte, im-**mod**-est, un-**luck**-y, ap-**pen**-dix, au-**tum**-nal, how-**ev**-er, em-**bär**-rass, in-**stall**-ment, in-**thrall**-ment, hy-**draul**-ics, en-**joy**-ment, a-**mass**-ment, em-**bär**-go, im-**prove**-ment, at-**tor**-nēy, an-**noy**-ançe.

WORDS OF TWO SYLLABLES, ACCENTED ON THE FIRST.

blan-dish, **bran**-dish, **fûr**-bish, **rub**-bish, **self**-ish, **chûrl**-ish, **fur**-nish, **blem**-ish, **skīr**-mish, **van**-ish, **fīn**-ish, **gär**-nish, **tar**-nish, **var**-nish, **bûr**-nish, **pŭn**-ish, **clown**-ish, **snap**-pish, **par**-ish, **cher**-ish, **floŭr**-ish, **noŭr**-ish, **skit**-tish, **slut**-tish, **lav**-ish, **rav**-ish, **pub**-lish, **pot**-ash.

Vain persons are fond of allurements of dress. Strong drink leads to the debasement both of the mind and the body. We look with amazement on the evils of strong drink. The gambler wishes to get money without earning it. An indorser indorses his name on the back of a note; and his indorsement makes him liable to pay the note. An archbishop is a chief dignitary of the church. Merchants often deposit money in the bank for safe-keeping. Autumnal fruits are the fruits that ripen in autumn. The wicked know not the enjoyment of a good conscience. Parents should provide useful employment for their children. Men devoted to mere amusement misemploy their time.

No. 65. – 32 Words

WORDS OF TWO SYLLABLES, ACCENTED ON THE FIRST.

THE UNMARKED VOWELS (EXCEPT **e** FINAL) IN THIS LESSON HAVE A
SOUND APPROACHING THAT OF SHORT **u**.

hôrse-băck, **lămp**-blăck, **băr**-rack, **răn**-săck, **hăm**-mock,
had-dock, **pad**-lock, **wĕd**-lŏck, **fīre**-lŏck, **hĭll**-ŏck, **bṳll**-
ŏck, **hĕm**-lŏck, **fĕt**-lŏck, **măt**-tock, **hōōd**-wĭnk, **bṳll**-wark,
pĭtch-fôrk, **dăm**-ask, **sy̆m**-bol, **vẽr**-bal, **mĕd**-al, **vẽr**-nal,
joûr-nal, **răs**-cal, **spī**-nal, **trĭb**-ūte, **stăt**-ūte, **cŏn**-cāve, **cŏn**-
clāve, **ŏc**-tāve, **rĕs**-cūe, **văl**-ūe.

No. 66. – 24 Words

WORDS OF TWO SYLLABLES, ACCENTED ON THE FIRST.

a IN **ate**, UNMARKED, DOES NOT HAVE THE FULL SOUND OF LONG **a**.

sĕn-ate, **in**-grāte, **pal**-ate, **stel**-lāte, **in**-māte, **mess**-māte,
stag-nāte, **fil**-trāte, **pros**-trate, **frus**-trāte, **dic**-tāte, **tes**-tāte,
clī-mate, **prel**-ate, **vī**-brāte, **pī**-rate, **cū**-rate, **prī**-vate, **fĭ**-
nīte, **pōst**-aġe, **plū**-maġe, **trī**-umph, **stāte**-ment, **rāi**-ment.

When an old house is pulled down, it is no small job to remove the
rubbish. Washington was not a selfish man. He labored for the
good of his country more than for himself. Exercises will give us
relish for our food. Riding on horseback is good exercise. Lamp-
black is fine soot formed from the smoke of tar, pitch, or pinewood. Granite is a kind of stone which is very strong, handsome,
and useful in building. The Senate of the United States is called the
Upper House of Congress. Water will stagnate, and then it is not
good. Heavy winds sometimes prostrate trees. Norway has a cold
climate. Medals are sometimes given as a reward at school. We
punish bad men to prevent crimes. The drunkard's face will publish his vice and his disgrace.

No. 67. – 90 Words

WORDS OF FOUR SYLLABLES, PRIMARY ACCENT ON THE FIRST.

lū-mi-na-ry, **cū**-li-na-ry, **mō**-ment-a-ry, **nū**-ga-to-ry, **nu**-mer-a-ry **brē**-vi-a-ry, **ef**-fi-ca-çy, **del**-i-ca-çy, **in**-tri-ca-çy, **con**-tu-ma-çy, **ob**-sti-na-çy, **ac**-cu-ra-çy, **ex**-i-ġen-çy, **ex**-çel-len-çy, **com**-pe-ten-çy, **im**-po-ten-çy, **mis**-çel-la-ny, **nec**-es-sa-ry, **ig**-no-min-y, **çer**-e-mo-ny, **al**-i-mo-ny, **mat**-ri-mo-ny, **pat**-ri-mo-ny, **pär**-si-mo-ny, **an**-ti-mo-ny, **tes**-ti-mo-ny, **drȯm**-e-da-ry, **preb**-end-a-ry, **sec**-ond-a-ry, **e͟x**-em-pla-ry, **an**-ti-qua-ry, **tit**-ū-la-ry, **cus**-tom-a-ry, *hon*-or-a-ry, **par**-çe-na-ry, **med**-ul-al-ry, **mer**-çe-na-ry, **mil**-li-na-ry, **or**-di-na-ry, **sem**-i-na-ry, **pul**-mo-na-ry, **sub**-lu-na-ry, **lit**-er-a-ry, **form**-u-al-ry, **ar**-bi-tra-ry, **ad**-ver-sa-ry, **em**-is-sa-ry, **com**-mis-sa-ry, **çem**-e-ter-y, **sec**-re-ta-ry, **mil**-i-ta-ry, **sol**-i-ta-ry, **sed**-en-ta-ry, **vol**-un-ta-ry, **trib**-u-ta-ry, **sal**-u-ta-ry, **an**-çil-la-ry, **cap**-il-la-ry, **ax**-il-la-ry, **cor**-ol-la-ry, **max**-il-la-ry, **al**-a-bas-ter, **plan**-et-a-ry, **stat**-ū-a-ry, **sanct**-ū-a-ry, **dy̆s**-en-ter-y, **pres**-by-ter-y, **prom**-is-so-ry, **pred**-a-to-ry, **pref**-a-to-ry, **pul**-sa-to-ry, **min**-a-to-ry, **a̤ud**-it-o-ry, **ex**-ce-to-ry, **jan**-i-za-ry, **mon**-as-ter-y, **al**-le-go-ry, **des**-ul-to-ry, **man**-da-to-ry, **pur**-ga-to-ry, **dil**-a-to-ry, **or**-a-to-ry, **dor**-mi-to-ry, **mon**-i-to-ry, **ter**-ri-to-ry, **tran**-si-to-ry, **in**-ven-to-ry, **con**-tro-ver-sy, **leġ**-is-la-tive, **leg**-is-la-tor.

The sun is the brightest luminary. The moon is the luminary of the night. The streets, houses, and shops of New York used to be illuminated with gaslights. Potatoes and turnips are common culinary roots used in our kitchens. We admire the rose for the delicacy of its colors and its sweet fragrance. There is a near intimacy between drunkeness, poverty, and ruin. The obstinate will should be subdued. Wedlock is an old Anglo-Saxon term for matrimony. Antimony is a hard mineral, and is used in making types for printing. A witness must give true testimony. A dromedary is a large quadruped. Worldly men make it their primary object to please themselves; duty holds but secondary place in their esteem. It is customary for tippers to visit taverns. Grammar is a difficult but ordinary study. A seminary means a place of instruction. Napoleon was an arbitrary emperor. He disposed kingdoms as he chose. Satan is a great adversary of God. Food is necessary for animal life. Alabaster is a kind of marble or limestone. An emissary is a secret agent employed to give information to an enemy, or to act as a spy. The planetary worlds are those stars, which go around the sun. A secretary is a writer or scribe. Our actions are voluntary, proceeding from free will. The Ohio River has many large tributary streams, which contribute to increase its waters. Pure water and good air are salutary. The church is called a sanctuary or holy place. The dysentery is a painful disease. A promissory note is a note by which a man promises to pay a sum of money. The remarks at the beginning of a discourse are called prefatory remarks. Dilatory people are such as delay doing their work. An orator makes orations; and oratory is the art of public speaking. The auditory is the company who attend as hearers of a discourse. They could not agree and had a bitter controversy.

WORDS OF THREE SYLLABLES, ACCENTED ON THE SECOND.

im-**môr**-tal, pa-**rent**-al, ac-**quit**-tal, en-**am**-el, im-**pan**-el, ap-**păr**-ent, ū-**ten**-sil, un-**çiv**-il, trī-**umph**-al, in-**form**-al, bap-**tis̠**-mal, hī-**bĕr**-nal, in-**fer**-nal, ma-**ter**-nal, pa-**ter**-nal, e-**ter**-nal, in-**ter**-nal, dī-**ûr**-nal, noc-**tur**-nal, pro-**con**-sul, un-**çer**-tain, in-**clem**-ent, de-**tĕr**-mĭne, as-**sas**-sin, re-**plev**-in, a-**ban**-don, pĭ-**as**-ter, pĭ-**las**-ter, as-**sev**-er, dis-**sev**-er, de-**liv**-er, e-**lix**-ir, pre-**cep**-tor, com-**pos̠**-ite, en-**am**-or, to-**bac**-co, si-**roc**-co, me-**men**-to, pĭ-**men**-to, mu-**lat**-to, pal-**met**-to, en-**vel**-ope, de-**vel**-op, De-**cem**-ber, Sep-**tem**-ber, No-**vem**-ber, en-**cum**-ber, con-**sid**-er, be-**wil**-der, mis-**fort**-ūne, me-**an**-der, en-**ġen**-der, sur-**ren**-der, dis̠-**ôr**-der, nar-**cis**-sus, co-**los**-sus, im-**pĕr**-fect, in-**ter**-pret, in-**hab**-it, pro-**hib**-it, dis-**cred**-it, de-**crep**-it, in-**her**-it, de-**mer**-it, pȯme-**gran**-ate, ex̠-**am**-ple, in-**tes**-tāte, a-**pos**-tāte, pro-**mul**-gate, in-**car**-nate, vol-**cā**-no, Oc-**tō**-ber, in-**clo̠**-sure, dis-**clo̠**-sure, ex-**po̠**-sure, fore-**clo**-sure, dis-**cȯv**-er, dis-**col**-or, re-**cov**-er, dis-**as̠**-ter, re-**pȧss**-ing.

The spirit is immortal; it will never die. Our bodies are mortal; they will soon die. Utensils are tools to work with. Plows, axes, and hoes are utensils for farming; needles and scissors are utensils for making garments. A formal meeting is one where the forms of ceremony are observed; when people meet without attending these formalities it is called an informal meeting. Children are sometimes bewildered and lost in the woods. Sons and daughters inherit the estate and sometimes the infirmities of their parents. The diurnal motion of the earth is its daily motion, and this gives us day and night. Pimento is the plant whose berries we call allspice. Paternal care and maternal love are great blessings to children, and should be repaid with their duty and affection. The blowing up of a steamship was a terrible disaster to us. Pomegranate is a fruit about the size of an orange.

No. 69. – 29 Words

bāy, day, fay, gay, hay, jay, lay, clay, fay, play, slay, may, nay, pay, ray, dray, fray, gray, pray, tray, stray, say, stay, way, sway, splay, prey, drey, bey.

No. 70. – 21 Words

boy, coy, hoy, joy, cloy, troy, toy, caw, daw, haw, jaw, draw, claw, flaw, maw, raw, craw, straw, saw, law, paw.

No. 71. – 30 Words

swamp, wasp, was, halt, malt, smalt, spalt, salt, want, wart, swart, quart, pōrk, fork, sport, port, mōst, dŏll, loll, gĭve, lĭve, come, some, dove, love, glove, work (*wŭrk*), worst (*wŭrst*), shove, monk.

No. 72. – 23 Words

bow, cow, how, plow, mow, now, brow, sow, vow, kēy, ley, worm (wŭrm), frŏnt, wont, wort (wŭrt), dĭrt, flirt, shirt, skirt, squirt, first, ward, warm.

The farmer cuts his grass to make hay. Bricks are made of clay baked in a kiln. You may play on a mow of hay. A dray is a kind of low cart. When we eat we move the under jaw; but the upper jaw of most animals is fixed. Little boys and girls are fond of toys. The sting of a wasp is very painful. A swamp is wet, spongy land. A monk lives in retirement from the world. Smalt is a blue glass of cobalt. Malt is barley steeped in water, fermented and dried in a kiln; of this are made ale and beer.

No. 73. – 127 Words

WORDS OF TWO SYLLABLES, ACCENTED ON THE FIRST.

lăd-der, blad-der, mad-der, fŏd-der, ŭl-cer, can-çer, ud-der, shud-der, rud-der, pud-der, gan-der, pan-der, ğĕn-der, slen-der, ren-der, ten-der, çĭn-der, hin-der, pŏn-der, ŭn-der, blun-der, plun-der, thun-der, sun-der, ôr-der, bor-der, mûr-der, dif-fer, shel-ter, fĭl-ter, mil-ler, chap-ter, suf-fer, pil-fer, bad-ğer, ledğ-er, ba<u>n</u>k-er, ca<u>n</u>k-er, ha<u>n</u>k-er, tum-bler, sad-dler, ant-ler, skim-mer, glim-mer, prop-er, clap-per, skip-per, crop-per, as-per, pros-per, less-er, dress-er, ȧft-er, rȧft-er, rănt-er, chärt-er, lob-ster, lit-ter, mon-ster, glis-ter, chat-ter, shat-ter, clut-ter, flut-ter, plat-ter, smat-ter, spat-ter, shiv-er, silv-er, quiv-er, cul-ver, tor-por, ĕr-ror, ter-ror, mĭr-ror, hŏr-ror, çen-sor, spon-sor, sec-tor, sach-el, flan-nel, chap-el, grav-el, chär-nel, băr-ren, flŏr-in, rob-in, cof-fin, muf-fin, bod-kin, wel-kin, nap-kin, pip-kin, bus-kin, gob-lin, mu<u>s</u>-lin, lū-çid, băr-on, flag-on, wag-on, fel-on, găl-lon, lem-on, gam-mon, mam-mon, com-mon, can-non, çit-ron, ten-on, can-ton, pis-ton, of-fer, cof-fer, scof-fer, prof-fer, proc-tor, chan-nel, cud-ğel, hatch-el, trav-el, pȯm-mel, bu̇sh-el, chan-çel, sex-ton, kim-bo, stuc-co, dit-to.

The farmer hatchels flax; he sells corn by the bushel, and butter by the firkin. Little boys and girls love to ride in a wagon. Four quarts make a gallon. A barrel is thirty gallons, more or less. Lemons grow on trees in warm climates. The robin is a pretty singing-bird. A napkin is a kind of towel. Brass is a compound of copper and zinc. The channel of a river is where the main current flows. Firemen have ladders to climb upon houses. The farmer fodders his cattle in winter. The sailor steers a vessel with a rudder. A gander is white and a goose gray. Broomcorn grows with a long slender stalk. The eye is a very tender organ, and one of the most useful members of the body.

WORDS OF TWO SYLLABLES, ACCENTED ON THE FIRST.

brāçe-let, dī-et, qui-et, sē-cret, pō-et, to-phet, eȳe-let, tū-mult, bōl-ster, hōl-ster, grā-ver, qua-ver, drī-ver, mā-jor, mī-nor, stū-por, ju-ror, prē-tor, tū-tor, prī-or, rā-zor, trē-mor, hū-mor, ru̩-mor, tū-mor, lā-bor, tā-bor, ō-dor, co-lon, dē-mon, ī-ron (*i-urn*), ā-pron, dew-lap, cru̩-et, bā-sis, ū-nit, crī-sis, grā-ter, fō-cus, mū-cus, bō-lus, fla-grant, vā-grant, tȳ-rant, de-çent, rē-cent, nō-cent, lū-cent, trī-dent, pru̩-dent, stū-dent, ā-ġent, rē-ġent, cō-ġent, sī-lent, cāse-ment, pave-ment, mo̩ve-ment, mō-ment, çī-pher, vā-cant, flū-ent, frē-quent, se-quent, rī-ot, pi-lot, bâre-foot, prē-çept, pōst-script, o-vert, ru̩-by, spī-çy, need-y, crō-ny, pū-ny, vā-ry, dū-ty, nā-vy, gra-vy, safe-ty, su̩re-ty, glō-ry, sto-ry, crā-zy, hā-zy, la-zy, dō-zy, slēa-zy, jas-per, bär-g*a*in, cap-t*a*in, çer-t*a*in, mŭr-r*a*in, vil-l*a*in, vī-s̭or, slan-der.

Ladies sometimes wear bracelets on their arms. Watts was a very good poet; he wrote good songs. Rabbit hide themselves in secret places. A bolster is put at the head of a bed. Men in old age love a quiet life. A graver is a tool for engraving. A holster is a case for carrying a pistol. A driver is one who drives a team. A minor is a young person not twenty-one years old. Miners work in mines under ground. A juror is one who sits to try causes and give verdict according to evidence. A rose emits a pleasant flavor. Labor makes us strong and healthy. A colon is one of the stops in reading. A pastor does not like to see vacant seats in his church. Girls wear aprons to keep their frocks clean. Nero was a wicked tyrant at Rome. Every person should wear a decent dress. A major is an officer next above captain. A vagrant is a wandering, lazy fellow. Cedar is the most durable species of wood. A postscript is something added to a letter. The streets of cities are covered with pavements.

No. 75. – 72 Words

WORDS OF THREE SYLLABLES, ACCENTED ON THE SECOND.

ar-**rī**-val, ap-**prọv**-al, co-ē-val, re-**fū**-ṣal, re-**pri**-ṣal, pe-**rụ**-ṣal, de-**crē**-tal, re-**çi**-tal, re-**qui**-tal, prī-**me**-val, un-**e**-qual co-**e**-qual, re-**new**-al, ī-**dē**-al, il-**le**-gal, de-**nī**-al, de-**cri**-al, tri-**bū**-nal, a-**cu**-men, le-**gu**-men, dis-**sēi**-zin, in-**çī**-ṣor, cre-**ā**-tor, spec-**ta**-tor, dic-**ta**-tor, tes-**ta**-tor, en-**vī**-ron, pa-**gō**-dȧ, tor-**pē**-do, bra-**vā**-do, tor-**na**-do, lum-**ba**-go, vī-**ra**-go, far-ra-go, pro-**vī**-ṣo, po-**tā**-to, oc-**ta**-vo, sub-**scrī**-ber, re-**vi**-val, en-**dān**-ġer, de-**çī**-pher, ma-**neū**-ver, hī-**ā**-tus, quī-**ē**-tus, con-**fess**-or, ag-**gress**-or, suc-**çess**-or, pre-**fig**-ūre, dis-**fig**-ūre, trans-**fi**-gūre, con-**ject**-ūre, de-**bent**-ūre, in-**dent**-ūre, en-**rapt**-ūre, con-**text**-ūre, com-**mixt**-ūre, con-**tin**-ūe, for-**bid**-ding, un-**ĕr**-ring, pro-**çeed**-ing, ex-**çeed**-ing, sub-**al**-tern, es-**pou**-ṣal, en-**coun**-ter, ren-**coun**-ter, a-**vow**-al, ad-**vow**-son, dis-**loy**-al, dis-**coŭr**-aġe, en-**cour**-aġe, mo-**las**-seṣ, de-**pärt**-ūre.

We often wait for the arrival of the mail. Coeval signifies of the same age. Reprisal is seizing anything from an enemy in retaliation. An incisor is a fore tooth. Our blood is often chilled at the recital of acts of cruelty. Primeval denotes what was first or original. A tribunal is a court for deciding causes. Acumen denotes quickness of perception. Illegal is the same as unlawful. It is illegal to steal fruit from another's orchard or garden. Molasses is the syrup, which drains from sugar when it is cooling. The potato is a native plant of America.

WORDS OF THREE SYLLABLES, ACCENTED ON THE LAST.

ap-per-**tāin**, su-per-**vene**, in-ter-**vene**, im-por-**tūne**, op-por-**tune**, in-se-**cure**, in-ter-**fēre**, pre-ma-**ture**, im-ma-**tūre**, ad-ver-**tīse**, re-com-**pōse**, de-com-**pose**, in-ter-**pose**, pre-dis-**pose**, re-in-**stāte**, im-po-**līte**, re-ū-**nite**, dis-u-**nite**, dis-re-**pūte,** in-ter-**lēave**, in-ter-**wēave**, mis-be-**hāve**, un-de-**çēive**, pre-con-**çēive**, o-ver-**drīve**, dis-ap-**prove**, o-ver-**look**, dis-in-**thrall**, re-in-**stall**, dis-es-**teem**, mis-de-**mēan**, un-fōre-**seen**, fōre-or-**dāin**, o-ver-**strain**, as-çer-**tain**, en-ter-**tain**, re-ap-**pēar**, dis-in-**tẽr**, in-ter-**spẽrse**, re-im-**bûrse**, cĩr-cum-**volve**, o-ver-**hang**, o-ver-**match**, dis-em-**bärk**, un-der-**sell**, dis-af-**fect**, o-ver-**whelm**, mis-in-**fôrm**, coun-ter-**act**, in-di-**rect**, in-cor-**rect**, in-ter-**sect**, con-tra-**dict**, o-ver-**set**, in-ter-**mit**, rep-re-**sent**, dis-con-**tent**, çĩr-cum-**vent**, un-der-**went**, o-ver-**shōōt**, in-ter-**çept**, in-ter-**rupt**, o-ver-**top**, re-ap-**point**, un-der-**gō**, o-ver-**lēap**, o-ver-**sleep**, dis-ap-**pēar**, moun-tain-**eer**, en-ġin-**eer**, dom-i-**neer**, mu-ti-**neer**, pī-o-**neer**, auc-tion-**eer**, o-ver-**seer**, prī-va-**teer**, vol-un-**teer**, gaz-et-**teer**, fīn-an-**çiēr**, brig-a-**diēr**, gren-a-**diēr**, bom-bar-**diēr**, deb-o-**nâir**, res-er-**voir**, o-ver-**joy**, mis-em-**ploy**, es-pla-**nāde**, in-ex-**pẽrt**, o-ver-**càst**, re-in-**vest**, co-ex-**ist**, prē-ex-**ist**, in-ter-**mix**, o-ver-**thrōw**, o-ver-**flōw**, o-ver-**lāy**, dis-o-**bey**, dis-al-**low**.

WORDS OF TWO SYLLABLES, ACCENTED ON THE FIRST.

at-las, **sŭc**-cor, *hon*-or, **ran**-cor, **can**-dor, **splen**-dor, **rig**-or, **vig**-or, **văl**-or, **fẽr**-vor, **sculp**-tor, **clam**-or, **ten**-nis, **clas**-sic, **ax**-is, **fan**-çy, **pen**-ny, **cop**-y, **hap**-py, **pop**-py, **pup**-py, **sun**-dry, **bel**-fry, **fel**-ly, **căr**-ry, **măr**-ry, **păr**-ry, **bĕr**-ry, **fer**-ry, **cher**-ry, **mer**-ry, **per**-ry, **sŏr**-ry, **cŭr**-ry, **hŭr**-ry, **flŭr**-ry, **här**-py, **en**-try, **sen**-try, **dusk**-y, **pạl**-try, **ves**-try, **pit**-y, **scan**-ty, **plen**-ty, **tes**-ty, **bet**-ty, **pet**-ty, **jet**-ty, **dit**-ty, **wit**-ty, **flab**-by, **shab**-by, **tab**-by, **lob**-by, **grit**-ty, **pŭt**-ty, **lev**-y, **priv**-y, **en**-vy, **dox**-y, **prox**-y, **cȯl**-or, **wȯr**-ry, **pär**-ty, **ar**-bor, **har**-bor.

An atlas is a book of maps. You must be good, or you cannot be happy. When you make letters, look at your copy. The poppy is a large flower. The puppy barks, as well as the dog. The place where the bell hangs in the steeple is called the belfry. Horses carry men on their backs. We cross the ferry in a boat. The cherry is an acid fruit. We are sorry when a good man dies. Never do your work in hurry. Boys like a warm fire in a wintery day. The farmer likes to have plenty of hay for his cattle, and oats for his horses. The lily is a very pretty flower. Glass is made fast in the window with putty.

WORDS OF THREE SYLLABLES, ACCENTED ON THE FIRST

ban-ish-ment, **blan**-dish-ment, **pun**-ish-ment, **rav**-ish-
ment, **ped**-i-ment, **sed**-i-ment, **ăl**-i-ment, **com**-pli-ment, **lin**-
i-ment, **mĕr**-ri-ment, **det**-ri-ment, **sen**-ti-ment, **doc**-ū-ment,
teg-ū-ment, **mon**-ū-ment, **in**-stru-ment, **con**-ti-nent, **căl**-a-
mint, **id**-i-ot, **găl**-i-ot, **chăr**-i-ot, **pol**-y-glot, **bĕr**-ga-mot,
an-te-pȧst, **pen**-te-cost, **haͅl**-i-but, **fûr**-be-lōw, **bed**-fel-lōw,
çic-a-trix, **păr**-a-dox, **sär**-do-nўx, **Sat**-ur-day, **hol**-i-day,
run-a-way, **căr**-a-way, **cȧst**-a-way, **leg**-a-çy, **făl**-la-cy, **pol**-
i-cy, **in**-fan-çy, **con**-stan-cy, **ten**-den-cy, **pun**-ġen-cy, **clem**-
en-cy, **cŭr**-ren-cy, **sol**-ven-cy, **ba**n**k**-rupt-cy, **sum**-ma-ry,
land-la-dy, **rem**-e-dy, **com**-e-dy, **pĕr**-fi-dy, **mel**-o-dy,
mon-o-dy, **păr**-o-dy, **pros**-o-dy, **cus**-to-dy, **crṳ**-çi-fix, **dī**-a-
lect, **ō**-ri-ent, **ā**-pri-cot, **vā**-can-çy, **va**-gran-cy, **lu**-na-cy,
dē-cen-cy, **pā**-pa-cy, **rē**-ġen-cy, **pī**-ra-cy, **cō**-ġen-cy, **sē**-cre-
cy, **prī**-va-cy, **pō**-ten-cy, **plī**-an-cy, **flū**-en-cy, **mu**-ti-ny,
scrṳ-ti-ny, **pē**-o-ny, **ī**-ron-y, **ob**-lo-quy, **dī**-a-ry, **rō**-ṣa-ry,
vo-ta-ry, **gro**-çer-y, **drā**-per-y, **ī**-vo-ry.

WORDS OF FOUR SYLLABLES, ACCENTED ON THE SECOND.

a-ē-ri-al, an-**nū**-i-ty, me-**mō**-ri-al, de-**mo**-ni-ac, am-**mo**-ni-ac, ad-**jū**-di-cāte, e-**lu**-çi-dāte, im-**mē**-di-ate, re-**pū**-di-āte, col-**lē**-ġi-ate, ex-**fō**-li-āte, in-**ē**-bri-āte (*v.*), ex-**co**-ri-ate, ap-**pro**-pri-āte, in-**fū**-ri-āte, al-**lē**-vi-āte, ab-**bre**-vi-āte, an-**nī**-hi-lāte, ac-**cū**-mu-lāte, il-**lu**-mi-nāte, e-**nu**-mer-āte, re-**mu**-ner-āte, in-**côr**-po-rāte, no-**tā**-ri-al, ma-**tē**-ri-al, im-**pe**-ri-al, ar-**te**-ri-al, är-**mō**-ri-al, mer-**cū**-ri-al, em-**pō**-ri-um, sen-**so**-ri-um, tra-**pē**-zi-um, crī-**te**-ri-on, çen-**tū**-ri-on, al-**lō**-di-al, al-**lo**-di-um, en-**co**-mi-um, tra-**ġē**-di-an, co-**me**-di-an, col-**le**-ġi-an, çe-**rụ**-le-an, bar-**bā**-ri-an, gram-**mā**-ri-an, in-**fē**-ri-or, su-**pe**-ri-or, an-**te**-ri-or, in-**te**-ri-or, pos-**te**-ri-or, ex-**te**-ri-or, pro-**prī**-e-tor, ex-**trā**-ne-oŭs, spon-**ta**-ne-ous, cu-**ta**-ne-ous, er-**rō**-ne-ous, ter-**rā**-que-ous, tär-**ta**-re-ous, com-**mō**-di-ous, fe-**lo**-ni-ous, här-**mo**-ni-ous, gra-**tū**-i-tous, for-**tu**-i-tous, lux̱-**u**-ri-ant, e-**lu**-so-ry, il-**lu**-so-ry, col-**lu**-so-ry, so-**çī**-e-ty, im-**pū**-ri-ty, se-**cu**-ri-ty, ob-**scu**-ri-ty.

All clouds float in the aërial regions. The aërial songsters are birds of the air. Gravestones are placed by graves, as memorials of the dead. They call to our remembrance our friends who are buried under them or near them. The blossoms of spring send forth an agreeable smell. There is an immediate communication between the heart and the brain. Men who have been instructed in colleges are said to have collegiate education. Laudanum is given to alleviate pain. The sun illuminates our world. Our bodies are material, and will return to dust; but our souls are immaterial, and will not die. Arterial blood is that which flows from the heart through the arteries. An actor of a tragedy upon the stage is called a tragedian. A collegian is a student at college. God has made two great lights for our world – the sun and the moon; the sun is the superior light, and the moon is the inferior light. The exterior part of a house is the outside; the interior is that within.

WORDS OF TWO SYLLABLES, ACCENTED ON THE FIRST.

mus̱-lin, **linch**-pin, **re̱s**-in, **ro̱s**-in, **mat**-in, **sat**-in, **spav**-in, **sav**-in, **wel**-kin, **ten**-don, **Lat**-in, **côr**-don, **côr**-ban, **kitch**-en, **chick**-en, **mär**-tin, **slŏv**-en, **grif**-fin, **ûr**-chin, **dol**-phin, **pip**-pin, **här**-ness, **wit**-ness, **in**-gress, **coṉ**-gress, **prog**-ress, **fôr**-tress, **mis**-tress, **but**-tress, **rick**-ets, **spĭr**-its, **non**-plus, **grăm**-pus, **mўs**-tic, **brick**-bat, **pẽr**-fect, **ab**-ject, **ob**-ject, **sub**-ject, **vẽr**-dict, **rel**-ict, **dis**-trict, **in**-stiṉct, **pre**-çinct, **ġib**-bet, **shẽr**-bet, **dul**-çet, **lan**-cet, **buf**-fet, **fidġ**-et, **budġ**-et, **rack**-et, **latch**-et, **fresh**-et, **jack**-et, **plack**-et, **brack**-et, **tick**-et, **crick**-et, **wick**-et, **dock**-et, **pock**-et, **sock**-et, **buck**-et, **blaṉk**-et, **mär**-ket, **bas**-ket, **cas**-ket, **bris**-ket, **mus**-ket, **val**-et, **tab**-let, **trip**-let, **gob**-let, **côrse**-let, **mal**-let, **pal**-let, **wạl**-let, **bil**-let, **fil**-let, **skil**-let, **mil**-let, **col**-let, **gul**-let, **mul**-let, **cam**-let, **ham**-let, **ḡim**-let, **in**-let, **bon**-net, **sŏn**-net, **run**-net, **gär**-ment, **côr**-net, **hor**-net, **bûr**-net, **trum**-pet, **lap**-pet, **tip**-pet, **cär**-pet, **clăr**-et, **gar**-ret, **fẽr**-ret, **tŭr**-ret, **off**-set, **on**-set, **côr**-set, **bụl**-let.

The old Romans used to write in the Latin language. The linchpin secures the cartwheel to the axletree. Satin is a rich glossy silk. The falcon is a bird of the hawk kind. Ladies should know how to manage a kitchen. The little chickens follow the hen. The martin builds its nest near the house. A witness must tell all the truth in court. Our Congress meets once a year to make laws. The sloven seldom keeps his hands clean. The dolphin is a sea fish. A boy can harness a horse and hitch him to a wagon. We harness horses for the coach or gig. A good mistress will keep her house in order. A grampus is a large fish living in the sea. Boys love to make a great racket. Brickbats are pieces of broken bricks. When large hailstones fall on a house they make a great racket. The little boy likes to have a new jacket.

WORDS OF THREE SYLLABLES, ACCENTED ON THE SECOND.

re-**venġe**-ful, for-**ġet**-ful, e-**vent**-ful, neg-**lect**-ful, dis-**gust**-ful, dis-**trust**-ful, suc-**çess**-ful, un-**skill**-ful, col-**lect**-ĭve, pros-**pect**-ive, per-**spect**-ive, cor-**rec**-tive, in-**vec**-tive, vin-**dic**-tive, af-**flict**-ive, at-**tract**-ive, dis-**tin̲ct**-ive, sub-**jun̲ct**-ive, con-**junc**-tive, in-**duct**-ive, pro-**duct**-ive, con-**struct**-ive in-**çen**-tive, re-**ten**-tive, at-**ten**-tive, pre-**vent**-ive, in-**vent**-ive, per-**çep**-tive, pre-**s̲ump**-tive, de-**çep**-tive, as-**sẽrt**-ive, a-**bôr**-tive, dĭ-**ġest**-ive ex-**plu**-sive, com-**pul**-sive, im-**pul**-sive, re-**puls**-ive, de-**fen**-sive, of-**fen**-sive, sub-**vẽr**-sive, dis-**cûr**-sive, ex-**cur**-sive, in-**cur**-sive, suc-**çess**-ive, ex-**çess**-ive, pro-**gress**-ive, ex-**press**-ive, im-**press**-ive, sub-**mis**-sive, per-**mis**-sive, trans-**mis**-sive, in-**ac**-tive, de-**fect**-ive, ef-**fect**-ive, ob-**ject**-ive, e-**lect**-ive, ad-**he**-sive, co-**he**-sive, de-**çi**-sive, cor-**ro**-sive, a-**bu**-sive, con-**clu**-sive, ex-**clu**-sive, in-**clu**-sive, e-**lu**-sive, de-**lu**-sive, al-**lu**-sive, il-**lu**-sive, col-**lu**-sive, ob-**tru**-sive, in-**tru**-sive, pro-**tru**-sive, e-**va**-sive, per-**sua**-sive, as-**sua**-sive, dis-**sua**-sive, un-**fad**-ing, un-**feel**-ing.

We are apt to live forgetful of our continual dependence on the will of God. We should not trust our lives to unskillful doctors or drunken sailors. Washington was a successful general. A prospective view means a view before us. Prospective glasses are such as we look through, to see things at distance. Telescopes are perspective glasses. Rum, gin, brandy, and whisky are destructive enemies of mankind. They destroy more lives than wars, famine, and pestilence. An attentive boy will improve in learning. Putrid bodies emit an offensive smell. The drunkard's course is progressive; he begins by drinking a little, and shortens his life by drinking to excess. The slouch is an inactive slow animal. The President of the United States is elected once every four years. He is chosen by electors who are selected by the people of the different states.

WORDS OF FOUR SYLLABLES, ACCENTED ON THE FIRST.

jū-di-ca-tūre,   **ex**-pli-ca-tĭve,   **pal**-li-a-tive,   **spec**-ū-la-tive, **cop**-ū-la-tive,   **nom**-i-na-tive,   **op**-er-a-tive,   **fĭg**-ū-ra-tive, **veġ**-e-tā-tive,   **im**-i-tā-tive,   spir-it-ū-oŭs,   spir-it-ū-al,   **lin**-e-a-ment,   **vis**-ion-ary,   **mis**-sion-a-ry,   **dic**-tion-a-ry,   **stā**-ti-on-ary,   **est**-ū-a-ry,   **mẽr**-çe-na-ry,   **mes**-en-ter-y,   **car**-i-ca-tūre, **tem**-per-a-ture,   **lit**-er-a-ture,   **ag**-ri-cul-ture,   **hôr**-ti-cul-ture, **pres**-by-ter-y,   **des**-ul-to-ry,   **prom**-on-to-ry,   **pĕr**-emp-to-ry, **cas**-ū-is-try.

WORDS OF THREE SYLLABLES, ACCENTED ON THE FIRST.

rel-a-tĭve,   **ab**-la-tive,   **năr**-ra-tive,   **lax**-a-tive,   **ex**-ple-tive, **neg**-a-tive,   **prim**-i-tive,   **pûr**-ga-tive,   **len**-i-tive,   **tran**-si-tive, **sen**-si-tive,   **sub**-stan-tive,   **ad**-jec-tĭve,   **ob**-vi-oŭs,   **en**-vi-ous, **pẽr**-vi-ous,   **păt**-ū-lous,   **pĕr**-il-ous,   **scŭr**-ril-ous,   **mär**-vel-ous,   **friv**-o-lous,   **fab**-ū-lous,   **neb**-u-lous,   **glob**-u-lous,   **cred**-u-lous,   **sed**-u-lous,   **gland**-u-lous,   **pend**-u-lous,   **scrof**-u-lous,   **em**-u-lous,   **trem**-u-lous,   **pop**-u-lous,   **quĕr**-u̧-ous,   **in**-fa-mous,   **blas**-phe-mous,   **dē**-vi-ous,   **pre**-vi-ous,   **lī**-bel-ous.

WORDS OF TWO SYLLABLES, ACCENTED ON THE FIRST.

bon-fīre, **sam**-phire, **sap**-phire (*saf-fire*), **quag**-mire, **em**-pire, **um**-pire, **wel**-fâre, **härd**-ware, **wind**-pipe, **bag**-pipe, **hôrn**-pipe, **brim**-stone, **san̲**-guĭne, **pris**-tine, **trib**-ūne, **fôrt**-une, **land**-scāpe, **pam**-phlet, **proph**-et, **con**-tract, **spend**-thrift, **sûr**-fei̯t, **des**-cant (*n.*), **ped**-ant, **pend**-ant, **vẽr**-dant, **sol**-em*n*, **col**-um*n*, **vol**-ume, **an**-sw*e*r, **con̲**-qu*e*r, **côr**-sâir, **grand**-eūr, **phy̲s**-ics, **tac**-tics, **op**-tics, **cal**-end̲s, **fôr**-ward, **rich**-e̲s, **ash**-e̲s, **căl**-dron, **chăl**-dron, saf-fron, **mod**-ern, **brick**-ern, **lan**-tern, **çis**-tern, **pat**-tern, **slat**-tern, **bit**-tern, **tav**-ern, **gȯv**-ern, **stub**-born, **check**-er, **vic**-ar, **hĕi̯f**-er, **cham**-fer, **pärs**-lēy, **frĭĕnd**-ship, **härd**-ship, **wor**-ship (*wur-ship*), **stär**-līght, **mid**-night, **up**-right, **in**-sight, **fôr**-feit, **non**-sūit, **pri̲s**-*on*, **gär**-d*e̅n*, **mẽr**-chant, *d*ou̯b-let, *fŏr*e-head, **vine**-yard, **cu̲ck**-oo̅, **co̅o̅p**-er, **wạ**-ter, **mawk**-ish, **awk**-ward, **dwarf**-ish.

Brimstone is a mineral, which is dug from the earth. Children should answer questions politely. When the sun shines with clearness, it is the most splendid object that we can see. Potashes and pearlashes are made from common ash. Thirty-six bushels of coal make one chaldron. Saffron is a well-known garden plant. To keep the wind from blowing the candle out, we put it into a lantern. A wooden cistern is not very durable. Many persons spend too much time in taverns. Mules are sometimes very stubborn animals. The cuckoo visits us early in the spring. Carrots have long tapering roots. Twelve o'clock at night is midnight. A merchant is one who exports and imports goods, or who buys and sells goods especially by wholesale. Water flows along a decent by force of gravity. God governs the world in infinite wisdom; the Bible teaches us that it is our duty to worship him. It is a solemn thing to die and appear before God.

No. 85. – 96 Words

WORDS OF THREE SYLLABLES, ACCENTED ON THE FIRST.

chĕr-u̯-bim, **ser**-a-phim, **mär**-tyr-dom, **id**-i-om, **drȧw**-ing-room, **cat**-a-plasm, **os**-tra-çism, **gal**-li-çism, **skep**-ti-çism, **syl**-lo-ġism, **hĕr**-o-ism, **bär**-ba-rism, **as**-ter-ism, **aph**-o-rism, **mag**-net-ism, **por**-cu-pīne, **or**-i-ġin, **jav**-e-lin, **rav**-e-lin, **här**-le-quin, **myr**-mi-don (*mer-mi-don*), **lex**-i-con, **dec**-a-gon, **oc**-ta-gon, **pen**-ta-gon, **hep**-ta-gon, **hex**-a-gon, **pol**-y-gon, **cham**-pi-on, **pȯm**-pi-on, **scôr**-pi-on, **băr**-ris-ter, **dul**-çi-mer, **măr**-i-ner, **cŏr**-o-ner, **can**-is-ter, **min**-is-ter, **sin**-is-ter, **pres**-by-ter, **quick**-sil-ver, **met**-a-phor, **bach**-e-lor, **chan**-çel-or, **em**-per-or, **con**-quer-or, **sen**-a-tor, **ŏr**-a-tor, **coun**-sel-or, **ed**-it-or, **cred**-it-or, **mon**-i-tor, **an**-çes-tor, **păr**-a-mo̯ur, **cop**-per-as, **pol**-i-tics, **hem**-or-rhoid̲s, **as**-ter-oids, **rē**-qui-em, **di**-a-phragm, **cham**-ber-lain, **in**-ter-im, **mē**-te-or, **cā**-pi-as, **ca**-ri-ēs̲, **a**-ri-ēs̲, **u**-ni-corn, **pōr**-ti-co, **au**-dit-or, **al**-ma-nac, **wa̯**-ter-fal̯l, **quad**-ra-ture, **cȯv**-ert-ūre, **wa̯**-ter-man, **salt**-çel-lar, **ē**-qui-nox, **con**-ter-poise̲, **coun**-ter-märch, **coun**-ter-sīgn, **boun**-ti-fu̯l, **pow**-er-ful, **că**-ve-at, **bāy**-o-net, **rōse**-ma-ry, **fru̯it**-er-y, **fōōl**-er-y, **drȫll**-er-y, **straw**-ber-ry, **qua̯l**-i-ty, **la̯u**-re-ate, **house**-wife-ry, **bu̯oy**-an-çy, **dent**-ist-ry, **soph**-ist-ry, **pôr**-phy-ry, **pro**-phe-cy, **off**-scour-ing.

Cherubim is a Hebrew word in the plural number. True heroism may sometimes be shown in everyday employment. We ought to pity the mistakes of the ignorant, and try to correct them. The porcupine can raise his sharp quills, in the same manner as a hog erects his bristles. All mankind have their origin from God. A lexicon is a dictionary explaining words. Goliath was the champion of the Philistines. Pompions are now commonly called *pumpkins*. The sting of a scorpion is poisonous and fatal. Mariners are sailors who navigate the ships on the high seas. We put tea into a canister to keep its flavor. Quicksilver is heavier than lead; and it flows like a liquid, but without moisture. Abraham was the great ancestor of the Hebrews. Cicero was the most celebrated of the Roman Orators. If John sells goods to James on credit, John is the creditor, and James is the debtor.

WORDS OF TWO SYLLABLES, ACCENTED ON THE SECOND.

com-**pĕl**, dis-**pel**, ex-**pel**, re-**pel**, im-**pel**, pro-**pel**, fōre-**tell**, fṳl-**fĭll**, dis-**till**, in-**still**, ex-**till**, ex-**tōl**, Ja-**pan**, tre-**pan**, rat-**tan**, dĭ-**van**, be-**ḡin**, with-**in**, un-**pin**, hēre-**in**, a-**non**, up-**on**, per-**haps**, re-**vōlt**, a-**dult**, re-**sult**, in-**sult** (*v.*), con-**sult**, de-**cant**, re-**cant**, a-**bĕt**, ca-**det**, be-**ḡet**, for-**ḡet**, re-**ḡret**, be-**set**, un-**fit**, sub-**mit**, e-**mit**, re-**mit**, trans-**mit**, com-**mit**, per-**mit**, re-**fit**, ac-**quit**, out-**wit**, re-**act**, en-**act**, com-**pact**, re-**fract**, in-**fract**, sub-**tract**, de-**tract**, re-**tract**, con-**tract** (*v.*), pro-**tract**, ab-**stract** (*v.*), dis-**tract**, ex-**tract** (*v.*), trans-**act**, re-**ject**, in-**ject**, pro-**ject** (*v.*), tra-**ject** (*v.*), ob-**ject** (*v.*), sub-**ject** (*v.*), de-**ject**, de-**fect**, af-**fect**, ef-**fect**, in-**fect**, e-**lect**, se-**lect**, re-**flect**, e-**ject**, in-**flect**, neg-**lect**, col-**lect**, con-**nect**, re-**spect**, sus-**pect**, e-**rect**, cor-**rect**, di-**rect**, de-**tect**, pro-**tect**, ad-**dict**, pre-**dict**, af-**flict**, in-**flict**, con-**flict** (*v.*), de-**pict**, re-**strict**, suc-**cinct**, dis-**tinct**, ex-**tinct**, de-**funct**, de-**coct**, de-**duct**, in-**duct**, con-**duct** (*v.*), ob-**struct**, in-**struct**, con-**struct**, re-**plant**, im-**plant**, sup-**plant**, dis-**plant**, trans-**plant**, le-**vant**, de-**sçent**, la-**ment**, ạug-**ment** (*v.*), af-**fix** (*v.*), pre-**fix** (*v.*), in-**fix**, trans-**fix**, pro-**lix**, com-**mix**, ce-**ment** (*v.*), con-**sent**, fo-**ment**, fer-**ment**, dis-**sent**, in-**tent**, con-**tent**, ex-**tent**, e-**vĕnt**, re-**prĭnt**, pre-**tĕxt**, re-**lăx**, per-**plĕx**, an-**nex**, de-**vour**, a-**loud**, com-**plāint**, re-**straint**, con-**straint**, dis-**traint**, ac-**quaint**, dis-**joint** a-**noint**, ac-**count**, al-**low**, en-**dow**, ba-**shạw**, be-**dew**, es-**chew**, re-**new**, fōre-**show**, be-**lōw**, be-**stōw**, af-**frȯnt**, con-**frȯnt**, re-**prọve**, dis-**prọve**, im-**prọve**, re-**plȳ**.

Heavy clouds foretell a shower of rain. The rattan is a long slender reed that grows in Java. Good children will submit to the will of their parents. Let all our precepts be succint and clear. We elect men to make our laws for us. Idle children neglect their books when young, and thus reject their advantage. The little busy bees collect honey from flowers; they never neglect their employment. The neck connects the head with the body. Children should respect and obey their parents. Parents protect and instruct their children. Satan afflicted Job with sore boils. The lady instructs her pupils how to spell and read. Teachers should try to implant good ideas in the minds of their pupils. The kind mother laments the death of dear a infant. A bashaw is a title of honor among the Turks; a governor. The word is now commonly spelled *pasha*. "If sinners entice thee, consent thou not," but withdraw from their company.

No. 87. – 107 Words

WORDS OF TWO SYLLABLES, ACCENTED ON THE FIRST.

fĭs-cal, of-fal, fôrm-al, dis-mal, chär-coal, pit-cōal, mŏr-al, çen-tral, vas-sal, men-tal, môr-tal, ves-tal, rev-el, gam-brel, tim-brel, mȯn-grel, quar-rel, squĭr-rel, min-strel, hand-sel, chis-el, dam-sel, trav-ail, ten-dril, ster-ĭle, nos-tril, tran-quil, hand-bill, wind-mill, gam-bol, sўm-bol, fŏot-stool, pis-tol, hand-ful, venġe-ful wish-ful, bash-ful, skill-ful, help-ful, bliss-ful, fret-ful, hurt-ful, wist-ful, lust-ful, mad-am, mill-dam, bed-lam, buck-ram, bạl-sam, em-blem prob-lem, sўs-tem, pil-grim, king-dom, sel-dom, ĕarl-dom, wis-dom, ven-mom, mush-rōom, tran-som, blos-som, phan-tom, sўmp-tom, cus-tom, bot-tom, plat-form, sär-casm, mī-asm, fan-tasm, sŏph-ism, bap-tism, ăl-um, vel-lum, min-im, nos-trum, frus-trum, tur-ban, or-gan, ôr-phan, horse-man, cär-man, pen-man, ġĕr-man, chûrch-man, work-man, kings-man, hunts-man, fŏot-man, grog-ram, cap-stan, sil-van, tur-ban, fam-ĭne, sär-dïne, en-ġĭne, mar-lĭne, ĕr-mĭne, ver-min, jas-mĭne, rap-ĭne, doc-trĭne, des-tĭne, phăl-anx sī-ren, in-grāin, pär-boil, breech-ing (*brĭch-ing*).

56

Charcoal is wood charred or burned to a coal. Pit coal is dug from the earth for fuel. Never quarrel with your playmates. A squirrel will climb a tree quicker than a boy. A ship is a vessel with three masts. The nose has two nostrils through which we breathe and smell. We sit in chairs and put or feet on a foot-stool. The farmer sows his grain by handfuls. Children may be helpful to their parents. Try to be a skillful workman (*wûrk-man*). An artist is one who is skillful in some art. The fox is said to be an artful animal. Little boys and girls must not be fretful. A kingdom is a country ruled by a king. A wise man will make a good use of his knowledge. A chill is a symptom of a fever. The chewing of tobacco is a useless habit.

No. 88. – 69 Words

WORDS OF TWO SYLLABLES, ACCENTED ON THE FIRST.

bōat-swain, **chiēf**-tain, **neū**-ter, **pew**-ter, **bēa**-ver, **clēav**-er, **sew**-er, **lāy**-er, **prâyer**-ful, **māy**-or, **ō**-yer, **col**-ter, **mō**-hair, **trāi**-tor, **hōme**-ward, **out**-ward, **wā**-ġes̲, **breech**-es [*brĭch-ĕz*], **crāy**-on, **hōme**-spun, **snōw**-drop, **fōre**-top, **māin**-top, **cham**-ber, **shōul**-der, **mōuld**-er, **rān**-ġer, **mān**-ġer, **strān**-ġer, **dān**-ġer, **çī**-pher, **twi**-light, **mōōn**-light, **dāy**-light, **skȳ**-light, **fore**-sight, **pōr**-trait, **bōw**-sprit, **ti**-dings, **do̤**-ings, **mōōr**-ings̲, **fire**-ärms̲, **twee**-zers̲, **heed**-less, **ē**-gress, **rē**-gress, **cȳ**-press, **fā**-mous, **spī**-nous, **vi**-nous, **sē**-rous, **pō**-rous, **ni**-trous, **griēv**-ous, **trēat**-ment, **wāin**-scot, **māin**-mast, **hīnd**-mōst, **fore**-most, **sīgn**-post, **bȳ**-la̤w, **rain**-bōw, **flȳ**-blōw, **cā**-lix, **phē**-nix, **rē**-flux, **week**-dāy, **Fri**-day, **pay**-day.

The boatswain takes care of the ship's rigging. Pewter is made chiefly of tin and lead. The fur of the beaver makes the best hats. The weaver weaves yarn into cloth. Oak trees produce acorns, and little animals eat them. Spring is the first season of the year. The planet Saturn has a bright ring around it. The mason puts a layer of mortar between bricks. The mayor of a city is the chief magistrate. Judas was a traitor: he betrayed his master; that is, he gave him up to his enemies. The hair that is over the forehead is called a foretop. The farmer feeds his horse in a manger. We should be attentive and helpful to strangers. Firearms were not known a few hundred years ago. Intemperance is a grievous sin of our country. Parents deserve the kind treatment of children. The United States have a large extent of seacoast. The rainbow is a token that the world will not be drowned again; but the regular seasons will continue. A portrait is a picture bearing the likeness of a person. Mohair is made of camels' hair. Pay the laborer his wages when he has done his work. Prayer is a duty, but it in vain to pray without a sincere desire of heart to obtain what we pray for; to repeat the words of a prayer, without such desire, is solemn mockery.

No. 89. – 91 Words

WORDS OF TWO SYLLABLES, ACCENTED ON THE SECOND.

du-**ress**, a-**mass**, re-**pass**, sur-**pass**, cui-**răss**, mo-**rass**, ac-**çess**, re-**çess**, ex-**çess**, con-**fess**, un-**less**, ca-**ress**, ad-**dress**, re-**dress**, ag-**gress**, trans-**gress**, de-**press**, re-**press**, im-**press**, op-**press**, sup-**press**, ex-**press**, dis-**tress**, as-**sess**, pos-**sess**, a-**miss**, re-**miss**, dis-**miss**, em-**boss**, a-**cross**, dis-**cuss**, ac-**cost**, ex-**haust**, ro-**bust**, ad-**just**, un-**just**, in-**trust**, dis-**trust**, mis-**trust**, un-**mixt**, be-**twixt**, a-**vĕrt**, sub-**vert**, re-**vert**, di-**vert**, con-**vert** (*v.*) per-**vert** (*v.*), a-**lert**, in-**ert**, ex-**pert**, de-**sert**, in-**sert**, as-**sert**, es-**côrt** (*v.*), de-**port**, re-**port**, im-**pōrt** (*v.*) com-**port**, sup-**port**, trans-**port** (*v.*), re-**sôrt**, as-**sort**, de-**tort**, re-**tort**, con-**tort**, dis-**tort**, ex-**tort** (*v.*), un-**hurt**, con-**trast** (*v*), a-**midst**, in-**fest**, sug-**ġest**, dī-**ġest** (*v.*), be-**hest**, mo-**lest**, ar-**rest**, de-**test**, con-**test** (*v.*), pro-**test** (*v.*), at-**test**, dĭ-**vest**, in-**vest**, be-**quest**, re-**quest**, sub-**sist**, de-**sist**, con-**sist**, per-**sist**, as-**sist**, un-**twist**, re-**sist**.

The miser amasses riches, and keeps his money where it will do no good. Confess your sins and forsake them. Unless you study you will not learn. The fond mother loves to caress her babe. Paul addressed Felix upon the subject of future judgment. Bridges are made across rivers. An unjust judge may give a false judgment. William Tell was an expert archer. The fearful man will desert his post in battle. Wolves infest new countries and destroy the sheep. We detest robbers and pirates. The wicked transgress the laws of God.

No. 90. – 57 Words

WORDS OF FOUR SYLLABLES, ACCENTED ON THE SECOND.

WORDS IN FINAL SYLLABLE **ATE**, IF UNMARKED HAVE **NOT** ITS FULL LONG SOUND

trī-**en**-ni-al, lĭx-**iv**-i-al, mil-**lĕn**-ni-al, quạd-**ren**-ni-al, per-**en**-ni-al, sep-**ten**-ni-al, sex-**ten**-ni-al, ter-**res**-tri-al, col-**lat**-er-al, de-**lĭr**-i-um, lix-**iv**-i-um, e-**ques**-tri-an, il-**lit**-er-ate, a-**dul**-ter-āte, as-**sev**-er-āte, de-**çem**-vi-rate, e-**lab**-o-rate, cor-**rob**-o-rāte, in-**vig**-or-āte, de-**lin**-e-āte, e-**vap**-o-rāte, in-**ac**-cu-rate, ca-**paç**-i-tāte, re-**sus**-çi-tāte, de-**bil**-i-tāte, fa-**çil**-i-tāte, de-**cap**-i-tāte, per-**çip**-i-tāte, in-**def**-i-nĭte, e-**rad**-i-cāte, çer-**tif**-i-cate, in-**del**-i-cate, pre-**var**-i-cāte, ạu-**then**-ti-cāte, do-**mes**-ti-cāte, prog-**nŏs**-ti-cāte, in-**tox**-i-cāte, re-**çip**-ro-cāte, e-**quiv**-o-cāte, in-**val**-i-dāte, con-**sŏl**-i-dāte, in-**tim**-i-dāte, di-**lap**-i-dāte, ac-**com**-mo-dạte, com-**men**-su-rate (*com-**mĕn**-shoo-rate*), in-**ves**-ti-gāte, re-**tal**-i-āte, con-**çil**-i-āte, ca-**lŭm**-ni-āte, de-**mŏn**-stra-tĭve, de-**rĭv**-a-tĭve, con-**sērv**-a-tĭve, de-**fin**-i-tĭve, in-**fin**-i-tĭve, re-**trib**-ū-tĭve, con-**sec**-ū-tĭve, e<u>x</u>-**ec**-ū-tĭve.

A triennial assembly is one that continues three years, or is held once in three years. The Parliament of Great Britain is septennial, that is, formed once in seven years. The sun will evaporate water on the ground. It is difficult to eradicate vicious habits. Never retaliate an injury, even on an enemy. Never equivocate or prevaricate, but tell the plain truth. A definitive sentence is one that is final. Liquors that intoxicate are to be avoided as poison. Love and friendship conciliate favor and esteem.

No. 91. – 116 Words

WORDS OF TWO SYLLABLES, ACCENTED ON THE SECOND.

ac-**quīre**, ad-**mire**, as-**pire**, re-**spire**, trans-**pire**, in-**spire**, con-**spire**, per-**spire**, sus-**pire**, ex-**pire**, de-**s̲ire**, re-**tire**, en-**tire**, at-**tire**, re-**quire**, in-**quire**, es-**quire**, a-**dōre**, be-**fore**, de-**plore**, im-**plore**, ex-**plore**, re-**store**, se-**cūre**, pro-**cure**, en-**dure**, ab-**jure**, ad-**jure**, al-**lure**, de-**mure**, im-**mure**, ma-**nure**, in-**ure**, im-**pure**, as-**s̲ure** (-*shur*), ma-**tūre**, de-**çēase**, de-**crease**, in-**crease**, pre-**çīse**, con-**çise**, mo-**rōse**, jo-**cose**, im-**brue**, dis-**cōurse**, ū-**nīte**, ig-**nite**, in-**vite**, re-**mōte**, pro-**mote**, de-**note**, re-**fūte**, con-**fute**, sa-**lute**, dĭ-**lute**, pol-**lute**, vo-**lute**, com-**pute**, de-**pute**, dis-**pute**, be-**hāve**, en-**slave**, for-**gave**, en-**grave**, de-**prave**, sub-**dūe**, in-**due**, a-**chiēve**, ag-**grieve**, re-**prieve**, re-**trieve**, re-**çeive**, per-**çēive**, de-**rive**, de-**prive**, ar-**rive**, con-**trive**, re-**vive**, sur-**vive**, un-**glūe**, al-**lūde**, re-**bāte**, un-**true**, re-**mọve**, be-**ho͞ove**, ap-**prọve**, ac-**crue**, dis-**sēize**, ap-**prīs̲e**, as-**size**, re-**liēf**, be-**ho͞of**, a-**loof**, re-**proof**, im-**pēach**, ap-**prōach**, en-**croach**, re-**proach**, be-**seech**, con-**ġēal**, re-**peal**, ap-**peal**, re-**veal**, ġen-**teel**, as-**sāil**, out-**sail**, de-**tail** (*v.*), re-**tail** (*v*), cur-**tail**, a-**vail**, pre-**vail**, be-**wail**, con-**trōl**, en-**roll**, pa-**trol**, ob-**līġe**.

WORDS OF TWO SYLLABLES, ACCENTED ON THE SECOND.

be-**tween**, ca-**reen**, cam-**pāign**, ar-**raign**, or-**dain**, dis-**dain**, re-**gain**, com-**plain**, ex-**plain**, a-**main**, ab-**stain**, do-**main**, re-**frain**, re-**strain**, dis-**train**, con-**strain**, con-**tain**, ob-**tain**, de-**tain**, per-**tain**, at-**tain**, dis-**tain**, su-**stain**, ca-**jole**, con-**sole**, pis-**tole**, mis-**r̲u̲le**, hu-**māne**, in-**sane**, ob-**sçēne**, ga̲n̲-**grene**, ter-**rene**, con-**vene**, com-**bīne**, de-**fīne**, re-**fīne**, con-**fine**, sal-**ine**, de-**cline**, ca-**nine**, re-**pine**, su-**pine**, en-**shrine**, dĭ-**vine**, en-**twine**, pōst-**pōne**, de-**throne**, a-**tone**, je-**jūne**, trī-**une**, com-**mune**, at-**tune**, es-**cāpe**, e-**lōpe**, de-**clâre**, in-**snare**, de-**spair**, pre-**pare**, re-**pair**, com-**pare**, im-**pair**, sin-**çēre**, ad-**here**, co-**here**, aus-**tere**, re-**vere**, se-**vere**, com-**peer**, ca-**reer**, bre-**viēr**, bab-**o͞on**, buf-**foon**, dra-**goon**, doub-**loon**, bal-**loon**, gal-**loon**, shal-**loon**, plat-**oon**, lam-**poon**, här-**poon**, mon-**soon**, bas-**soon**, fes-**toon**, pol-**troon**, di̲s̲-**ōwn**, un-*knōwn*, un-**sōwn**, a-**d̲o̲**, out-**d̲o̲**, a-**gō**, a-**līg̲h̲t**, de-**lig̲h̲t**, a-**rig̲h̲t**, af-**frig̲h̲t**, a-**wāit**, de-**çēit**, con-**çeit**, a-**m̲o̲ur**, con-**t̲o̲ur**, be-**sīde̲s̲**, re-**çēipt**, re-**liēve**.

When the moon passes between the earth and the sun, we call it new; but you must not think that it is more new at that time, than it was when it was full; we mean, that it begins anew to show us the side on which the sun shines. God ordained the sun to rule the day and the moon to give light by night. The laws of nature are sustained by the immediate presence and agency of God. The heavens declare an Almighty power that made them. The science of astronomy explains the causes of day and night and why the sun, and moon, and stars appear to change their places in the heavens. Air contains the vapors that rise from earth; and it sustains them, till the fall in dews, and in showers of rain, or in snow or hail.

Grapevines entwine their tendrils round the branches of trees. Laws are made to restrain the bad, and project the good. Glue will make pieces of wood adhere. The careful ant prepares food for the winter. We often compare childhood to the morning: morning is the first part of the day, and childhood is the first stage of human life. Do not postpone for tomorrow what you should do today. A harpoon is an instrument for striking whales. Monsoon is a wind in the East Indies that blows six months from one quarter, and then six months from another. Be careful to keep your house in good repair. Refrain from all evil, keep no company with immoral men. Never complain of unavoidable calamities. Let your words be sincere, and never deceive. A poltroon is an arrant coward, and deserves the contempt of all brave men. Never practice deceit for this is sinful. To revere a father is to regard him with fear mingled with respect and affection. Brevier is a small kind of printing letter.

No. 93. – 61 Words

WORDS OF FOUR SYLLABLES, THE FULL ACCENT ON THE THIRD AND A WEAK ON THE FIRST.

an-te-**çēd**-ent, dis-a-**gree**-ment, çĩr-cum-**jā**-çent, re-en-**fōrçe**-ment, pre-en-**gāġe**-ment, en-ter-**tāin**-ment, in-co-**hēr**-ent, in-de-**çī**-sive, su-per-**vi**-s̠or, con-ser-**vā**-tor, des-pe-**ra**-do, bas-ti-**na**-do, brag-ga-**dō**-çi-o (-*shi-o*), mis-de-**mēan**-or, ap-pa-**rā**-tus, af-fi-**da**-vit, e̱x-ul-**ta**-tion, ad-a-**man**-tĭne, man-ū-**fact**-ūre, su-per-**struct**-ure, per-ad-**vent**-ure, met-a-**môr**-phōse, in-nu-**en**-do, su-per-**cär**-go, in-ter-**nŭn**-çi-o (-*shi-o*), är-ma-**dĭl**-lo, man-i-**fĕs**-to, laz-a-**ret**-to, dis-en-**cum**-ber, pred-e-**çes**-sor, in-ter-**çes**-sor, mal-e-**făc**-tor, ben-e-**fac**-tor, met-a-**phy̆s̠**-ics, math-e-**mat**-ics, dis-in-**hĕr**-it, ev-a-**nes**-çent, con-va-**les**-çent, ef-flo-**res**-çent, cor-res-**pond**-ent, in-de-**pend**-ent, re-im-**bûrse**-ment, dis-con-**tent**-ment, om-ni-**pres**-ent, in-ad-**vẽrt**-ent, pre-e̱x-**ist**-ent, in-ter-**mit**-tent, in-ter-**măr**-ry, ō-ver-**shad**-ōw, ac-çi-**dent**-al, in-ci-**dent**-al, o-ri-**ent**-al, fun-da-**ment**-al, or-na-**men**-tal, sac-ra-**ment**-al, reġ-i-**ment**-al, det-ri-**ment**-al, mon-ū-**ment**-al, in-stru̱-**ment**-al, hor-i-**zŏn**-tal, dis-a-**vow**-al.

Gage is a French word, and signifies to pledge. The banks engage to redeem their notes with species, and they are obliged to fulfill their engagements. To preëngaged means to engage beforehand. I am not at liberty to purchase goods when they are preëngaged to another person. To disengage, is to free from a previous engagement. A mediator is a third person who interposes to adjust a dispute between parties at variance. How can a young man cleanse his ways? Oh, how I love thy law!

No. 94. – 101 Words

WORDS OF THREE SYLLABLES, ACCENTED ON THE FIRST.
LEFT UNMARKED FOR EXERCISE IN NOTATION

çin-na-mon, et-y-mon, grid-i-ron, and-i-ron, skel-e-ton, sim-ple-ton, buf-fa-lo, cap-ri-corn, cal-i-co, in-di-go, ver-ti-go, cal-i-ber, bed-cham-ber, çin-na-bar, of-fi-çer, col-an-der, lav-en-der, prov-en-der, çyl-in-der, in-te-ġer, scav-en-ger, har-bin-ġer, por-rin-ġer, stom-a-cher, ob-se-quines, prom-i-ses, com-pass-es, in-dex-es, am-ber-gris, em-phas-is, di-o-çese o-li-o, o-ver-plus, nu-cle-us, ra-di-us, ter-min-nus, blun-der-buss, syl-la-bus, in-cu-bus, ver-bi-aġe, sir-i-us, cal-a-mus, mit-ti-mus, du-te-ous, a-que-ous, du-bi-ous, te-di-ous, o-di-ous, stu-di-ous, co-pi-ous, se-ri-ous, cu-ri-ous, fu-ri-ous, spu-ri-ous, lu-mi-nous, glu-ti-nous, ru-in-ous, lu-di-crous, dan-ġer-ous, hid-e-ous, in-fa-mous, ster-to-rous, nu-mer-ous, o-dor-ous, hu-mor-ous, ri-ot-ous, trai-tor-ous, per-vi-ous, treach-er-ous, haz-ard-ous, pit-e-ous, plen-te-ous, im-pi-ous, vil-lain-ous, mem-bra-nous, rav-en-ous, om-i-nous, res-in-ous, glut-ton-ous, bar-ba-rous, ul-cer-ous, slan-der-ous, pon-der-ous, mur-der-ous, ġen-er-ous, pros-per-ous, ran-cor-ous, rig-or-ous vig-or-ous, val-or-ous, am-or-ous, clam-or-ous, tim-or-ous, sul-phur-ous, ven-tu-rous, rapt-ur-ous, ar-du-ous, mis-chiev-ous, stren-u-ous, sin-u-ous, tyr-an-nous.

No. 95. – 65 Words

WORDS OF TWO SYLLABLES, ACCENTED ON THE SECOND.

ap-**pēase**, dis-**please**, dis-**ease**, e-**rāse**, pre-**mīse**, sur-**mise**, de-**spise**, a-**rise**, com-**prise**, chas-**tise**, ad-**vise**, de-**vise**, re-**vise**, dis-**ḡuīse**, fōre-**clōse**, in-**close**, dis-**close**, re-**pose**, pro-**pose**, im-**pose**, com-**pose**, trans-**pose**, a-**būse** (*v.*), ac-**cuse**, ex-**cuse** (*v.*), re-**fuse**, ef-**fuse**, dif-**fuse**, suf-**fuse**, in-**fuse**, con-**fuse**, a-**muse**, re-**cruit**, de-**fēat**, es-**chēat**, re-**pēat**, en-**trēat**, re-**trēat**, un-**lōōse**, de-**bauch**, re-**call**, be-**fall**, with-**al**, fore-**stall**, fore-**warn**, de-**fault**, as-**sault**, pa-**paw**, a-**sleep**, en-**dēar**, re-**hear**, be-**smear**, ap-**pear**, tat-**tōō**, en-**trap**, in-**wrap**, un-**ship**, e-**quip**, en-**camp**, un-**stop**, ū-**sûrp**, un-**clasp**, de-**bär**, un-**bar**, ap-**plause**.

No. 96. – 110 Words

MONOSYLLABLES IN th, HAS THE ASPIRATED SOUND, AS IN THINK, THIN.

theme, three, thane, thrīçe, thrōne, thrōw, truth, youth, hēath, Ruth, shēath, bōth, oath, quoth, growth, blowth, forth, fourth, thiēf, thieve, fāith, thīgh, thrōat, dȯth, thōle, throe, throve, teeth, threw (*thrōō*), thrive, mēath, thrĕad, thresh thrift, thrust, thrum, dĕpth, width, filth, frith, plinth, spilth, thwack, broth, cloth, froth, lōth, mŏth, troth, nôrth, sloth, thought, thôrn, thrŏb, throng, thĭng, think, thin, thank, thick, thrill, thumb, thump, lĕngth, strength, hăth, wĭthe, thătch, thill, theft, thrush, tilth, smith, truths, thaw, thrall, thwart, warmth, swatch päth, bäth, läth wräth, heärth, tooth, bĭrth, mirth, third, thirst, thirl, worth, mȯnth, south, mouth, drouth.

IN THE FOLLOWING, THE NOUNS HAVE THE ASPIRATED, AND THE VERBS THE VOCAL SOUND OF th.

Nouns: clŏth, bath, mouth, brĕath, shēath, wreath, swäth, teeth.

Verbs: clōthe, bāthe, mouth, brēathe, shēathe, wreathe, swāthe, teeth.

Cambric is a kind of thin muslin. A fire was burning on the hearth. Many kings have been thrown down from their thrones. A tiger has great strength, and is very ferocious. A manly youth will speak the truth. Keep your mouth clean, and save your teeth. The water in the canal is four feet in depth. A toothbrush is good to brush your teeth. The length of a square figure is equal to its breadth. The breadth of an oblong square is less than its length. Plants will not thrive among thorns and weeds. The thresher threshes grain, as wheat, rye, and oats. A severe battle thins the ranks of an army. Youth may be thoughtful, but it is not very common. One good action is worth many good thoughts. A piece of cloth, if good, is worth what it will bring. Drunkards are worthless fellows, and despised. Bathing houses have baths to bathe in. We breathe fresh air at every breath.

No. 97. – 72 Words

WORDS OF TWO SYLLABLES, ACCENTED ON THE FIRST.

băl-last, **fĭl**-bert, **cŏn**-çert, **ĕf**-fort, **pûr**-pōrt, **tran**-script, **con**-script, **ba͟nk**-rupt, **eld**-est, **neph**-ew (*nef-yụ*), **sin**-ew, **land**-tax, **sy̆n**-tax, **in**-dex, **comp**-lex, **vĕr**-tex, **vôr**-tex, **con**-vex, **lăr**-y̆͟nx, **af**-flux, **con**-flux, **ĕf**-flux, **in**-flux, **con**-text, **bōw**-line, **mid**-day, **Sun**-day, **Mon**-day, **Tues**-day, **We***d***nes**-day, **Thurs**-day, **mid**-wāy, **gang**-way, **päth**-way, **es**-say, **cȯm**-fort, **cȯv**-ert, **bȯm**-bast, **cōurt**-ship, **flim**-sy, **clum**-sy, **swel**-try, **vĕr**-y, **driz**-zly, **ḡir͟s**-ly, **g***u***ilt**-y, **pan**-s͟y, **fren**-zy, **quĭn**-s͟y, **ġip**-sy, **ti**-psy, **drop**-sy, **scrub**-by, **shrub**-by, **stub**-by, **nut**-meg, **ŏff**-ing, **stuff**-ing, **bri**-ny, **nōse**-gāy, **hēar**-say, **drēar**-y, **wēar**-y, **quē**-ry, **dāi**-ly, **dai**-sy, **ēa**-sy, **trēa**-ty, **frail**-ty, **dain**-ty, **cām**-bric, **shōul**-der.

No. 98. – 37 Words

WORDS OF TWO SYLLABLES, ACCENTED ON THE FIRST.

THE O OF THE DIGRAPH HAS ITS FIRST OR LONG SOUND.

bor-rōw, **el**-bow, **fel**-low, **fol**-low **căl**-low, **mĕad**-ow, **shad**-ow, **hal**-low, **bel**-low, **bil**-low, **hol**-low, **ăr**-row, **făr**-row, **năr**-row, **mal**-low, **pil**-low, **min**-now, **măr**-row, **hăr**-row, **spăr**-row, **yăr**-row, **yel**-low, **tăl**-low, **fal**-low, **shal**-low, **fur**-row, **wid**-ow, **win**-dōw, **win**-now, **wil**-low, **mil**-low, **mel**-low, **mŏr**-row, **sŏr**-row, **bŭr**-row, **swạl**-low, **wạl**-low.

Filberts are small nuts growing in hedges. A ship or boat must have a ballast to prevent it from oversetting. The sinews are the tendons that move the joints of the body. The tendon of the heel is the main sinew that moves the foot. From the shoulder to the elbow to the hand there are two bones in the arm, but from the elbow to the hand there are two bones. The light is on one side of the body, and the shadow on the other. In old times there were no glass for windows. The farmer winnows chaff from the grain. The callow young means the young bird before it has feathers. Fallow ground is that which has lain without being plowed and sowed. A shallow river will not float ships. Some places on the Ohio River are at times too shallow for large boats. Cattle in South America are hunted for their hides and tallow.

No. 99. – 137 Words

WORDS OF TWO SYLLABLES, ACCENTED ON THE FIRST.

rās-ūre, sēiz-ure, trēa-tĭse, līke-wise, dōor-case, stair-case, sēa-hôrse, brī-dal, feū-dal, ōat-meal, spī-ral, flō-ral, neū-tral, plū-ral, pōrt-al, brū-tal, vī-tal, ē-qual, sûr-feĭt, ān-ġel, ān-çient, wēa-sel, jew-el, new-el, crew-el (*krу-el*), trē-foil, wee-vil, snōw-ball, brīde-well, mōle-hill, fē-rīne, mīnd-ful, pēace-ful, hāte-ful, wake-ful, guīle-ful, dole-ful, shame-ful, bane-ful, tūne-ful, hōpe-ful, câre-ful, īre-ful, dire-ful, ūse-ful, grāte-ful, spīte-ful, wāste-ful, fāith-ful, youth-ful, gāin-ful, pain-ful, spōon-ful, mōurn-ful, fēar-ful, cheer-ful, rīght-ful, frŭit-ful, bōast-ful, aw-ful, law-ful, plāy-dāy, thrall-dom, watch-man, watch-ful, free-dom, bo-som, luke-warm, trī-form, glōw-worm, dē-ism, ōak-um, stra-tum, sēa-man, free-man, fōre-man, yeō-man, sāles-man, spōrts-man, brāin-pan, mŏn-ster, free-stōne, mīle-stone, grāve-stone, hāil-stone, hȳ-phen, au-tum*n*, au-burn, sauçe-pan, war-fare, faç-ĭle, sērv-ĭle, dac-tўl, duc-tĭle, mis-sĭle, doç-ĭle, rep-tĭle, fēr-tĭle, hos-tĭle, sex-tĭle, flex-ĭle, vērd-ūre, ôrd-ure, fig-ure, in-jure, con-jure, pēr-jure, plĕas-ure, mĕas-ure, trĕas-ure, çen-sure, press-ure, fis-sure, fract-ure, cult-ure, fixt-ure, cam-phor, grand-sīre, prom-ĭse, an-ĭse, tur-kēy, mor-tĭse, prac-tĭce, trav-erse, ad-verse, pack-hôrse, ref-ūse, man-dāte, ag-ate, leg-ate, frig-ate, in-grāte, phўs-ic, jon-quil, sub-tĭle, fer-ule, con-dor.

A treatise is a written composition on some particular subject. Oatmeal is a meal of oats, and is very good food. An egg is nearly oval in shape. A newel is the post round which winding stairs are formed. Crewel is a kind of yarn, or twisted worsted. Trefoil is a grass of three leaves. Weevils in grain are very destructive vermin. To be useful is more honorable than to be showy. A hyphen is a little mark between syllables or words, thus hy-phen, attorney-general. A spiral line winds and rises at the same time. It is a mean act to deface the figure on milestone. No pleasure is equal that of a quiet conscience. Let us lay up for ourselves treasures in heaven where neither moth nor rust can corrupt.

No. 100. – 75 Words

WORDS OF FOUR SYLLABLES, ACCENTED ON THE SECOND.

ad-**vent**-ūr-oŭs, a-**non**-y-mous, sў-**non**-y-mous, un-**ġen**-er-ous, mag-**nan**-i-mous, ū-**nan**-i-mous, as-**păr**-a-gus, pre-**çip**-i-toŭs, ne-**çes**-si-tous, am-**phib**-i-ous, mĭ-**rac**-ū-lous, a-**nal**-o-gous, per-**fĭd**-i-ous, fas-**tid**-i-ous, in-**sid**-i-ous, in-**vid**-ious, con-**spic**-u-ous, per-**spic**-u-ous, pro-**mis**-cū-ous, as-**sid**-ū-ous, am-**big**-ū-ous, con-**tig**-ū-ous, mel-**lif**-lu-ous, su-**pẽr**-flu-ous, in-**ġen**-ū-ous, con-**tin**-ū-ous, in-**con**-gru̯-ous, im-**pet**-ū-ous, tu-**mult**-u-ous, vo-**lupt**-u-ous, tem-**pest**-u-ous, sig-**nif**-i-cant, ex-**trav**-a-gant, pre-**dom**-i-nant, in-**tol**-er-ant ī-**tin**-er-ant, in-**hab**-i-tant, con-**com**-i-tant, ir-**rel**-e-vant, be-**ne**-fi-çent, mag-**nif**-i-çent, co-in-**çi**-dent, non-**res**-i-dent, im-**prov**-i-dent, in-**tel**-li-ġent, ma-**lev**-o-lent, be-**nev**-o-lent, pre-**dic**-a-ment, dis-**par**-aġe-ment, en-**cour**-aġe-ment, en-**fran**-chĭse-ment, dis-**fan**-chĭse-ment, en-**tan**-gle-ment, ac-**knŏwl**-edġ-ment, es-**tab**-lish-ment, em-**bel**-lish-ment, ac-**com**-plish-ment, as-**ton**-ish-ment, re-**lin**-quish-ment, im-**ped**-i-ment, ha-**bil**-i-ment, im-**pris**-*on*-ment, em-**băr**-rass-ment, in-**teg**-ū-ment, e-**mol**-ū-ment, pre-**em**-i-nent, in-**con**-ti-nent, im-**pẽr**-ti-nent, in-**dif**-fer-ent, ir-**rev**-er-ent, om-**nip**-o-tent, mel-**lif**-lu-ent, çĩr-**cum**-flu-ent, ac-**cou̯**-ter-ment, com-**mū**-ni-cant.

An anonymous author writes without signing his name to his composition. Synonymous words have the same signification. Very few words in English are exactly synonymous. Precipitous signifies steep; the East and West rocks in New Haven are precipitous. An amphibious animal can live in different elements. The frog lives in the air, and can live in water for a long time. A miraculous event is one that cannot take place according to the ordinary laws of nature. It can only take place by the agency of divine power. Assiduous study will accomplish almost any thing that is within human power. An integument is a cover. The skin is the integument of animal bodies. The bones also have integuments. Young persons are often improvident – far more improvident than the little ants.

No. 101. – 79 Words

WORDS OF FOUR SYLLABLES, ACCENTED ON THE SECOND.
MOSTLY LEFT UNMARKED

as-**per**-i-ty, se-**ver**-i-ty, pros-**per**-i-ty, aus-**ter**-i-ty, dex-**ter**-i-ty, in-**teḡ**-ri-ty, ma-**jor**-i-ty, pri-**or**-i-ty, mi-**nor**-i-ty, plu-**ral**-i-ty, fa-**tal**-i-ty, vi-**tal**-i-ty, mo-**ral**-i-ty, mor-**tal**-i-ty, bru-**tal**-i-ty, fi-**del**-i-ty, sta-**bil**-i-ty, mo-**bil**-i-ty, no-**bil**-i-ty, fa-**cil**-i-ty, do-**cil**-i-ty, a-**ġil**-i-ty, fra-**ġil**-i-ty, ni-**hil**-i-ty, ste-**ril**-i-ty, scur-**ril**-i-ty, duc-**til**-i-ty, ġen-**til**-i-ty, fer-**til**-i-ty, hos-**til**-i-ty, tran-**quil**-i-ty, ser-**vil**-i-ty, pro-**pin**-qui-ty, ca-**lam**-i-ty, ex-**trem**-i-ty, sub-**lim**-i-ty, prox-**im**-i-ty, con-**form**-i-ty, e-**nor**-mi-ty, ur-**ban**-i-ty, cu-**pid**-i-ty, tur-**ġid**-i-ty, va-**lid**-i-ty, ca-**lid**-i-ty, so-**lid**-i-ty, ti-**mid**-i-ty, hu-**mid**-i-ty, ra-**pid**-i-ty, stu-**pid**-i-ty, a-**rid**-i-ty, flo-**rid**-i-ty, fe-**cun**-di-ty, ro-**tun**-di-ty, com-**mod**-i-ty, ab-**surd**-i-ty, lo-**cal**-i-ty, vo-**cal**-i-ty, re-**al**-i-ty, le-**ḡal**-i-ty, fru-**gal**-i-ty, for-**mal**-i-ty, car-**nal**-i-ty, neu-**tral**-i-ty, as-**cend**-en-çy, de-**spond**-en-cy, e-**mer**-ġen-cy, in-**clem**-en-cy, in-**solv**-en-cy, de-**lin**-quen-cy, mo-**not**-o-ny, a-**pos**-ta-sy, hy-**poc**-ri-sy, ti-**moc**-ra-cy, im-**pi**-e-ty, va-**ri**-e-ty, e-**bri**-e-ty, so-**bri**-e-ty, pro-**pri**-e-ty, sa-**ti**-e-ty.

The winters in Lapland are severe. The people of that country dress in furs, to protect themselves from the severity of the cold. Major signifies more or greater; minor means less. A majority is more than half; a minority is less than half. Plurality denotes two or more; as a plurality of worlds. In grammar, the plural number expresses more than one; as two *men*, ten *dogs*. A majority of votes means more than half of them. When we say a man has a plurality of votes, we mean he has more than any one else. Members of Congress and Assembly are often elected by a plurality of votes. Land is valued for its fertility and nearness to market. Many parts of the United States are noted for the fertility of the soil. The rapidity of a stream sometimes hinders its navigation. Consistency of character, in just men, is a trait that commands esteem. Humility is the prime ornament of a Christian.

No. 102. – 42 Words

WORDS OF FIVE SYLLABLES, ACCENTED ON THE SECOND.

con-**tem**-po-ra-ry, ex-**tem**-po-ra-ry, de-**rog**-a-to-ry, ap-**pel**-la-to-ry, con-**sol**-a-to-ry, de-**fam**-a-to-ry, de-**clam**-a-to-ry, ex-**clam**-a-to-ry, in-**flam**-ma-to-ry, ex-**plan**-a-to-ry, de-**clar**-a-to-ry, pre-**par**-a-to-ry, dis-**pen**-sa-to-ry, sub-**sid**-i-a-ry, in-**çen**-di-a-ry, stī-**pen**-di-a-ry, e-**pis**-to-la-ry, vo-**cab**-u-la-ry, im-**aġ**-i-na-ry, pre-**lim**-i-na-ry, con-**fec**-tion-er-y, un-**neç**-es-sa-ry, he-**re**-di-ta-ry, in-**vol**-un-ta-ry, re-**sid**-ū-a-ry, tu-**mult**-ū-a-ry, vo-**lupt**-ū-a-ry, ob-**sẽrv**-a-to-ry, con-**serv**-a-to-ry, pro-**hib**-it-o-ry, pre-**mon**-i-to-ry, re-**pos**-i-to-ry, sup-**pos**-i-to-ry, le-**ġit**-i-ma-çy, in-**vet**-er-a-çy, sub-**serv**-i-en-çy, de-**ġen**-er-a-çy, con-**fed**-er-a-çy, ef-**fem**-i-na-çy, in-**del**-i-ca-cy, in-**hab**-it-an-çy, ac-**com**-pa-ni-ment.

Addison and Pope were contemporary authors, that is, they lived at the same time. A love of trifling amusements is derogatory to Christian character. Epistolary correspondence is carried on by letters. Imaginary evils make no small part of the troubles of life. Hereditary property is that which descends from ancestors. The Muskingum is a subsidiary stream of the Ohio. A man who willfully sets fire to a house is an incendiary. An observatory is a place for observing heavenly bodies with telescopes. An extemporary discourse is one spoken without notes or premeditation. Christian humility is never derogatory to character. Inflame, signifies to heat, or excite. Strong liquors inflame the blood and produce disease. The prudent good man will govern his passions, and not suffer them to be inflamed with anger. A conservatory is a large greenhouse for the preservation and culture of exotic plants.

No. 103. – 40 Words

WORDS OF SIX SYLLABLES, ACCENTED ON THE FOURTH, OR ANTEPENULT.

ma-te-ri-**ăl**-i-ty, il-lib-er-**al**-i-ty, u-ni-ver-**sal**-i-ty, ho-sp-i-**tal**-i-ty, in-stru-ment-**al**-i-ty, spir-it-u-**al**-i-ty, im-prob-a-**bĭl**-i-ty, im-pla-ca-**bil**-i-ty, mal-le-a-**bil**-i-ty, in-flam-ma-**bil**-i-ty, in-ca-pa-**bil**-i-ty, pen-e-tra-**bil**-i-ty, im-mu-ta-**bil**-i-ty, in-cred-i-**bil**-i-ty, il-leġ-i-**bil**-i-ty, re-fran-ġi-**bil**-i-ty, in-fal-li-**bil**-i-ty, di-vis-i-**bil**-i-ty, in-sen-si-**bil**-i-ty, im-pos-si-**bil**-i-ty, com-press-i-**bil**-i-ty, com-pat-i-**bil**-i-ty, de-struct-i-**bil**-i-ty, per-çep-ti-**bil**-i-ty, re-sist-i-**bil**-i-ty, com-bus-ti-**bil**-i-ty, in-flex-i-**bil**-i-ty, dis-sim-i-**lar**-i-ty, par-tic-u-**lar**-i-ty, ir-reg-ū-**lar**-i-ty, in-fe-ri-**ŏr**-i-ty, su-pe-ri-**or**-i-ty im-pet-u-**os**-i-ty, ġen-er-al-**ĭs**-si-mo, dis-çi-plin-**a**-ri-an, pre-des-ti-**na**-ri-an, ante-di-**lū**-vi-an, het-e-ro-**ġē**-ne-ous, me-di-a-**tō**-ri-al, in-quis-i-**to**-ri-al.

WORDS OF THREE SYLLABLES, ACCENTED ON THE FIRST.

ben-e-fīt, **ăl**-pha-bet, **păr**-a-pet, **sum**-mer-set **min**-u-et,
pol-y̆-pus, **im**-pe-tus, **cat**-a-ract, **in**-tel-lect, **çir**-cum-spect,
pick-pock-et, **flow**-er-et, **lev**-er-et, **pen**-ny-weight, **cat**-a-
pult, **men**-di-cant, **sup**-pli-cant, **per**-ma-nent, **mis**-cre-ant,
tẽr-ma-gant, **el**-e-gant, **lit**-i-gant, **ar**-ro-gant, **el**-e-phant,
sy̆c-o-plant, **pet**-ū-lant, **ăd**-a-mant, **cȯv**-e-nant, **cŏn**-so-nant,
per-ti-nent, **tol**-er-ant, **cȏr**-mo-rant, **ig**-no-rant, **con**-ver-
sant, **mil**-i-tant, **ad**-ju-tant, **rel**-e-vant, **in**-no-çent, **ac**-çi-
dent, **dif**-fī-dent, **con**-fī-dent, **res̲**-i-dent, **pres̲**-i-dent, **prov**-
i-dent, **in**-di-ġent, **neg**-li-gent, **am**-bi-ent, **prev**-a-lent, **pes**-
ti-lent, **ex**-çel-lent, **red**-o-lent, **in**-do-lent, **tȗr**-bu-lent, **suc**-
cu-lent, **fec**-u-lent, **es**-cu-lent, **op**-ū-lent, **vir**-u̬-lent, **flat**-ū-
lent, **lig**-a-ment, **pär**-li*a*-ment, **fil**-a-ment, **ärm**-a-ment, **sac**-
ra-ment, **test**-a-ment, **man**-aġe-ment, **im**-ple-ment, **com**-
ple-ment, **bat**-tle-ment, **set**-tle-ment, **ten**-e-ment, **in**-cre-
ment, **em**-bry-o, **pärt**-ner-ship, **fel**-lōw-ship, **cal**-en-dar,
vin-e-gar, **in**-su-lar, **sim**-i-lar, **pop**-ū-lar, **tab**-u-lar, **glob**-u-
lar, **sec**-u-lar, **oc**-u-lar, **joc**-u-lar, **çir**-cu-lar, **mus**-cu-lar,
reg-u-lar, **çel**-lu-lar, **an**-nu-lar, **scap**-u-lar, **spec**-u-lar, **con**-
su-lar, **cap**-su-lar, **tit**-u-lar, **sub**-lu-nar, **çim**-e-ter, **bas̲**-i-
lisk, **can**-ni-bal, **coch**-i-nēal **mär**-tin-gal, **hos**-pi-tal, **ped**-
es-tal, **tū**-bu-lar, **jū**-gu-lar, **fū**-ner-al.

WORDS OF FIVE SYLLABLES, ACCENTED ON THE THIRD.

am-bi-**gū**-i-ty, con-ti-**gu**-i-ty, con-tra-**rī**-e-ty, im-por-**tū**-ni-ty, op-por-**tu**-ni-ty, per-pe-**tu**-i-ty, su-per-**flu**-i-ty, in-cre-**du**-li-ty, in-se-**cu**-ri-ty, im-ma-**tu**-ri-ty, per-spi-**cu**-i-ty, as-si-**du**-i-ty, con-ti-**nu**-i-ty, in-ġe-**nu**-i-ty, in-con-**gru**-i-ty, fran-ġi-**bil**-i-ty, fal-li-**bil**-i-ty, fea-s̲i-**bil**-i-ty, vis̲-i-**bil**-i-ty, sen-si-**bil**-i-ty, pos-si-**bil**-i-ty, pla̬u-s̲i-**bil**-i-ty, im-be-**çil**-i-ty, in-do-**çil**-i-ty, vol-a-**til**-i-ty, ver-sa-**til**-i-ty, ca-pa-**bil**-i-ty, in-si-**pid**-i-ty, il-le-**găl**-i-ty, prod-i-**gal**-i-ty, cor-di-**al**-i-ty, per-son-**al**-i-ty, prin-çi-**pal**-i-ty, lib-er-**al**-i-ty, ġen-er-**al**-i-ty, im-mor-**tal**-i-ty, hos-pi-**tal**-i-ty, in-e-**qual**-i-ty, sen-sū-**al**-i-ty (*sen-shu-*), pun̲ct-u-**ăl**-i-ty, mūt-ū-**al**-i-ty, in-fi-**del**-i-ty, prob-a-**bil**-i-ty, in-a-**bil**-i-ty, du-ra-**bil**-i-ty, dis-a-**bil**-i-ty, in-sta-**bil**-i-ty, mu-ta-**bil**-i-ty, cred-i-**bil**-i-ty, tan-ġi-**bil**-i-ty, so-çia-**bil**-i-ty (*so-aha-*), tract-a-**bil**-i-ty, pla-ca-**bil**-i-ty, in-ū-**til**-i-ty, in-çi-**vil**-i-ty, non-con-**fôrm**-i-ty, con-san-**guĭn**-i-ty, sin̲-gu-**lăr**-i-ty, joc-u-**lar**-i-ty, reg-u-**lar**-i-ty, pop-u-**lar**-i-ty, me-di-**oc**-ri-ty, in-sin-**çẽr**-i-ty, sin-u-**os**-i-ty, cu-ri-**os**-i-ty, an-i-**mos**-i-ty, ġen-er-**os**-i-ty, flex-i-**bil**-i-ty, im-mo-**bil**-i-ty, vol-u-**bil**-i-ty, mag-na-**nim**-i-ty, ū-na-**nim**-i-ty, in-hu-**man**-i-ty, ar-is-**toc**-ra-çy, in-ad-**vẽr**-ten-çy, phra-s̲e-**ŏl**-o-ġy, os-te-**ol**-o-ġy, a-er-**ol**-o-ġy, no-to-**rī**-e-ty.

WORDS OF THREE SYLLABLES, ACCENTED ON THE SECOND.

çes-**sā**-tion, lī-**ba**-tion, pro-**ba**-tion, va-**ca**-tion, lo-**ca**-tion, vo-**ca**-tion, gra-**da**-tion, foun-**da**-tion, cre-**a**-tion, ne-**ga**-tion, pur-**ga**-tion, mi-**gra**-tion, ob-**la**-tion, re-**la**-tion, trans-**la**-tion, for-**ma**-tion, stag-**na**-tion, dam-**na**-tion, cär-**na**-tion, vi-**bra**-tion, nar-**ra**-tion, pros-**tra**-tion, du-**ra**-tion, pul-**sa**-tion, sen-**sa**-tion, dic-**ta**-tion, çi-**ta**-tion, plan-**ta**-tion, no-**ta**-tion, ro-**ta**-tion, quo-**ta**-tion, temp-**ta**-tion, pri-**va**-tion, sal-**va**-tion, e-**qua**-tion, vex-**a**-tion, tax-**a**-tion, sa-**na**-tion, com-**plē**-tion, se-**cre**-tion, con-**cre**-tion, ex-**cre**-tion, e-**mō**-tion, pro-**mo**-tion, de-**vo**-tion, pro-**pōr**-tion, ap-**por**-tion, ab-**lū**-tion, so-**lu**-tion, di-**lu**-tion, at-**trăc**-tion, re-**frac**-tion, sub-**trac**-tion, de-**trac**-tion, con-**trac**-tion, pro-**trac**-tion, dis-**trac**-tion, ex-**trac**-tion, con-**nec**-tion, af-**fec**-tion, con-**fec**-tion, per-**fec**-tion, in-**fec**-tion, sub-**jec**-tion, de-**jec**-tion, re-**jec**-tion, in-**jec**-tion, ob-**jec**-tion, pro-**jec**-tion, e-**lec**-tion, se-**lec**-tion, re-**flec**-tion, col-**lec**-tion, in-**spec**-tion, dĭ-**rec**-tion, cor-**rec**-tion, dis-**sec**-tion, de-**tec**-tion, af-**flic**-tion, re-**stric**-tion, con-**vic**-tion, com-**pŭl**-sion, ex-**pul**-sion, con-**vul**-sion, ex-**pan**-sion, as-**çen**-sion, de-**sçen**-sion, di-**men**-sion, sus-**pen**-sion, dis-**sen**-sion, pre-**ten**-sion, sub-**mẽr**-sion, e-**mer**-sion, im-**mer**-sion, as-**per**-sion, dis-**per**-sion, a-**ver**-sion sub-**ver**-sion, re-**ver**-sion, dĭ-**ver**-sion, in-**ver**-sion, con-**ver**-sion, per-**ver**-sion, com-**pas**-sion, ac-**çes**-sion, se-**çes**-sion, con-**çes**-sion, pro-**çes**-sion con-**fes**-sion, pro-**fes**-sion, ag-**gres**-sion, di-**gres**-sion, pro-**gres**-sion, re-**gres**-sion, de-**pres**-sion, im-**pres**-sion, op-**pres**-sion, sup-**pres**-sion, ex-**pres**-sion, pos-**ses**-sion, sub-**mis**-sion, ad-**mis**-sion, e-**mis**-sion, re-**mis**-sion, com-**mis**-sion, o-**mis**-

sion, per-**mis**-sion, dis-**mis**-sion, con-**cul**-sion, dis-**cus**-sion, re-**act**-ion, con-**junc**-tion, in-**junc**-tion, com-**punc**-tion, de-**coc**-tion, con-**coc**-tion, in-**frac**-tion, ab-**duc**-tion, de-**duc**-tion, re-**duc**-tion, se-**duc**-tion, in-**duc**-tion, ob-**struc**-tion, de-**struc**-tion, in-**struc**-tion, con-**struc**-tion, de-**ten**-tion, in-**ten**-tion, re-**ten**-tion, con-**ten**-tion, dis-**ten**-tion, at-**ten**-tion, in-**ven**-tion, con-**ven**-tion, de-**çep**-tion, re-**cep**-tion, con-**çep**-tion, ex-**cep**-tion, per-**çep**-tion, a-**scrip**-tion, de-**scrip**-tion, in-**scrip**-tion, pre-**scrip**-tion, pro-**scrip**-tion, re-**demp**-tion, con-**sump**-tion, a-**dop**-tion, ab-**sôrp**-tion, e-**rup**-tion, cor-**rup**-tion, de-**sẽr**-tion, in-**ser**-tion, as-**ser**-tion, ex-**er**-tion, con-**tôr**-tion, dis-**tor**-tion, ex-**tinc**-tion, ex-**ten**-sion, ex-**tôr**-tion, ir-**rup**-tion, com-**plex**-ion, de-**flux**-ion.

No. 107. – 60 Words

WORDS OF FOUR SYLLABLES, ACCENTED ON THE THIRD.

pub-li-**cā**-tion, rep-li-**ca**-tion, im-pli-**ca**-tion, com-pli-**ca**-tion, ap-pli-**ca**-tion, sup-pli-**ca**-tion, ex-pli-**ca**-tion, re-pro-**ba**-tion, ap-pro-**ba**-tion, per-tur-**ba**-tion, in-cu-**ba**-tion, ab-di-**ca**-tion, ded-i-**ca**-tion, med-i-**ta**-tion, in-di-**ca**-tion, vin-di-**ca**-tion, del-e-**ga**-tion, ob-li-**ga**-tion, al-le-**ga**-tion, ir-ri-**ga**-tion, lit-i-**ga**-tion, mit-i-**ga**-tion, in-sti-**ga**-tion, nav-i-**ga**-tion, pro-mul-**ga**-tion, pro-lon-**ga**-tion, ab-ro-**ga**-tion, sub-ju-**ga**-tion, fas-çi-**na**-tion, me-di-**a**-tion, pal-li-**a**-tion, ex-pi-**a**-tion, va-ri-**a**-tion, de-vi-**a**-tion, ex-ha-**la**-tion, con-ġe-**la**-tion, mu-ti-**la**-tion, in-stąl-**la**-tion, ap-pel-**la**-tion, con-stel-**la**-tion, dis-til-**la**-tion, per-co-**la**-tion, vi-o-**la**-tion, im-mo-**la**-tion, des-o-**la**-tion, con-so-**la**-tion, con-tem-**pla**-tion, leġ-is-**la**-tion, trib-ū-**la**-tion, pec-u-**la**-tion, spec-u-**la**-tion, cal-cu-**la**-tion cir-cu-**la**-tion, mod-u-**la**-tion, reg-u-**la**-tion, gran-u-**la**-tion, stip-u-**la**-tion, pop-u-**la**-tion, grat-u-**la**-tion, re-tar-**da**-tion.

Legislation is the enacting of laws, and a legislator is one who makes laws. God is the divine legislator. He proclaimed his ten commandments from Mount Sinai. In free governments the people choose their legislators. We have legislators for each State, who make laws for the State where they live. The town, in which they meet to legislate, is called the seat of government. These legislators, when they are assembled to make laws, are called the legislature. The people should choose their best and wisest men for their legislators. It is the duty of every good man to inspect the moral conduct of the man who is offered as legislator at our yearly elections. If the people wish for good laws, they may have them by electing good men. The legislative councils of the United States should feel their dependence on the will of a free and virtuous people. Or farmers, mechanic, and merchants, compose the strength of our nation. Let them be wise and virtuous, and watchful of their liberties. Let them trust no man to legislate for them, if he lives in the habitual violation of the laws of his country.

No. 108. – 57 Words

WORDS OF THREE SYLLABLES, ACCENTED ON THE FIRST.

def-i-nĭte, **ap**-po-sĭte, **op**-po-sĭte, **in**-fi-nĭte, **hȳp**-o-crĭte, **păr**-a-sīte, **ob**-so-lēte, **ex**-pe-dīte, **rec**-on-dīte, **sat**-el-līte, **ĕr**-e-mite, **ap**-pe-tite, **an**-ec-dōte, **pros**-e-cūte, **pĕr**-se-cute, **ex**-e-cute, **ab**-so-lute, **dis**-so-lute, **sub**-sti-tute, **des**-ti-tute, **in**-sti-tute, **con**-sti-tute, **pros**-ti-tute, **pros**-e-lȳte, **bär**-be-cue, **res**-i-due, **ves**-ti-bule, **rid**-i-cule, **mus**-ca-dine, **brig**-an-tine, **cal**-a-mine, **çel**-an-dine, **sĕr**-pen-tine, **tûr**-pen-tine, **pôr**-cu-pine, **an**-o-dȳne, **tel**-e-scope, **hŏr**-o-scope, **mī**-cro-scope, **an**-te-lope, **prō**-to-type, **hem**-is-phēre, **at**-mos-phere, **com**-mo-dōre, **syc**-a-mōre, **vol**-a-tĭle, **vĕr**-sa-tĭle, **mer**-can-tĭle, **in**-fan-tĭle, **dis**-çi-plĭne, **mas**-cu-lĭne, **fem**-i-nĭne, **nec**-tar-ĭne, **ġen**-u-ĭne, **ber**-yl-ĭne, **fā**-vo-rĭte, **pū**-er-ĭle.

An anecdote is a short story, or the relation of a particular incident. Ridicule is not often the test of truth.

WORDS OF TWO SYLLABLES, ACCENTED ON THE SECOND.

con-**dĕnse**, im-**mense**, de-**fense**, pre-**pense**, of-**fense**, dis-**pense**, pre-**tense**, col-**lăpse**, im-**mērse**, as-**perse**, dis-**perse**, a-**verse**, re-**verse**, in-**verse**, con-**verse**, per-**verse**, trans-**verse**, in-**dôrse**, un-**horse**, dis-**bûrse**, de-**tērge**, dĭ-**verge**, mis-**gĭve**, out-**lĭve**, for-**give**, ab-**sŏlve**, re-**solve**, dis-**solve**, e-**volve**, de-**volve**, re-**volve**, con-**volve**, a-**bōde**, un-**nērve**, ob-**serve**, sub-**serve**, de-**serve**, re-**serve**, pre-**serve**, con-**serve**, her-**sĕlf**, my-**self**, at-**tăch**, de-**tach**, en-**rich**, re-**trench**, in-**trench**, dis-**patch**, mis-**match**, a-**fresh**, re-**fresh**, de-**bärk**, em-**bark**, re-**mark**, un-**mask**, ca-**bal**, reb-**el**, fâre-**well**, un-**fûrl**, de-**fôrm**, re-**form**, in-**form**, con-**form**, per-**form**, trans-**form**, con-**demn**, in-**tēr**, a-**ver**, ab-**hôr**, oc-**cûr**, in-**cur**, con-**cur**, re-**cur**, de-**mur**, a-**làs**, a-**mend**, de-**fẽ r**, re-**fer**, pre-**fer**, in-**fer**, con-**fer**, trans-**fer**, se-**çern**, con-**çern**, dis-**çern**, sub-**ôrn**, a-**dorn**, for-**lorn**, ad-**joûrn**, re-**turn**, fōre-**run**, cra-**văt**, co-**quĕt**, a-**bàft**, be-**set**, a-**loft**, un-**apt**, con-**tempt**, at-**tempt**, a-**dŏpt**, ab-**rupt**, cor-**rupt**, a-**pärt**, de-**part**, im-**part**, a-**mòng**, be-**long**.

The fixed stars are at immense distances from us. They are so distant that we cannot measure the number of miles. When fogs and vapors rise from the earth and ascend one or two miles high, they come to a cold part of the air. The cold there condenses these vapors into thick clouds, which fall in showers of rain. Noah and his family outlived all the people who lived before the flood. The brave sailors embark on board of ships, and sail over the great and deep seas. The time will soon come when we must bid a last farewell to this world. The bright stars without number adorn the skies. When our friends die, they will never return to us; but we must soon follow them. God will forgive those who repent of their sins, and live a holy life. Thy testimonies, O Lord, are very sure; holiness becomes thine house forever. Do not attempt to deceive God; nor to mock him with solemn words, whilst your heart is set to do evil. A holy life will disarm death of its sting. God will impart grace to the humble penitent.

No. 110. – 80 Words

WORDS OF THREE SYLLABLES, ACCENTED ON THE SECOND.

de-**mēan**-or, re-**māin**-der, en-**tīçe**-ment, en-**fōrçe**-ment, di-**vorçe**-ment, in-**duçe**-ment, a-**gree**-ment, en-**ġaġe**-ment, de-**fīle**-ment, in-**cite**-ment, re-**fine**-ment, con-**fine**-ment, e-**lōpe**-ment, re-**tīre**-ment, ac-**quire**-ment, im-**pēach**-ment, en-**crōach**-ment, con-**çēal**-ment, at-**tāin**-ment, de-**pō**-nent, op-**po**-nent, com-**po**-nent, ad-**jā**-cent, in-**dē**-çent, viçe-**ġe**-rent, en-**rōll**-ment, im-**pru**-dent, in-**hēr**-ent, ad-**her**-ent, co-**hēr**-ent, at-**tend**-ant, as-**çend**-ant, in-**tes**-tĭnes, pro-**bos**-çis, el-**lip**-sis, syn-**op**-sis, com-**mand**-ment, a-**mend**-ment, bȯm-**bärd**-ment, en-**hance**-ment, ad-**vance**-ment, a-**merce**-ment, in-**frĭnġe**-ment, de-**tach**-ment, at-**tach**-ment, in-**trench**-ment, re-**trench**-ment, re-**fresh**-ment, dis-**cern**-ment, (-*zẽrn*-) pre-**fer**-ment, a-**mass**-ment, al-**lot**-ment, a-**pärt**-ment, de-**pärt**-ment, ad-**just**-ment, in-**vest**-ment, a-**but**-ment, as-**sist**-ant, in-**çes**-sant, re-**luc**-tant, im-**pôr**-tant, re-**sis**-tant, in-**con**-stant, in-**cum**-bent, pu-**tres**-çent, trans-**çend**-ent, de-**pend**-ent in-**dul**-ġent, re-**ful**-ġent, ef-**ful**-ġent, e-**mul**-ġent, as-**trin**-ġent, e-**mēr**-ġent, de-**ter**-ġent, ab-**hŏr**-rent, con-**cŭr**-rent, con-**sist**-ent, re-**solv**-ent, de-**lin**-quent, re-**cum**-bent.

Demeanor signifies behavior or deportment. Remainder is that which remains or is left. An enticement is that which allures. Divorcement signifies an entire separation. Elopement is a running away or private departure. Impeachment signifies accusation. Retirement is a withdrawing from company. A deponent is one who makes oath to any thing. A vicegerent is one who governs in place of another. A proboscis is a long tube of snout from the mouth of a jar. An ellipsis is an omission of a word. Amercement is a penalty imposed for a wrong done, not a fine fixed, but at the mercy of the court. A synopsis is a collective view. Refulglent is applied to things that shine. A contingent event is that which happens, or which is not expected in the common course of things.

No. 111. – 85 Words

WORDS OF THREE SYLLABLES, ACCENTED ON THE FIRST.

THE ENDING ate WITH OUT A MACRON HAS THE SHORT ĭ sound.

des-o-lāte (*v.*), **ad**-vo-cāte (*v.*), **ven**-ti-lāte, **tit**-il-lāte, **sçin**-til-lāte, **per**-co-lāte, **im**-mo-lāte, **spec**-ū-lāte, **cal**-cu-lāte, **çĭr**-cu-lāte, **reg**-u-lāte, **un**-du-lāte, **em**-u-lāte, **stim**-u-lāte, **gran**-u-lāte, **stip**-u-lāte, **pop**-u-lāte, **con**-su-lāte, **sub**-li-māte (*v.*), **an**-i-māte (*v.*), **in**-ti-māte (*v.*), **es**-ti-māte (*v*), **fas**-çi-nāte, **ôr**-di-nate, **ful**-mi-nāte, **nom**-i-nāte, **ġer**-mi-nāte, **per**-son-āte, **pas**-sion-ate, **fôrt**-ū-nate, **dis**-si-pāte, **sep**-a-rāte (*v.*), **çel**-e-brāte, **des**-e-crāte, **con**-se-crāte, **ex**-e-crāte, **vẽr**-ber-āte, **ul**-çer-āte, **mod**-er-āte, **ag**-gre-gate, **vẽr**-te-brāte, **ġen**-er-āte, **ven**-er-āte, **tem**-per-ate, **op**-er-āte, **as**-per-āte, **des**-per-ate, **it**-er-āte, **em**-i-grāte, **trans**-mi-grāte, **as**-pi-rāte (*v.*), **dec**-o-rāte, **pẽr**-fo-rāte, **côr**-po-rate, **pẽr**-pe-trate, **pen**-e-trāte, **är**-bi-trāte, **ac**-cu-rate, **lam**-i-nate, **in**-du-rāte (*v.*), **sat**-ū-rāte, **sus**-çi-tāte, **med**-i-tāte, **im**-i-tāte, **ir**-ri-tāte, **hes̱**-i-tāte, **grav**-i-tāte, **am**-pu-tāte, **ex**-ca-vāte, **ag**-gra-vāte, **grad**-u-āte, **sal**-i-vāte, **cul**-ti-vāte, **cap**-ti-vāte, **ren**-o-vāte, **in**-no-vāte, **ad**-e-quate, **fluct**-ŭ-āte, **sit**-u-āte, **est**-u-āte, **ex**-pi-āte, **dē**-vi-āte, **vī**-o-lāte, **ru̱**-mi-nāte, **lū**-cu-brāte.

An advocate is one who defends the cause or opinion of another, or who maintains a party in opposition to another. Ardent spirits stimulate the system for a time, but leave it more languid. Men often toil all their lives to get property, which their children dissipate and waste. We should emulate the virtuous actions of great and good men. Moderate passions are most conductive to happiness, and moderate gains are most likely to be durable. Abusive words irritate the passions, but "a soft answer turneth away wrath." Discontent aggravates the evils of calamity. Violent anger makes one unhappy, but a temperate state of the mind is pleasant.

WORDS OF TWO SYLLABLES, ACCENTED ON THE FIRST.

ain UNMARKED IS SOUNDED AS **in**; **ot** UNMARKED, AS **ut**.

chil-blāin, **vil**-lain, **môrt**-māin, **plant**-ain, **vẽr**-vāin, **cûr**-tain, **dŏl**-phin, **sȯme**-tīmes̲, **tress**-es̲, **trap**-pings, **ăn**-nals̲, **ĕn**-trails, **mit**-tens̲, **sum**-mons̲, **fôr**-çepts̲, **pinch**-ers̲, **glan**-ders̲, **jaun**-dĭçe, **snuf**-fers̲, **stag**-ḡers̲, **man**-ners̲, **nip**-pers, **sçis**-sors, **cär**-cass, **cut**-lass, **cȯm**-pass, **mat**-rass, **mat**-tress, **ab**-s̲çess, **lär**-ġess, **end**-less, **zĕal**-ous, **jĕal**-ous, **pomp**-ous, **wȯn**-drous, **lep**-rous, **mon**-strous, **nẽrv**-ous, **tôr**-ment, **vest**-ment, **sẽr**-pent, **tŏr**-rent, **cŭr**-rent, **ab**-sent, **pres̲**-ent, **ad**-vent, **solv**-ent, **con**-vent, **fẽr**-ment, **sun**-bûrnt, **ab**-bot, **tûr**-bot, **fag**-ot, **mag**-got, **spig**-ot, **in**-got, **blȯod**-shŏt, **red**-hŏt, **zĕal**-ot, **tap**-rōot, **gràss**-plot, **buck**-et, **bū**-gloss.

Chilblains are sores caused by cold. A curtain is used to hide something from the view. The colors of the dolphin in the water are very beautiful. The ladies adorn their heads and necks with tresses. A matrass is a chemical vessel used for distilling, etc.; but a mattress is a quilted bed. Annals are history in the order of years. A cutlass is a broad curved sword. A largess is a donation or gift. A bigot is one who is too strongly attached to some religion or opinion. An abscess is a collection of matter under the skin. Good manners are always becoming; ill manners are evidence of low breeding. A solvent is that which dissolves something. Warm tea and coffee are solvents of sugar. Solvent, an adjective, signifies able to pay all debts. A summons is a notice or citation to appear.

No. 113. – 86 Words

WORDS OF THREE SYLLABLES, ACCENTED ON THE FIRST

căl-o-mel, **çit**-a-del, **in**-fĭ-del, **sen**-ti-nel, **mack**-er-el, **cock**-er-el, **cod**-i-cil, **dom**-i-çĭle, **daf**-fo-dil, **ăl**-co-hol, **vit**-ri-ol, **păr**-a-sol, **sī**-ne-cūre, **ep**-i-cūre, **lig**-a-tūre, **sig**-na-tūre, **cûr**-va-tūre, **for**-feit-ūre, **gär**-ni-tūre, **fûr**-ni-tūre, **sep**-ul-tūre, **păr**-a-dīse, **mer**-chan-dīse, **en**-ter-prīse, **hand**-ker-chĭef [*hank-er-chif*], **sem**-i-brēve, **an**-ti-pōde, **rec**-om-pense, **hŏl**-ly-hock, **ăl**-ka-lī, **hem**-i-stich, **au**-to-graph, **păr**-a-graph, **ep**-i-taph, **av**-e-nūe, **rev**-e-nūe, **ret**-i-nūe, **des**-pot-ism, **păr**-ox-ysm, **mī**-crō-cŏsm, **min**-i-mum, **pend**-ū-lum, **max**-i-mum, **tўm**-pa-num, **pel**-i-can, **guär**-di-an, **Stўġ**-i-an, **hôrt**-ū-lan, **hus**-band-man, **ġen**-tle-man, **mus**-sul-man, **ạl**-der-man, **joûr**-ney-man, **bish**-op-ric, **cler**-ġy-man, **coŭn**-try-man, **vet**-er-an, **ăl**-co-ran, **wȯn**-der-fụl, **sŏr**-rōw-ful, **an**-a-gram, **ep**-i-gram, **mŏn**-o-gram, **dī**-a-gram, **ū**-ni-verse, **sēa**-fâr-ing, **wāy**-fâr-ing, **fū**-ġi-tĭve, **pū**-ni-tĭve, **nu**-tri-tĭve, **ē**-go-tism, **prō**-to-col, **dū**-pli-cāte, **ro**-ṣe-ate, **fu**-mi-gate, **mē**-di-ate, **me**-di-um, **ō**-di-um, **ō**-pi-um, **prē**-mi-um, **spō**-li-āte, **o**-pi-ate, **o**-vert-ure, **jū**-ry-man, **pu**-ri-tan, **phil**-o-mel.

Calomel is a preparation of mercury made by sublimation, that is, by being raised into vapor by heat and then condensed. A citadel is a fortress to defend a city or town. A codicil is a supplement or addition to a will. An infidel is one who disbelieves revelation. An epicure is one who indulges his appetite to excess, and is fond of delicacies. Alcohol is spirit highly refined by distillation. Despotism is tyranny or oppressive government. The despotism of government can often be overthrown; but for despotism of fashion there is no remedy. A domicile is the place of a man's residence. Mackerel signifies spotted. The glanders is a disease of horses. The jaundice is a disease characterized by a yellow skin. A loaquacious companion is sometimes a great torment.

THE SOUNDS OF a IN ạll (= aw), AND IN whạt (= ŏ).

ạu-thor, sau-cy, gaud-y, taw-ny, taw-dry, fault-y, pau-per, squạd-ron, sạu-cer, squan-der, plaud-it, brawn-y, quar-ry, flaw-y, saw-pit law-sūit, wạ-ter, dau*gh*-ter, slau*gh*-ter, al-ter, fal-ter, quar-ter, law-yer, saw-yer, haw-thôrn, scạl-lop, wạl-lop, wạn-der, draw-ers, wạl-nut, cau-sey, pal-try, draw-back, al-mōst, want-ing, wạr-ren.

The saucy stubborn child displeases his parents. The peacock is a gaudy, vain, and noisy fowl. The skin of the Indiana is of a tawny color. Paupers are poor people who are supported by a public tax. Twenty-five cents are equal to one quarter of a dollar. It is the business of a lawyer to give counsel on questions of law, and to manage law suits. Walnuts are the seeds of walnut trees. The Tartars wander from place to place without any settled habitation.

WORDS OF TWO SYLLABLES, ACCENTED ON THE FIRST.

mis-sĭve, cap-tĭve, fes-tĭve, cos-tĭve, mag-pīe, sȯme-thing, stock-ing, mid-dling, world-ling, sprin̲k-ling, twin̲k-ling, shil-ling, sap-ling, strip-ling, dump-ling, där-ling, star-ling, stēr-ling, gos-ling, nûrs-ling, fat-ling, bant-ling, scant-ling, nest-ling, hĕr-ring, ob-long, hĕ*ad*-long, fûr-long, hĕ*ad*-āche, tōōth-āche, heärt-āche, os-trich, găl-lant, dôr-mant, ten-ant, preg-nant, rem-nant, pen-nant, flip-pant, quad-rant, ăr-rant, wạr-rant, pärch-ment, plĕ*as*-ant, pĕ*as*-ant, dis-tant, in-stant, con-stant, ex-tant, sex-tant, lam-bent, ac-çent, ad-vent, cres-çent, sĕr-aph, stā-tĭve, nā-tĭve, plāin-tĭve, mō-tĭve, spōrt-ĭve, hīre-ling, yē*ar*-ling, day-spring, trī-umph, tri-glўph, trụ-ant, är-dent, mȧs-sĭve, pas-sĭve, stat-ūe, stat-ūte, vĩr-tūe.

WORDS OF TWO SYLLABLES, ACCENTED ON THE FIRST.

mō-tion (*-shun*), **no**-tion, **lo**-tion, **po**-tion, **pōr**-tion, **na**-tion, **ra**-tion, **sta**-tion, **man**-sion, **pas**-sion, **fac**-tion, **ac**-tion, **frac**-tion, **trac**-tion, **men**-tion, **pen**-sion, **çes**-sion, **ten**-sion, **mẽr**-sion, **ver**-sion, **ses**-sion, **lec**-tion, **dic**-tion, **fic**-tion, **un̲c**-tion, **fun̲c**-tion, **jun̲c**-tion, **suc**-tion, **spon**-sion, **tôr**-sion, **mis**-sion, **cap**-tion, **op**-tion, **flec**-tion, **a̤uc**-tion, **cau**-tion.

Lection is reading, and lecture is discourse. Lectures on chemistry are delivered in our colleges. A lotion is a washing or a liquid preparation. A ration is an allowance daily for a soldier. A mansion is a place of residence, or dwelling. A fraction is part of a whole number. Fiction is a creature of the imagination. Caution is prudence in the avoidance of evil. Auction is a sale of goods by outcry to the highest bidder. Option is choice. It is at our option to make ourselves respectable or contemptible.

WORDS OF FOUR SYLLABLES, ACCENTED ON THE SECOND.

su-**prem**-a-çy, the-**oc**-ra-çy, de-**moc**-ra-çy, con-**spir̆**-a-çy, ġe-**og**-ra-phy, bi-**og**-ra-phy, cos-**mog**-ra-phy, ste-**nog**-ra-phy, zo-**og**-ra-phy, to-**pog**-ra-phy, tȳ-**pog**-ra-phy, hȳ-**drog**-ra-phy, phĭ-**los**-o-phy, a-**cad**-e-my, e-**con**-o-my, a-**nat**-o-my, zo-**ot**-o-my, e-**piph**-a-ny, phĭ-**lan**-thro-py, mis-**an**-thro-py, pe-**riph**-e-ry, är-**til**-le-ry, hȳ-**drop**-a-thy, de-**liv**-e-ry, dis-**cȯv**-er-y, com-**pŭl**-so-ry, ol-**fac**-to-ry, re-**frac**-to-ry, re-**fec**-to-ry, di-**rec**-to-ry, con-**sis**-to-ry, ī-**dŏl**-a-try, ġe-**om**-e-try, im-**men**-si-ty, pro-**pen**-si-ty, ver-**bos**-i-ty, ad-**vẽr**-si-ty, ne-**çes**-si-ty, ī-**den**-ti-ty, con-**cav**-i-ty, de-**prav**-i-ty, lon-**ġev**-i-ty, ac-**cliv**-i-ty, na-**tiv**-i-ty, ac-**tiv**-i-ty, cap-**tiv**-i-ty, fes-**tiv**-i-ty, per-**plex**-i-ty, con-**vex**-i-ty, pro-**lix**-i-ty, un-**çer**-t*a*in-ty, im-**mod**-es-ty, dis̲-***h*on**-est-y, so-**lil**-o-quy, hu-**man**-i-ty, a-**men**-i-ty, se-**ren**-i-ty, vĭ-**cin**-i-ty, af-**fin**-i-ty, dĭ-**vin**-i-ty, in-**dem**-ni-ty, so-**lem**-ni-ty, fra-**ter**-ni-ty, e-**ter**-ni-ty, bär-**băr**-i-ty, vul-**găr**-i-ty, dis-**par**-i-ty, çe-**leb**-ri-ty, a-**lac**-ri-ty, sin-**çer**-i-ty, çe-**ler**-i-ty, te-**mer**-i-ty, in-**teg**-ri-ty, dis-**til**-ler-y.

Theocracy is government by God himself. The government of the Israelites was a theocracy. Democracy is a government by the people. Hydropathy, or water cure, is a mode of treating diseases by the copious use of pure water. Geography is a description of the earth. Biography is a history of a person's life. Cosmography is a description of the world. Stenography is the art of writing in shorthand. Zoögraphy is a description of animals; but zoölogy means the same things, and is generally used. Topography is the exact delineation of a place or region. Topography is the art of printing with types. Hydrography is the description of seas and other waters, or the art of forming charts. Philanthropy is a love of mankind; but misanthropy signifies a hatred of mankind. The olfactory nerves are the organs of smell. Idolatry is the worship of idols. Pagans worship gods of wood and stone. These are their idols. But among Christians many worship other sorts of idols. Some worship a gay and splendid dress, consisting of silks and muslins gauze and ribbons; some worship pearls and diamonds; but all excessive fondness for temporal things is idolatry.

WORDS OF FOUR SYLLABLES, ACCENTED ON THE SECOND.

ju-**rid**-i-cal, con-**viv**-i-al, di-**ag**-on-al, pen-**tag**-o-nal, tra-**dĭ**-tion-al, in-**ten**-tion-al, per-**pet**-ū-al, ha-**bit**-u-al, e-**vent**-u-al, un-**mer**-çi-ful, fa-**nat**-i-çi̱sm, ex-**ôr**-di-um, mil-**len**-ni-um, re-**pub**-lic-an, me-**rid**-i-an, un-**nat**-u-ral, con-**ject**-ūr-al, cen-**trip**-e-tal, con-**tin**-ū-al, ef-**fect**-u-al, ob-**liv**-i-on, in-**cog**-ni-to, co-**pärt**-ner-ship, dis-**sim**-i-lar, ver-**nac**-ū-lar, o-**rac**-u-lar, or-**bic**-u-lar, par-**tic**-u-lar, ir-**reg**-u-lar, bī-**vălv**-u-lar, un-**pop**-u-lar, tri-**an̲**-gu-lar, pa-**rish**-*i*on-er, dī-**am**-e-ter, ad-**min**-is-ter, em-**bas**-sa-dor, pro-**ġen**-i-tor, com-**po̱s**-i-tor, me-**trop**-o-lis, e-**phem**-e-ris, a-**nal**-y̆-sis, de-**lĭr**-i-oŭs, in-**dus**-tri-ous, il-**lus**-tri-ous, las-**civ**-i-ous, ob-**liv**-i-ous, a-**nom**-a-lous, e-**pit**-o-mīze, a-**pos**-ta-tīze, im-**môr**-tal-īze, ex-**tem**-po-re, en-**tab**-la-tūre, dis-**cȯm**-fit-ure, pro-**con**-sul-ship, dis-**con**-so-late, a-**pos**-to-late, ob-**sē**-qui-oŭs, oc-**ca**-s̱ion-al, pro-**pōr**-tion-al, heb-**dŏm**-a-dal.

WORDS OF FOUR SYLLABLES, ACCENTED ON THE SECOND.

A, UNMARKED, IN ate, DOES NOT HAVE ITS FULL LONG SOUND

as-**sim**-i-lāte, prog-**nos**-tic-āte, per-**am**-bu-lāte, e-**jac**-ū-lāte, im-**mac**-u-lāte, ma-**tric**-u-lāte, ġes-**tic**-u-lāte, in-**oc**-u-lāte, co-**aġ**-u-lāte, de-**pop**-u-lāte, con-**grat**-u-lāte, ca-**pit**-u-lāte, ex-**pŏst**-u-lāte, a-**mal**-ga-māte, ex-**hil**-a-rāte, le-**ġit**-i-māte (*v.*), ap-**prox**-i-māte, con-**cat**-e-nāte, sub-**ôr**-di-nate (*v.*), o-**rig**-i-nāte, con-**tam**-i-nāte, dis-**sem**-i-nāte, re-**crim**-i-nāte, a-**bom**-i-nāte, pre-**dom**-i-nāte, in-**tem**-per-ate, re-**ġen**-er-āte (*v*), co-**op**-er-āte, ex̱-**as**-per-āte, com-**miṣ**-er-āte, in-**vet**-er-ate, re-**it**-er-āte, ob-**lit**-er-āte, e-**vac**-u-āte, ex-**ten**-u-āte, in-**ad**-e-quate, ef-**fect**-ū-āte, per-**pet**-u-āte, as-**sas**-sin-āte, pro-**cras**-ti-nāte, pre-**des**-ti-nāte (*v.*), com-**pas**-sion-āte (*v.*), dis-**pas**-sion-ate, af-**fec**-tion-ate, un-**fort**-u-nate, e-**man**-çi-pāte, de-**lib**-er-āte (*v*), in-**car**-çer-āte, con-**fed**-er-āte (*v.*), con-**sid**-er-ate, pre-**pon**-der-āte, im-**mod**-er-ate, ac-**çel**-er-āte, in-**dic**-a-tĭve, pre-**rog**-a-tĭve, ir-**rel**-a-tive, ap-**pel**-la-tĭve, con-**tem**-pla-tĭve, su-**pēr**-la-tĭve, al-**ter**-na-tĭve, de-**clăr**-a-tĭve, com-**par**-a-tĭve, im-**pĕr**-a-tĭve, in-**dem**-ni-fȳ, per-**sŏn**-i-fy, re-**stōr**-a-tĭve, dis-**quaḷ**-i-fȳ.

WORDS OF FOUR SYLLABLES, ACCENTED ON THE SECOND.

al-**lū**-vi-on, pe-**trō**-le-um, çe-**ru̬**-le-an, le-**vī**-a-than, li-**brā**-ri-an, a-**grā**-ri-an, pre-**ca**-ri-oŭs, vī-**ca**-ri-ous, ne-**fa**-ri-ous, gre-**ga**-ri-ous, o-**va**-ri-oŭs, op-**prō**-bri-ous, sa-**lū**-bri-oŭs, im-**pē**-ri-ous, mys-**te**-ri-ous, la-**bō**-ri-ous, in-**glo**-ri-ous, çen-**so**-ri-ous, vic-**to**-ri-ous, no-**to**-ri-ous, ux̱-**o**-ri-ous, in-**jū**-ri-ous, pe-**nū**-ri-ous, ū-**s̱ū**-ri-ous (*yoo-zhoo-ri-oŭs*), lux̱-**ū**-ri-oŭs, vo-**lu**-mi-nous, o-**bē**-di-ent, ex-**pe**-di-ent, in-**gre**-di-ent, im-**mū**-ni-ty, com-**mu**-ni-ty, im-**pu**-ni-ty, com-**plā**-çen-çy, in-**dē**-çen-çy, di-**plō**-ma-çy, trans-**pâr**-en-çy.

A library is a collection of books. A librarian is a person who has charge of a library. The laborious bee is a pattern of industry. That is precarious which is uncertain. Life and health are precarious. Vicarious punishment is that which one person suffers in place of another. Gregarious animals are such as herd together, as sheep and goats. Salubrious air is favorable to health. A covetous man is called penurious. Escape or exemption from punishment is impunity. Do nothing that is injurious to religion, to morals, or to the interest of others. We speak of the transparency of glass, water, etc.

WORDS OF SEVEN SYLLABLES, ACCENTED ON THE FIFTH.

im-ma-te-ri-**ăl**-i-ty, in-di-vis̱-i-**bĭl**-i-ty, in-di-vid-ū-**ăl**-i-ty, im-con-pat-i-**bĭl**-i-ty, in-de-struct-i-**bil**-i-ty, im-per-çep-ti-**bil**-i-ty, ir-re-sist-i-**bil**-i-ty, in-com-bus-ti-**bil**-i-ty, im-pen-e-tra-**bil**-i-ty, in-el-i-ġi-**bil**-i-ty, im-mal-le-a-**bil**-i-ty, per-pen-dic-ū-**lăr**-i-ty, in-com-press-i-**bĭl**-i-ty, in-de-fen-si-**bil**-i-ty, val-e-tu-di-**nā**-ri-an, an-ti-trin-i-**ta**-ri-an.

WORDS OF EIGHT SYLLABLES, ACCENTED ON THE SIXTH.

un-in-tel-li-ġi-**bil**-i-ty, in-com-pre-hen-si-**bil**-i-ty.

The immateriality of the soul has rarely been disputed. The indivisibility of matter is supposed to be demonstrably false. It was once a practice in France to divorce husband and wife for incompatibility of tempers; a practice soon found to be incompatible with social order. The incompressibility of water has been disproven. We can not doubt the incomprehensibility of the divine attributes. Stones are remarkable for their immalleability. The indestructibility of matter is generally admitted. Asbestos is noted for its incombustibility. A Valetudinarian is a sickly person.

No. 122. – 92 Words

WORDS IN WHICH th HAS ITS ASPIRATED SOUND.

ē-ther, jā-çinth, thē-sis, ze-nit h, thick-et, thun-der, this-*t*le, thros-*t*le, throt-*t*le, thĭrst-y, thrif-ty, length-wīse, thrĕ*at*-*e*n-ing, au-thor, au-thor-īze, au-thŏr-i-ty, au-thŏr-i-ta-tĭve, meth-od, an-them, diph-thong (*dif-thong*), eth-ics, pan-ther, Sab-bath, thim-bl*e*, Thûrs-day, triph-thong, in-thrall, a-thwart, be-trŏth, thĭr-ty, thȯr-ough, thĭr-teen, thou-sand, ā-the-ism, thē-o-ry, the-o-rem, hȳ-a-çinth, cath-o-lic, ap-o-thegm, thŭn-der-bōlt, ep-i-thet, lab-y̆-rinth, leth-ar-ġy, pleth-o-ry, pleth-o-ric, sy̆m-pa-thy, am-a-ranth, am-e-thy̆st, ap-a-thy, aes-thet-ics, thĭr-ti-eth, sy̆n-the-sis, pan-thē-on, e-the-re-al, can-tha-ris, ca-thē-dral, ū-re-thra̍, au-then-tic, pa-thet-ic, syn-thet-ic, a-can-thus, ath-let-ic, me-theg-lin, ca-thär-tic, a-the-ist-ic, the-o-ret-ic-al, me-thod-ic-al, math-e-mat-ics, le-vī-a-than, en-thu-si-asm, an-tip-a-thy, a-rith-me-tic, an-tith-e-sis, mis-an-thro-py, phi-lan-thro-py, can-thär-i-dēs, the-oc-ra-çy, the-ol-o-ġy, the-od-o-līte, ther-mom-e-ter, ca-thol-i-con, my̆-thol-o-ġy, or-thog-ra-phy, hȳ-poth-e-sis, lĭ-thog-ra-phy, lĭ-thot-o-my, a-poth-e-ca-ry, ap-o-thē-o-sis, pol-y̆-the-ism, bib-li-o-thē-cal, ich-thy-ŏl-o-ġy, or-ni-thol-o-ġy.

No. 123. – 41 Words

WORDS IN WHICH th HAS ITS VOCAL SOUND.

ēi-ther, **nei**-ther, **hēa**-then, **clōth**-ier (*-yer*), **răth**-er, **fath**-om, **gath**-er, **hith**-er, **fur**-ther, **brĕth**-ren, **whith**-er, **wheth**-er, **lĕath**-er, **feath**-er, **nĕth**-er, **weth**-er, **prĭth**-ee, **bûr**-then, **soŭth**-ern, **teth**-er, **thith**-er, **with**-er, **lăth**-er, **fä**-ther, **far**-thing, **fûr**-thest, **pŏth**-er, **broth**-el, **broth**-er, **wor**-thy (*wur-thy*), **moth**-er, **smoth**-er, **oth**-er, **with**-ers, be-**nĕath**, be-queath, **with**-draw, an-**oth**-er, to-**ḡeth**-er, thêre-**with**-al, **nev**-er-the-less.

The heathen are those people who worship idols or know not the true God. Those who enjoy the light of the gospel, and neglect to observe its precepts, are more criminal than the heathen. All mankind are brethren, descendants of common parents. How unnatural and wicked it is to make war on our brethren, to conquer them, or to plunder and destroy them. It is every man's duty to bequeath to his children a rich inheritance of pious precepts.

No. 124. – 29 Words

WORDS OF THREE SYLLABLES, ACCENTED ON THE SECOND.

ac-**com**-plish, es-**tab**-lish, em-**bel**-lish, a-**bŏl**-ish, re-**plen**-ish, dĭ-**min**-ish, ad-**mon**-ish, pre-**mon**-ish, as-**ton**-ish, dis-**tin**-guish, ex-**tin**-guish, re-**lin**-quish, ex-**cul**-pāte, con-**trib**-ūte, re-**mon**-strançe, em-**broid**-er, re-**join**-der

ADJECTIVES: e-**nôr**-moŭs, dis-**as**-trous, mo-**ment**-ous, por-**tent**-ous, a-**bun**-dant, re-**dun**-dant, dis-**cor**-dant, trī-**umph**-ant, as-**sail**-ant, so-**nō**-roŭs, a-**çē**-tous, con-**cā**-vous.

A man, who saves the fragments of time, will accomplish a great deal in the course of his life. The most refined education does not embellish the human character like piety. Laws are abolished by the same power that made them. Wars generally prove disastrous to all parties. We are usually favored with abundant harvests. Most persons are ready to exculpate themselves from blame. Discordant sounds are harsh, and offend the ear.

WORDS OF FIVE SYLLABLES, ACCENTED ON THE THIRD.

in-ter-**mē**-di-ate, dis-pro-**pōr**-tion-ate, çĕr-e-**mo**-ni-al, mat-ri-**mo**-ni-al, pat-ri-**mo**-ni-al, an-ti-**mo**-ni-al, tes-ti-**mo**-ni-al, im-ma-**tē**-ri-al, maġ-is-**te**-ri-al, min-is-**te**-ri-al, im-me-**mō**-ri-al, sen-a-**to**-ri-al, dic-ta-**to**-ri-al, e-qua-**to**-ri-al, in-ar-**tĭc**-ū-late, il-le-**ġit**-i-mate, in-de-**tĕrm**-i-nate, e-qui-**pon**-der-ate, pär-ti-**çip**-i-al, in-di-**vid**-ū-al, in-ef-**fect**-ū-al, in-tel-**lect**-ū-al, pu-sil-**lan**-i-moŭs, dis-in-**ġen**-ū-ous, in-sig-**nif**-i-cant, e-qui-**pon**-der-ant, çĩr-cum-**am**-bi-ent, an-ni-**vĕr**-sa-ry, pär-li*a*-**ment**-a-ry, tes-ta-**ment**-a-ry, al-i-**ment**-a-ry, sup-ple-**ment**-a-ry, el-e-**ment**-a-ry, sat-is-f**ac**-to-ry, con-tra-**dic**-to-ry, val-e-**dic**-to-ry, in-tro-**duc**-to-ry, trig-o-**nom**-e-try, a-re-**om**-e-try, mis-çel-**lā**-ne-oŭs, sub-ter-**ra**-ne-ous, suc-çe-**da**-ne-ous, sī-mul-**ta**-ne-ous, in-stan-**ta**-ne-ous, hom-o-**ġē**-ne-ous, con-tu-**me**-li-ous, ac-ri-**mō**-ni-ous, par-si-**mo**-ni-ous, del-e-**tē**-ri-ous, mer-i-**tō**-ri-ous, dis-o-**bē**-di-ent, in-ex-**pe**-di-ent, con-ti-**nū**-i-ty, im-pro-**prī**-e-ty.

Senate originally signified a council of elders; for the Romans committed the public concerns to men of age and experience. The maxim of wise men was – old men for counsel, young men for war. But in modern times the senatorial dignity is not always connected with age. The bat is the intermediate link between quadrupeds and fowls. The orangoutang is intermediate between man and quadrupeds. Bodies of the same kind or nature are called homogeneous. Reproachful language is contumelious or contemptuous. Bitter and sarcastic language is acrimonious. Simultaneous acts are those that happen at the same time. Many things are lawful but not expedient.

No. 126. – 113 Words

dĕlve, twelve, nĕrve, cûrve, elf, shelf, self, pelf, ash, cash, dash, gash, hash, lash, flash, plash, slash, mash, smash, rash, crash, trash, flesh, mesh, fresh, dish, fish, pish, wish, gush, hush, blush, crush, frush, tush, next, text, twixt, mi<u>n</u>x, sphi<u>n</u>x, chānġe, mānġe, rānġe, grānġe, fōrġe, bāste, chaste, haste, waste, lūte, flute, mute, brṳte, fīght, bright, light, blight, plight, sight, slight, night, wight, right, tight, blowze, frounçe, rounçe, trounçe, *ch*a<u>s</u>m, pri<u>s</u>m.

MONOSYLLABLES WITH **th** VOCAL.

the, thōse, this, that, thīne, thȳ, then, thus, thou, thee, them, thençe, thē<u>s</u>e, th<u>a</u>n, blīthe, tīthe, līthe, wrīthe, sçȳthe, thō*ugh*, smōōth, sōōth, th<u>e</u>y, thêre, thêir.

THE FOLLOWING, WHEN NOUNS, HAVE THE ASPIRATED SOUND OF **th** IN THE SINGULAR NUMBER, AND THE VOCAL IN THE PLURAL.

bath, **baths**; lath, **laths**; path, **path<u>s</u>**; swath, **swath<u>s</u>**; cloth, **cloths**; moth, **moth<u>s</u>**; mouth, **mouth<u>s</u>**; wrēath, **wrēathe<u>s</u>**; shēath, **shēathe<u>s</u>**.

Twelve things make a dozen. To delve is to dig in the ground. When the nerves are affected the hands shake. Turf is a clod of earth held together by the roots of grass. Surf is the swell of the sea breaking on the shore. Cash formerly meant a chest, but now signifies money. An elf is an imaginary being or being of the fancy. A flash of lightening sometimes hurts the eyes. Flesh is the soft part of animal bodies. Blushes often manifest modesty, sometimes shame. Great and sudden changes sometimes do hurt. A grange is a farm and farmhouse. A forge is a place where iron is hammered. A rounce is the handle of a printing press. To frounce is to curl or frizzle the hair. Great haste often makes waste. It is no more right to steal apples or watermelons from another's garden or orchard, than it is to steal money from a desk. Besides, it is the meanest of all low tricks to creep into a man's enclosure to take his property. How much more manly is it to ask a friend for cherries, peaches, pears, or melons, than it is to sneak privately into his orchard and steal them! How must a boy, and much more a man, blush to be detected in so mean a trick!

No. 127. – 70 Words

IN THE FOLLOWING WORDS, **h** IS PRONOUNCHED BEFORE **W**; THUS *whale* IS PRONOUNCED hwale; *when*, hwen.

whāle, whēat, wharf, what, wheel, wheeze, **whee**-dle, whine, while, white, **whi**-t*e*n, **white**-wash, **whi**-tish, **whi**-ting, whȳ, whet, which, whilk, whiff, whig, whim, whin, whip, whelm, whelp, when, whençe, whisk, whist, whit, whiz, whêre, whe̱y, **whĕr**-ry, **wheth**-er, **whet**-stōne, **whif**-fle, **whig**-g̱ish, **whig**-g̱i̱sm, **whim**-per, **whim**-sēy, **whin**-ny, **whip**-côrd, **whip**-gràft, **whip**-saw, **whip**-stock, **whis**-per, **whis**-ky, **whis**-k̲er, **whis**-*t*le, **whith**-er, **whit**-lōw, **whit**-tle, whirl, **whirl**-pōol, **whirl**-wind, **whirl**-bat, **whirl**-i-g̱ig, **wharf**-aġe, **wharf**-in-ġer.

IN THE FOLLOWING WORDS **W** IS SILENT.

*wh*o̱, *wh*om, *wh*o̱se, *wh*ōle, *wh*o͞op, *wh*o̱-**ev**-er, *wh*o-so-**ev**-er, *wh*om-so-**ev**-er, **whōle**-sale, **whole**-sȯme.

Whales are the largest of marine animals. They afford us oil for lamps and other purposes. Wheat is a species of grain that grows in most climates, and the flour makes our finest bread. Wharves are structures built for the convenience of lading and unlading ships. Wheels are most admirable instruments of conveyance; carts, wagons, gigs, and coaches run on wheels. Whey is the thin watery part of milk. Bad boys sometimes know what a whip is by their feelings. This is a kind of knowledge, which good boys dispense with. One of the first things a little boy tries to get is a knife that he may whittle with it. If he asks for a knife and it is refused, he is pretty apt to whimper. The love of whisky has brought many a strong fellow to a disgraceful death. Whiskers are though by some to afford projection from the throat in cold weather.

No. 128. – 30 Words

IN THE FOLLOWING WORDS, **X** PASSES INTO THE SOUND OF **GZ**.

e**x**-**ăct**, e**x**-**ạlt**, ex-**em***p***t**, e**x**-**ẽrt**, e**x**-**hạust**, e**x**-**hôrt**, e**x**-**īle** (*v.*), e**x**-**ist**, e**x**-**ult**, e**x**-**hāle**, e**x**-**ăġ**- ġer-āte, e**x**-**am**-ĭne, e**x**-**am**-ple, e**x**-**an**-i-māte, e**x**-**as**-per-āte, e**x**-**ec**-ū-tĭve, e**x**-**ec**-ū-tor, e**x**-**ec**-ū-trix, e**x**-**hib**-it, e**x**-**ist**-ençe, e**x**-**ôr**-di-um, e**x**-**ot**-ic, e**x**-**em**-plar, e**x**-**em**-pla-ry, e**x**-**em**-pli-fӯ, e**x**-**emp**-tion, e**x**-**ŏn**-er-āte, e**x**-**ôr**-bi-tançe, e**x**-**ôr**-bi-tant, e**x**-**ū**-ber-ant.

The word exact is an adjective signifying nice, accurate, or precise; it is also a verb signifying to demand, require, or compel to yield. Astronomers can, by calculating, foretell the exact time of an eclipse, or the rising and setting of the sun. It is useful to keep very exact accounts. A king or a legislature must have power to exact taxes or duties to support the government. An exordium is a preface or preamble. To exist signifies to be, or to have life. The spirit is immortal; it will never cease to exist. We must not exalt ourselves, or exult over the fallen rival. It is our duty to exert our talents in doing good. We are not to expect to be exempt from evils. Exhort one another to the practice of virtue. Water is exhausted from the earth in vapor, and in time the ground is exhausted of water. An exile is one who is banished from his country. In telling a story be careful not to exaggerate. Examine the Scriptures daily and carefully, and set an example of good words. An executor is one appointed by a will to settle an estate after the death of the testator who makes the will. The President of the United States is the chief executive officer of the government. Officers should not exact exorbitant fees for their services. Charitable societies exhibit proofs of much benevolence. The earth often produces exuberant crops. Every man wishes to be exonerated from burdensome services.

No. 129. – 69 Words

IN THE FOLLOWING WORDS,
tian AND **tion** ARE PRONUNCED NEARLY **chun.**

băs-tion, **Chris**-tian, **mix**-tion, **quĕs**-tion, **fŭs**-tian, con-**ġes**-tion, dĭ-**ġes**-tion, ad-**mix**-tion, com-**bus**-tion, in-dĭ-**ġes**-tion, ex-**haus**-tion, suḡ-**ġes**-tion.

IN THE FOLLOWIN WORDS, **i** IN AN UNACCENTED SYLLABLE AND FOLLWING BY A VOWEL, A LIQUID SOUND, LIKE **y** CONSONANT; THUS *alien* IS PRONOUNCED **āl**-yen, AND *clothier, clōthier,* **clōth**-yer.

āl-ien (*-yen*), **cōurt**-ier, **clōth**-ier, **sāv**-ior (*-yur*), **pāv**-ior, **jūn**-ior, **sēn**-ior, **bĭl**-ioŭs, **bill**-ion, **bĭll**-iards, **cull**-ion, **mill**-ion, **min**-ion, **mill**-ionth, **pill**-ion, **pin**-ion, **rȯn**-ion, **scull**-ion, **trill**-ion, **trunn**-ion, **brill**-iant, **fil**-ial, **coll**-ier, **pann**-ier, **pon**-iard, **văl**-iant, **ȯn**-ion, **bṳll**-ion, **āl**-ien-āte, **bil**-ia-ry, **brill**-ian-çy, **brill**-iant-ly, **mil**-ia-ry, **văl**-iant-ly, **val**-iant-ness, com-**mūn**-ion, ver-**mil**-ion, pa-**vil**-ion, pōs-**till**-ion, fa-**mil**-iar, bat-**tăl**-ion, com-**pan**-ion, ras-**cal**-ion, do-**min**-ion, mo-**dill**-ion, o-**pin**-ion, re-**bell**-ion, re-**bell**-ioŭs, cĭ-**vil**-ian, dis-**ūn**-ion, be-**hāv**-ior, pe-**cūl**-iar, in-**tagl**-io, se-**ragl**-io, fa-**mĭl**-iar-īze, o-**pin**-ion-ist, o-**pin**-ion-ā-ted.

No. 130. – 56 Words

IN THE FOLLOWING WORDS, THE SYLLABLES **sier** and **zier** ARE PRO-
NOUNCED LIKE **zher** OR **zhur**, **sion** ARE PRONOUNCED **zhun**,
AND **sia** ARE PRONOUNCED **zha**.

brā-sier, **gla**-zier, **gra**-zier, **hō**-sier, **o**-sier, **cro**-sier, **fū**-sion, af-**fu**-sion, co-**hē**-sion, ad-**he**-sion, de-**lu**-sion, e-**ro**-sion, e-**va**-sion, pro-**fu**-sion, a-**bra**-sion, col-**lu**-sion, con-**clu**-sion, con-**fu**-sion, cor-**ro**-sion, oc-**ca**-sion, per-**va**-sion, e-**lu**-sion, dif-**fu**-sion, dis-**plo**-sion, ex-**plo**-sion, ef-**fu**-sion, il-**lu**-sion, in-**fu**-sion, in-**va**-sion, suf-**fu**-sion, dis-**suā**-sion, per-**sua**-sion, am-**bro**-sià, ob-**trụ**-sion, de-**trụ**-sion, in-**trụ**-sion, pro-**trụ**-sion, ex-**trụ**-sion.

**IN SOME OF THE FOLLOWING WORDS, THE TERMINATING SYLLABLE
IS PRONOUNCED** zhun, **AND IN OTHER THE VOWEL** i **MAY BE
CONSIDERED TO HAVE THE SOUND OF** y.

ab-**sçis**-sion, col-**lis**-ion, de-**çis**-ion, de-**ris**-ion, e-**lis**-ion, pre-**çis**-ion, pro-**vis**-ion, re-**vis**-ion, re-**sçis**-sion, con-**çis**-ion, ex-**çis**-ion, di-**vis**-ion, in-**çis**-ion, mis-**pris**-ion, pre-**vis**-ion, e-**lўs**-ian, cir-cum-**çis**-ion, sub-dĭ-**vis**-ion.

No. 131. – 81 Words

WORDS IN WHICH c BEFORE h HAS THE SOUND OF k.

Christ, chyle, scheme, āche, chasm, chrism, chôrd, chȳme, loch, school, choir (*kwīr*), **chō**-rus, **cho**-ral, **är**-chīves, **chā**-os, **ep**-och, **ī**-chor, **ō**-cher, **tro**-chee, **an**-chor, **chem**-ist, **Christ**-mas, **Chris**-tian, **dis**-tich, **ech**-o, **chron**-ic, **sched**-ūle, **pas**-chal, **chol**-er, **chō**-rist, **schol**-ar, **mon**-arch, **stȯm**-ach, **an**-ar-chy, **chrȳs**-o-līte, **chăr**-ac-ter, **cat**-e-chism, **pen**-ta-teūch, **sep**-ul-cher, **tech**-nic-al, **an**-cho-rīte, **arch**-i-tect, **arch**-i-trāve, **arch**-e-tȳpe, **hep**-tar-chy, **mach**-i-nāte, **Chris**-ten-dom, **brach**-i-al, **lach**-rȳ-mal, **sac**-cha-rĭne, **sȳn**-chro-nism, **Mich**-ael-mas, **chŏr**-is-ter, **chron**-i-cle, **ôr**-ches-trȧ, **pā**-tri-arch, **eū**-cha-rist, chi-**mē**-rȧ, pa-**rō**-chĭ-al, cha-**mē**-le-on, chro-**mat**-ic, me-**chan**-ic, cha-**ot**-ic, scho-**las**-tic, ca-**chex**-y, cha-**lȳb**-e-ate, a-**nach**-ro-nism, syn-**ec**-do-che, mo-**närch**-ic-al, bron-**chot**-o-my, chro-**nol**-o-ġy, chī-**rog**-ra-phy, chō-**rog**-ra-phy chro-**nom**-e-ter, the-**om**-a-chy, **mel**-an-chol-y, **pā**-tri-ärch-y, **hī**-er-arch-y, **ol**-i-gar-chy, cat-e-**chĕt**-ic-al, ich-thȳ-**ŏl**-o-ġy.

Experience keeps a dear school, but fools will learn in no other. Chyle is the milky fluid separated from food by digestion, and from this are formed blood and nutriments for the support of animal life. An epoch is a fixed point of time from which years are recorded. The departure of the Israelites from Egypt is a remarkable epoch in their history. Sound striking against an object and returned, is an echo. The stomach is the great laboratory of animal bodies, in which food is digested and prepared for entering the proper vessels, and nourishing the body. If the stomach is impaired and does not perform its proper functions, the whole body suffers.

No. 132. – 107 Words

WORDS IN WHICH g BEFORE e, i, AND y HAS ITS HARD OR CLOSE SOUND.

ḡēar, ḡeese, ḡeld, ḡift, ḡĭve, ḡig, ḡĭld ḡimp, ḡĩrd, ḡĩrth, **ēa-ḡer**, **mēa-ḡer**, **ḡew-gaw**, **tī-ḡer**, **tō-ḡed**, **big-ḡin**, **brag-ḡer**, **dag-ḡer**, **crag-ḡy**, **bug-gy**, **crag**-ged, **dig**-ger, **dig**-ging, **rig**-ging, rigged (*rĭgd*), **rig-ḡer**, **flag-ḡing**, **flag-ḡy**, **sog-ḡy**, ḡib-ber-ish, ḡib-boŭs, ḡid-dy, ḡig-gle, ḡig-gling, ḡig-gler, ḡiz-zard, ḡim-let, ḡĩrl-ish, **jag-ḡed**, **jag-ḡy**, legḡed*, **leg-ḡin**, **pig-ḡer-y**, **quăg-ḡy**, **rag-ḡed**, **trig-ḡer**, **scrag-ḡed**, **scrag-ḡy**, **shag-ḡy**, **shag-ḡed**, **slug-ḡish**, **lug-ḡer**, **snag-ḡed**, **snag-ḡy**, **sprig-ḡy**, **stag-ḡer**, **stag-ḡers**, twigḡed*, **twig-ḡy**, **wag-ḡish**, au-ḡer, **bŏg-ḡy**, **fog-ḡy**, clogḡed*, **clog-ḡing**, **clog-ḡy**, cogḡed*, **bag-ḡy**, **dog-ḡed**, **dog-ḡish**, jogḡed*, **jog-ḡing**, **jog-ḡer**, **nog-ḡin**, **tär-ḡet**, flogḡed*, **flog-ḡing**, **ḡift-ed**, hugḡed*. **hug-ḡing**, shrugḡed*, **shrug-ḡing**, **rug-ḡed**, tugḡed*, **tug-ḡing**, lugḡed*, **lug-ḡing**, **mug-ḡy**, fagḡed*, **fag-ḡing**, **gag-ḡing**, bragḡed*, **brag-ḡing**, **bag-ḡing**, **ḡeld**-ing, **ḡild-ing**, **ḡild-ed**, **ḡild-er**, **swag-ḡer**, **swag-ḡy**, **ḡĩrd-le**, **ḡĩrd-er**, **be-ḡin**, wagḡed*, **wag-ḡer-y**, **log-ḡer-hĕ**ad, to-ḡeth-er.

---

* The starred words are pronouncd as one syllable.

IN THE FOLLOWING, c OR g ENDING A SYLLABLE HAVING A PRIMARY OR A SECONDARY ACCENT, IS SOUNDED AS s AND j RESPECTIVELY.

maġ-ic, **traġ**-ic, **aġ**-ĭle, **aç**-id, **diġ**-it, **faç**-ĭle, **fraġ**-ĭle, **friġ**-id, **riġ**-id, **plaç**-id, **viġ**-il, **taç**-it, **aġ**-i-tāte, **leġ**-i-ble, **viġ**-i-lant, **reġ**-i-ment, **preç**-e-dent, **preç**-i-pĭçe, **reç**-i-pe, **deç**-i-mal, **deç**-i-māte, **laç**-er-āte, **paç**-i-fȳ, **paġ**-i-nal, **reġ**-i-çide, **reġ**-i-men, **reġ**-is-ter, **speç**-i-fȳ, **maç**-er-āte, **maġ**-is-trāte, **maġ**-is-tra-çy, **traġ**-e-dy, **viç**-i-naġe, **veġ**-e-tāte, **veġ**-e-ta-ble, **lŏġ**-ic, **proç**-ess, **coġ**-i-tāte, **proġ**-e-ny, il-**liç**-it, im-**pliç**-it, e-**liç**-it, ex-**pliç**-it, so-**liç**-it, im-**aġ**-ĭne, au-**daç**-i-ty, ca-**paç**-i-ty, fu-**gaç**-i-ty, lo-**quaç**-i-ty, men-**daç**-i-ty, il-**leġ**-i-ble, o-**riġ**-i-nate, so-**liç**-i-tor, fe-**liç**-i-ty, mu-**niç**-i-pal, an-**tiç**-i-pāte, par-**tiç**-i-pāte, sim-**pliç**-i-ty, me-**diç**-i-nal, so-**liç**-i-tūde, trī-**pliç**-i-ty, ver-**tiç**-i-ty, rus-**tiç**-i-ty, ex-a**ġ**-**ġer**-āte, mor-**daç**-i-ty, pub-**liç**-i-ty, o-**paç**-i-ty, ra-**paç**-i-ty, sa-**gaç**-i-ty, bel-**liġ**-er-ent, o-**riġ**-i-nal, ar-**miġ**-er-oŭs, ver-**tiġ**-i-nous, re-**friġ**-er-ate, reç-i-**tā**-tion, veġ-e-**ta**-tion, aġ-i-**ta**-tion, coġ-i-**ta**-tion, o-le-**ăġ**-i-noŭs, au-then-**tiç**-i-ty, e-las-**tiç**-i-ty, du-o-**deç**-i-mo, in-ca-**paç**-i-tāte, ab-o-**riġ**-i-nal, ec-çen-**triç**-i-ty, mu-çi-**laġ**-i-noŭs, mul-ti-**pliç**-i-ty, per-spi-**caç**-i-ty, per-ti-**naç**-i-ty, taç-i-**tur**-ni-ty, maġ-is-**tē**-ri-al, a-**troç**-i-ty, fe-**roç**-i-ty, ve-**loç**-i-ty, r*h*ī-**noç**-e-rŏs, rec-i-**proç**-i-ty, im-aġ-in-**ā**-tion, ex-aġ-ġer-**ā**-tion, re-friġ-er-**ā**-tion, so-liç-i-**tā**-tion, leġ-er-de-**māin**.

No. 134. – 63 Words

WORDS IN WHICH ce, ci, ti, **AND** si, **ARE SOUNDED AS** sh.

Grē-cian, **grā**-cioŭs, **spa**-cious, **spē**-cious, **spe**-ciēs̱ **sō**-cial, **ġen**-tian, **tĕr**-tian, **con**-scienҫe, **cap**-tioŭs, **fac**-tious, **fic**-tious, **lus**-cious, **frac**-tious, **cạu**-tious, **con**-scious, **nup**-tial, **pär**-tial, es-**sen**-tial, po-**ten**-tial, pro-**vin**-cial, pru-**den**-cial, com-**mĕr**-cial, im-**pär**-tial, sub-**stan**-tial, con-fi-**den**-tial, pen-i-**ten**-tial, prov-i-**den**-tial, rev-e-**ren**-tial, e-qui-**noc**-tial, in-flu-**en**-tial, pes-ti-**len**-tial, au-**dā**-cioŭs, ca-**pa**-cious, fa-**cē**-tious, fal-**lā**-cious, a-**trō**-cious, fe-**rō**-cioŭs, lo-**quā**-cious, ra-**pa**-cious, sa-**ga**-cious, te-**na**-cious, vex-**a**-tious, vī-**va**-cious, vo-**ra**-cious, ve-**ra**-cious, crus-**ta**-ceous, con-**ten**-tious, in-**fec**-tious, sen-**ten**-tious, lī-**cen**-tioŭs, in-**cạu**-tious, ef-fi-**cā**-cious, os-ten-**ta**-tious, per-spi-**ca**-cious, per-ti-**na**-cious, con-**sci**-en-tious, **pā**-tient, **quō**-tient, **ān**-cient, **tran**-sient, pär-ti-**al**-i-ty, im-par-ti-**al**-i-ty.

No. 135. – 99 Words

WORDS IN WHICH ci, ti, **ARE SOUNDED AS** sh,
AND IN PRONOUNCIATION ARE UNITED TO THE PRECEEDING SYLLABLE.

prĕ-cioŭs (*prĕsh-*), **spĕ**-cial (*spĕsh-al*), **vĭ**-cioŭs, ad-**dĭ**-tion, am-**bĭ**-tion, ạus-**pĭ**-cious, of-**fĭ**-cious, ca-**prĭ**-cious, nu-**trĭ**-tious, de-**lĭ**-cious, am-**bĭ**-tious, fac-**tĭ**-cious, fic-**tĭ**-tious, den-**tĭ**-tion, fru-**ĭ**-tion, es-**pĕ**-cial, op-**tĭ**-cian, mo-**nĭ**-tion, mu-**nĭ**-tion, con-**trĭ**-tion, at-**trĭ**-tion, nu-**trĭ**-tion, cog-**nĭ**-tion, ig-**nĭ**-tion, con-**dĭ**-tion, de-**fĭ**-cient, de-**lĭ**-cious, dis-**crĕ**-tion, e-**dĭ**-tion, ef-**fĭ**-cient, fla-**ġĭ**-tioŭs, fru-**ĭ**-tion, ju-**dĭ**-cial, lo-**ġĭ**-cian, ma-**ġĭ**-cian, ma-**lĭ**-cioŭs, mi-**lĭ**-tiȧ, mu-**sĭ̱**-cian, of-**fĭ**-cial, pa-**trĭ**-cian, pär-**tĭ**-tion, per-**dĭ**-tion, per-**nĭ**-cious, pe-**tĭ**-tion, pro-**fĭ**-cient, phy-**sĭ̱**-cian, po-**sĭ̱**-tion, pro-**pĭ**-tioŭs, se-**dĭ**-tion, se-**dĭ**-tioŭs, sol-**stĭ**-tial, suf-**fĭ**-cient, sus-**pĭ**-cioŭs, vo-**lĭ**-tion, ab-o-**lĭ**-tion, ac-qui-**sĭ**-tion, ad-mo-**nĭ**-tion, ad-ven-**tĭ**-tioŭs, am-mu-**nĭ**-tion, pre-mo-**nĭ**-tion, dis-qui-**sĭ**-tion in-qui-**sĭ**-tion, rep-e-**tĭ**-tion, in-hi-**bĭ**-tion, ex-po-**sĭ**-tion, ap-pa-**rĭ**-tion, är-ti-**fĭ**-cial, ap-po-**sĭ**-tion, eb-ul-**lĭ**-tion, er-ụ-**dĭ**-tion, ex-hi-**bĭ**-tion, im-po-**sĭ**-tion, op-po-**sĭ**-tion, prej-ū-**dĭ**-cial, pol-i-**tĭ**-cian, prep-o-**sĭ**-tion, prop-o-**sĭ**-tion, pro-hi-**bĭ**-tion, su-per-**fĭ**-cial, su-per-**stĭ**-tion, sup-po-**sĭ**-tion, sur-rep-**tĭ**-tioŭs, mer-e-**trĭ**-cioŭs, av-a-**rĭ**-cioŭs, in-ạu-**spĭ**-cioŭs, ben-e-**fĭ**-cial, co-a-**lĭ**-tion, com-pe-**tĭ**-tion, com-po-**sĭ**-tion, def-i-**nĭ**-tion, dem-o-**lĭ**-tion, dep-o-**sĭ**-tion, dis-po-**sĭ**-tion, prac-**tĭ**-tion-er, a-rith-me-**tĭ**-cian, ac-a-de-**mĭ**-cian, ġe-om-e-**trĭ**-cian, in-ju-**dĭ**-cioŭs, de-**fĭ**-cien-çy.

No. 136. – 21 Words

IN THE FOLLOWING WORDS, ci **AND** ti **ARE PRONOUNCE**
LIKE shi **AS** *associate* (as-so-**shĭ**-āte)

as-**sō**-ci-āte, con-**sō**-ci-āte, ap-**prē**-ci-āte, de-**pre**-ci-āte, e-**mā**-ci-āte, ex-**pa**-ti-āte, in-**gra**-ti-āte, ne-**gō**-ti-āte, in-**sā**-ti-āte, an-**nun**-ci-āte, lī-**çen**-ti-ate, sub-**stan**-ti-āte, no-**vĭ**-ti-ate, of-**fĭ**-ci-āte, ex-**crụ**-ci-āte, pro-**pĭ**-ti-āte, e-**nun**-ci-āte, de-**nun**-ci-āte, dis-**sō**-ci-āte, **sā**-ti-āte, **vĭ**-ti-āte

No. 137. – 307 Words

THE FOLLOWING WORDS, ENDING IN ic, **MAY HAVE, AND SOME OF THEM OFTEN DO HAVE, THE SYLLABLE** al **ADDED AFTER** ic, as *comic, comical;* **AND THE ADVERBS IN** ly **DERIVED FROM THESE WORDS ALWAYS HAVE** al, **AS IN** *classically.*

cau̯-stie, çen-tric, clas-sic, clin-ic, com-ic, con-ic, crit-ic, cū-bic, çy̆n-ic, eth-ic, eth-nic, loġ-ic, ly̆r-ic, maġ-ic, mū-sic, my̆s-tic, op-tic, *phthis-ic,* skep-tic, sphĕr-ic, stat-ic, stō-ic, sty̆p-tic, top-ic, traġ-ic, ty̆p-ic, rus-tic, graph-ic.

WORDS OF THREE SYLLABLES, ACCENTED ON THE SECOND. THESE MAY RECEIVE THE TERMINATION al **FOR THE ADJECTIVE, AND TO THAT MAY BE ADDED** ly **TO FORM THE ADVERB; AS,** *agrestic, agrestical,* **and** *agrestically.*

a-crŏn-y, a-grĕs-tic, al-ehem-ic, as-çet-ic, ath-let-ic, äu-then-tic, bär-băr-ic, bo-tan-ic, ca-thär-tic, clas-sif-ic, cos-met-ic, dī-dac-tic, do-mes-tic, dog-mat-ic, dra-mat-ic, Drụ-id-ic, dys-pep-tic, ec-çen-tric, ec-lec-tic, ec-stat-ic, e-lec-tric, em-pĭr-ic, er-rat-ic, fa-nat-ic, fo-ren-sic, ġe-nĕr-ic, ġym-nas-tic, har-mŏn-ic, He-brā-ic, hĕr-met-ic, hy̆s-ter-ic, ī-ron-ic, in-trin-sic, la-con-ic, lu-çif-ic, mag-net-ic, mag-nif-ic, ma-jes-tic, me-ehan-ic, mo-nas-tic, mor-bif-ic, nu-mĕr-ic, ob-stet-ric, or-gan-ic, os-sif-ic, pa-çif-ic, pa-thet-ic, pe-dant-ic, phleg-mat-ic, phre-net-ic, Pla-ton-ic, *p*neū-mat-ic, po-lem-ic, prag-mat-ic, pro-lif-ic, pro-phet-ic, *r*hap-sod-ic, ro-man-tic, ru-bif-ic, sa-tĭr-ic, *s*chis-mat-ic, scho-las-tic, scor-bū-tic, so-phis-tic, sper-mat-ic, sta-lac-tic, stig-mat-ic, sy̆m-met-ric, syn-od-ic, ter-rĭf-ic, thē-ist-ic, ty̆-ran-nic, e-las-tic, bȯm-bast-ic, sta-tist-ic.

ac-a-**dem**-ic, al-chem-**ist**-ic, al-pha-**bet**-ic, ap-o-**plec**-tic, an-a-**loġ**-ic, an-a-**lўt**-ic, an-a-**tom**-ic, ap-os-**tol**-ic, a-rith-**met**-ic, as-tro-**loġ**-ic, as-tro-**nom**-ic, a-the-**ist**-ic, at-mos-**phĕr**-ic, bar-o-**met**-ric, be-a-**tif**-ic, bī-o-**graph**-ic, cab-a-**list**-ic, cal-vin-**ist**-ic, ca̱s-ū-**ist**-ic, cat-e-**ehet**-ic, cat-e-**gŏr**-ic, chro-no-**loġ**-ic, dem-o-**crat**-ic, dī-a-**bŏl**-ic, dī-a-**lec**-tic, dip-lo-**mat**-ic, dī-a-**met**-ric, dī-ū-**ret**-ic, dol-o-**rif**-ic, em-blem-**at**-ic, en-er-**ġet**-ic, e-nig-**mat**-ic, ep-i-**lep**-tic, ep-i-**dem**-ic, ep-i-**sŏd**-ic, eū-eha-**rist**-ic, ex-e-**ġet**-ic, friġ̄-or-**if**-ic, ġe-o-**loġ**-ic, ġe-o-**met**-ric, hem-is-**phĕr**-ic, his-tri-**on**-ic, hyp-o-**crit**-ic, hȳ-per-**bŏl**-ic, hȳ-po-**stat**-ic, hȳ-po-thet-ic, id-i-**ot**-ic, in-e-**last**-ic, Jac-o-**bin**-ic, math-e-**mat**-ic, met-a-**phŏr**-ic, met-a-**phy̱s**-ic, myth-o-**loġ**-ic, ne-o-**tĕr**-ic, or-tho-**graph**-ic, pan-the-**ist**-ic, par-a-**lўt**-ic, par-a-**phrast**-ic, par-a-**sit**-ic, par-en-**thet**-ic, par-a-**bŏl**-ic, path-o-**loġ**-ic, pe-ri-**od**-ic, phil-o-**loġ**-ic, phil-o-**soph**-ic, phil-an-**throp**-ic, Phar-i-**sā**-ic, prob-lem-**at**-ic, pu-ri-**tan**-ic, pyr-a-**mid**-ic, pyr-o-**tec**_h_-nic, sçī-en-**tif**-ic, syc-o-**phant**-ic, syl-lo-**ġis**-tic, sym-pa-**thet**-ic, sys-tem-**at**-ic, tal-is-**man**-ic, the-o-**lŏġ**-ic, the-o-**crăt**-ic, the-o-**ret**-ic, to-po-**graph**-ic, tȳ-po-**graph**-ic, zo-o-**loġ**-ic, ġe-o-**çen**-tric.

Thermometrical observations show the temperature of the air in winter and summer. The mineralogist arranges his specimens in a scientific manner.

WORDS OF FIVE SYLLABLES, ACCENTED ON THE FOURTH

an-ti-scor-**bū**-tic, ar-is-to-**crat**-ic, ehar-ac-ter-**is**-tic, ec-cle-si-**as**-tic, en-thu-si-**as**-tic, en-to-mo-**lŏġ**-ic, e-pi-gram-**mat**-ic, ġen-e-a-**loġ**-ic, lex-i-co-**graph**-ic, mon-o-syl-**lab**-ic, or-ni-tho-**loġ**-ic, os-te-o-**loġ**-ic, phy̱s-i-lo-**loġ**-ic, ieh-thy̆-lo-**loġ**-ic.

THE FOLLOWING WORDS RARELY OR NEVER TAKE THE TERMINATION al.

quạd-**rat**-ic, **cath**-o-lic, çe-**phal**-ic, eha-**ot**-ic, con-**çen**-tric, e-**lē**-ġĭ-ac, ec-**stat**-ic, **ep**-ic, e̱x-**ot**-ic, **găl**-lic, **Gŏth**-ic, **hy̆m**-nic, ī-**tăl**-ic, me-**dal**-ic, me-te-**ŏr**-ic, me-**tăl**-lic, O-**ly̆m**-pic, par-e-**gŏr**-ic, **plas**-tic, **pub**-lic, **Pū**-nic, re-**pub**-lic, **tac**-tic, **ärc**-tic, **pep**-tic, e-**las**-tic, **çy̆s**-tic.

THE FOLLOWING WORDS USUALLY OR ALWAYS END IN al.

bib-lic-al, ca-**non**-ic-al, ehĭ-**mer**-ic-al, **cler**-ic-al, **co̱s**-mic-al, **côr**-ti-cal, do-**min**-i-cal, **fin**-i-cal, il-**lŏġ**-ic-al, in-**im**-i-cal, me-**thod**-ic-al, **fär**-çi-cal, **med**-i-cal, **trop**-ic-al, **top**-ic-al, **drop**-si-cal, **com**-ic-al, **met**-ri-cal, **phy̆s̱**-ic-al, **prac**-ti-cal, **rad**-i-cal, **ver̃**-ti-cal, **vôr**-ti-cal, **whim**-s̱i-cal.

THE FOLLOWING WORDS NEVER TAKE THE TERMINATION al.

ap-o-**stroph**-ic, **ehol**-er-ic, **lū**-na-tic, **pleth**-o-ric, car-**bol**-ic, sul-**phū**-ric, car-**bon**-ic, **tûr**-mer-ic, oph-**thal**-mic.

WORDS ENDING IN an, en, OR on, IN WHICH THE VOWEL IS MUTE OR SLIGHTLY PRONOUNCED.

ärt-i-s̱an, **ben**-i-s̱on, ca-**păr**-i-son, com-**păr**-i-son **co̱ûr**-te-s̱an, **gär**-ri-son, **çit**-i-zen, **den**-i-zen, **ŏr**-i-son, **pär**-ti-s̱an, **ū**-ni-son, **ven**-i-s̱on.

WORDS ENDING IN ism, RETAINING THE ACCENT ON THE PRIMATIVES.

mo-**nas**-ti-çiṣm, ne-**ŏl**-o-ġiṣm, **at**-ti-çism, **goth**-i-çiṣm, pa-**răl**-o-ġiṣm, A-**mer**-i-can-iṣm, **ep**-i-cū-riṣm, **Jes**-ū-it-iṣm, **lib**-er-tin-iṣm, ma-**tē**-ri-al-iṣm, **mon**-o-the-iṣm, **nat**-ū-ral-iṣm, **pā**-tri-ot-iṣm, **pŏl**-y̆-the-iṣm, **pros**-e-lȳt-iṣm, **phăr**-i-sa-iṣm, **Prot**-est-ant-iṣm, prop-a-**gand**-iṣm, per-i-pa-**tet**-i-çiṣm, pro-**vin**-çial-iṣm, **an**-gli-çiṣm **van**-dal-iṣm, **gal**-li-çiṣm, **ped**-a-gog-iṣm, **pū**-ri-tan-iṣm, Pres-by-**tē**-ri-an-iṣm, **par**-a-sit-iṣm, **par**-al-lel-iṣm, **fā**-vor-it-iṣm, so-**çin**-i-an-iṣm, pa-**raeh**-ro-niṣm, re-**pub**-lic-an-iṣm, sec-**ta**-ri-an-iṣm, seho-**las**-ti-çiṣm.

No. 138. – 48 Words

WORDS IN ize, ACCENED ON THE FIRST SYLLABLE

au-thor-īze, **bas**-tard-ize, **çiv**-il-ize, **can**-on-ize, **lē**-gal-ize, **mŏr**-al-ize, **drăm**-a-tize, **em**-pha-size, **găl**-va-nize, **hẽr**-bo-rize, **mag**-net-ize, **mod**-ern-ize, **ag**-o-nize, **pul**-ver-ize, **stĕr**-il-ize, **sub**-si-dize, **ty̆r**-an-nize, **sy̆s**-tem-ize, **meth**-od-ize, **jo͝ur**-nal-ize, **bru̟**-tal-ize, **cŏl**-o-nize, **en**-er-ġize, **ē**-qual-ize, **hū**-man-ize, **Ju**-da-ize, **ôr**-gan-ize, **pat**-ron-ize, **sat**-ir-ize **tan**-tal-ize, **vō**-cal-ize, **cau̟**-ter-ize, **bär**-bar-ize, **bot**-a-nize, **das**-tard-ize, **det**-o-nize, **dŏg**-ma-tize, **dram**-a-tize, **fẽr**-til-ize, **ī**-dol-ize, **mel**-o-dize, **mes**-mer-ize, **pō**-lar-ize, **rē**-al-ize, **the**-o-rize, **tran**-quil-ize, **tem**-po-rize, **Rō**-man-ize.

No. 139. – 27 Words

WORDS OF FOUR AND FIVE SYLLABLES, RETAINING THE ACCENTS OF THEIR PRIMITIVES.

al-co-hol-īze, **ăl**-le-go-rize, a-**năth**-e-ma-tize, **an**-i-mal-ize, e-**pis**-to-lize, **bes**-tial-ize, e-**nig**-ma-tize, e**hăr**-ac-ter-ize, e-**the**-re-al-ize, ġen-er-al-ize, **lib**-er-al-ize, ma-**tē**-ri-al-ize, me-**mō**-ri-al-ize, **min**-er-al-ize, mo-**nop**-o-lize, **nat**-u-ral-ize, **ox**-y-ġen-ize, par-**tic**-ū-lar-ize, **pan**-e-ġyr-ize, **pop**-ū-lar-ize, **pros**-e-ly-tize, **pū**-ri-tan-ize, re-**pub**-lic-an-ize, **sec**-ū-lar-ize, **sen**-sū-al-ize (*sĕn-shu̯-al-ize*), **spĭr**-it-ū-al-ize, **vŏl**-a-til-ize.

We should never tyrannize over those weaker than ourselves

No. 140. – 118 Words

THE COMBINATION ng **REPRESENTS IN SOME WORDS, A SIMILAR ELEMENTARY SOUND, AS HEARD IN** *sing, singer, long*; **IN OTHER WORDS, IT REPRESENTS THE SAME ELEMENARY SOUND FOLLOWED BY THAT OF** g **HARD (HEARD IN** *go, get* **) AS IN** *finger, linger, longer*.

THE FOLLOWING HAVE THE SIMPLE SOUND.

a-mȯng, bang, bring, **bring**-ing, bung, clang, cling, **cling**-ing, clung, dung, fang, fling, **fing**-er, **fling**-ing flung, gang, hang, hanged **hang**-er, **hang**-man, **hang**-nail, hung, king, ling, long, lung̲s, pang, prong, rang, ring, **ring**-ing, **ring**-let, rung, sang, sing, **sing**-er **sing**-ing, song, sung, slang, sling, **sling**-er, slung, spring, sprang, **spring**-er **spring**-ing, sting, **sting**-er, **sting**-ing, stung, string, stringed, **string**-er, strung, **string**-ing, strong, **strong**-ly, swing, **swing**-er, **swing**-ing, swung, tang, thing, thong, **tȯn**-g*ue*, twang, *w*ring, ***w*ring**-er, ***w*ring**-ing, *w*rong, *w*ronged.

IN THE FOLLOWING WORDS, n, ALONE REPRESENTS THE SOUND OF ng, AND IS MARKED THUS n̲.

a̲n-ḡer, a̲n-gry, a̲n-gle, a̲n-gler, a̲n-gli-can, a̲n-gli-çism, a̲n-gli-çīze, a̲n-guish, a̲n-gu-lar, bra̲n-gle, bu̲n-gle, cla̲n-gor, **co̲n-go, da̲n-gle, di̲n-gle, fa̲n-gle, fi̲n-ḡer, fu̲n-**gus **hu̲n-ger, hu̲n-gry, i̲n-gle, ja̲n-gle, ja̲n-gler ja̲n-gling, ji̲n-**gle, **la̲n-guid, la̲n-guish, lo̲n-ger, lo̲n-gest, ma̲n-gle, ma̲n-**gler, **ma̲n-go, mi̲n-gle, mo̲n-ger, mȯn-grel, strŏ̲n-ger, stro̲n-ḡest, li̲n-ḡer, ta̲n-gle, ti̲n-gle, wra̲n-gle, e-lo̲n-gate, li̲n-ḡer-ing, sy̆-ri̲n-ḡȧ, stra̲n-gu-ry.**

No. 141. – 32 Words

IN THE FOLLOWING WORDS THE d, t, AND u. PREFERABLY TAKE THEIR REGULAR SOUNDS; AS IN *capture, verdure,* PRONOUNCED *capt-yoor,* MANY SPEAKERS HOWEVER, SAY, *kap-choor, vēr-jur.*

capt-ūre, çi̲nct-ure, crēat-ure, cult-ure, fēa-ture, fract-ure, fūt-ure, joint-ure, ju̲nct-ure, lect-ure, mixt-ure, moist-ure, nāt-ure, nûrt-ure, ôrd-ure, pȧst-ure, pict-ure, pŏst-ure, pu̲nct-ure, rapt-ure, script-ure, sculpt-ure, stat-ure, ġest-ure, **strict-ure, struct-ure, sūt-ure, text-ure, ti̲nct-ure, tôrt-**ure, **vent-ure, vĕrd-ure.**

The lungs are organs of respiration. If any substance, except air is inhaled and comes in contact with the lungs, we instantly cough. This cough is an effort of nature to free the lungs. A finger signifies a taker, as does fang. We take or catch things with the fingers, and fowls and rapacious quadrupeds seize other animals with their fangs. A pang is a severe pain. Anguish is violent distress. A lecture is a discourse read or pronounced on any subject; it is also formal reproof. The Bible, that is the Old and the New Testament contains the Holy Scriptures. Discourage cunning in a child: cunning is the ape of wisdom. Whatever is wrong is a deviation from right, or from the just laws of God or man. Anger is a tormenting passion, and so are envy and jealously. To be doomed is to suffer these passions long, would be as severe a punishment as confinement in a state prison. An anglicism is a peculiar mode of speech among the English. Love is an agreeable passion, and love is something stronger than death. How happy men would be if they always love what is right and hate what is wrong.

No. 142. – 52 Words

g AND k BEFORE n ARE ALWAYS SILENT.

gnär, gnärl, gnash, gnat, gnạw, **gnō**-mon, **gnŏs**-tics, **gnŏs**-ti-çis̱m, knab, knack, knag, **knag**-g̱y, knap, **knap**-sack, **knap**-weed, kneel, knāve, **knāv**-er-y, **knāv**-ish, **knāv**-ish-ly, **knāv**-ish-ness, knēad, knee, kneel, knīfe, knight, knight-ĕr-rant, **knight**-hŏ͝od, **knight**-ly, knit, **knit**-ter, **knit**-ting, knob, knobbed, **knob**-by, knock, **knock**-er, knŏll, knŏt, **knōt**-grass, **knŏt**-ty, **knot**-ti-ly, **knot**-ti-ness, knout, knōw, **know**-a-ble, known, **know**-ing, **knŏwl**-edg̱e, **knuck**-le, knûrl, **knurl**-y.

Knead the dough thoroughly, if you would have good bread. The original signification of *knave* was 'a boy'; but the word now signifies 'a dishonest person.' In Russia, the knout is used to inflict stripes on the bare back.

No. 143. – 27 Words

IN THE FOLLOWING WORDS, ch HAS THE SOUND OF sh, AND IN MANY OF THEM i HAS THE SOUND OF e LONG.

çhāise, çha-**grin**, çham-**pāign**, çhĭ-**cāne**, çhĭ-**cān**-er-y, çhev-a-**liēr**, **çhĭv**-al-ry, çhan-de-**liēr**, çhe-**mĭs̱e**, cap-ū-**çhĭn**, mag-a-**zĭne**, sub-ma-**rĭne**, trans-ma-**rĭne**, bȯm-ba-**zĭne**, brig-a-**diēr**, can-non-**iēr**, cap-a-**piē**, cär-bin-**iēr**, cav-a-**liēr**, **quạr**-an-tïne, man-da-**rĭn**, cash-**iēr**, ma-**rĭne**, ca-**prĭçe**, po-lïçe, fas-**çĭne**, fron-**tiēr**.

107

No. 144. – 62 Words

IN THE FOLLOWING WORDS, THE VOWEL a IN THE DIGRAPH ea, HAS NO SOUND AND e IS EITHER SHORT, OR PRONOUNCED LIKE e IN *term;* THUS, *bread, tread, earth, dearth, ARE PRONOUNCED brĕd, trĕd, ĕrth, dĕrth.*

brĕad, dead, head, tread, dread, thread, spread, breast, breadth, breath, ẽarth, dearth, thrĕat, sweat, sẽarch, hĕalth, wealth, stealth, cleanse, ẽarl, pearl, earn, learn, yean, mĕant, dreamt, realm, **ĕar**-ly, **earn**-est, re-**sẽarch**, **clĕan**-ly, **hĕav**-*e*n, **leav**-*e*n, **heav**-y, **read**-y, **health**-y, **wealth**-y, **feath**-er, **leath**-er, **leath**-ern, **tread**-l*e*, **jeal**-oŭs, **jeal**-oŭs-y, **zeal**-oŭs, **zeal**-ot, **pleas**-ant, **pĕas**-ant, **pleas**-ure, **meas**-ūre, **treas**-ūre, **treach**-er-y, en-**dĕav**-or, re-**hẽarse**, **thrĕat**-*e*n, **break**-fast, **stead**-fast, **mead**-ōw, **pẽarl**-ash, **stĕalth**-y, **stead**-y, **stealth**-fu̸l, **health**-fu̸l.

No. 145. – 70 Words – Counting Suffixes

IN THE FOLLOWING, g IS SILENT.

P. *stands for past tense;* PPR. *for participle of the present tense.*

VERBS.	P.	PPR.	AGENT.	VERBS.	P.	PPR.	AGENT.
sīgn	ed	ing	er	re-**sīgn**	ed	ing	er
as-**sign**	ed	ing	er	im-**pūgn**	ed	ind	er
con-**sign**	ed	ing	er	op-**pūgn**	ed	ing	er
de-**sign**	ed	ing	er	ar-**rāign**	ed	ing	er
ma-**lign**	ed	ing	er	**coun**-ter-sign	ed	ing	er

Adjectives and Nouns.

con-**dīgn**, be-**nīgn**, **poign**-ant, ma-**līgn**, **fŏr**-eign, **sȯv**-er-eign, **ĕn**-sīgn, cam-**pāign**.

IN THE FOLLOWING, THE SOUND OF g IS RESUMED.

as-sig-**nā**-tion, des-ig-**nā**-tion, re<u>s</u>-ig-**nā**-tion, be-**nĭg**-nant, be-**nig**-ni-ty, ma-**lig**-ni-ty, ma-**lig**-nant, in-**dig**-ni-ty, in-**dig**-nant, **dig**-ni-ty, **dig**-ni-fȳ, **preg**-nant, **preg**-nan-çy, im-**preg**-nāte, im-**preg**-na-ble, op-**pug**-nan-çy, re-**pug**-nant, re-**pug**-nan-çy, **sig**-ni-fȳ, sig-ni-fi-**cā**-tion, sig-**nif**-i-cant.

No. 146. – 21 Words

**WORDS IN WHICH e, i, AND o, BEFORE n, ARE MUTE, THOSE WITH *v*
ANNEXED, ARE OR MAY BE USED AS VERBS, ADMITTING ed FOR THE
PAST TIME, AND ing FOR THE PARTICIPLE.**

bā-con, **bēa**-con, **beech**-en, **bā**-sin, **bēat**-en, **bĭt**-ten, **blā**-zon, **brā**-zen, **brō**-ken, **black**-en (*v*), **bat**-ten (*v*), **bĕck**-on (*v*), **bûr**-den (*v*), **bur**-then, **bid**-den, **slack**-en (*v*), **bound**-en, **bŭt**-ton, **bro̭ad**-en (*v*), **chō**-<u>s</u>en, **clō**-ven.

109

Table 147.

Three Animal Descriptions and Seven Fables

THE DOG.

This dog is a mastiff. He is active, strong, and used as a watchdog. He has a large head and pendent ears. He is not very apt to bite; but he will sometimes take down a man and hold him down. Three mastiffs once had a combat with a lion, and the lion was compelled to save himself by flight.

THE STAG.

The stag is the male of the red deer. He is a mild and harmless animal, bearing a noble attire of horns, with are shed and renewed every year. His form is light and elegant, and he runs with great rapidity. The female is called a hind; and the fawn or young deer, when his horns appear, is called picket or brocket.

THE SQUIRREL.

The squirrel is a beautiful little animal. The gray and black squirrels live in the forest and make a nest of leaves and sticks on the high branches. It is amusing to see the nimble squirrel spring from branch to branch, or run up and down the stem of a tree, and dart behind it to escape from sight. Little ground squirrels burrow in the earth. They subsist on nuts, which they hold in their paws, using them as little boys use their hands.

FABLE 1.

OF THE BOY THAT STOLE APPLES.

An old man found a rude boy upon one of his trees stealing apples, and desired him to come down; but the young saucebox told him plainly that he would not. "Won't you?" said the old man, "then I will fetch you down;" so he pulled some turf for grass and threw it at him; but only this made the youngster laugh, to think the old man should pretend to beat him down the tree with grass only.

"Well, well," said the old man, "if neither words nor grass will do, I must try what virtue there is in the stones;" so the old man pelted him down heartily with stones, and soon made the young chap hasten down from the tree and beg the old man's pardon.

MORAL.

If good words and gentle means will not reclaim the wicked they must be dealt with in a more severe manner.

FABLE 2.

THE COUNTRY MAID AND HER MILK PAIL.

When men suffer their imagination to amuse them with the prospect of distant and uncertain improvements of their condition, they frequently sustain real looses, buy their inattention to those affairs in which they are immediately concerned.

A country maid was walking very deliberately with a pail of milk upon her head, when she fell into the following train of reflection: "The money for which I shall sell this milk, will enable me to increase my stock of eggs by three hundred. These eggs, allowing for what may prove addle, and what may be destroyed by vermin, will produce at least two hundred and fifth chickens. The chickens will be fit to carry to market about Christmas, when poultry always bears a good price; so that by May Day I cannot fail of having money enough to purchase a new gown. Green! – Let me consider – yes, green becomes my complexion best, and green it shall be. In this dress I will go to the fair, where all the young fellows will strive to have me for a partner; but I shall refuse every of them, and, with an air of distain, toss them." Transported with this triumphant thought, she could not forbear acting with her head what thus passed in her imagination, when down came the pail of milk, and with it all her imaginary happiness.

Fable 3.

The Two Dogs.

Hasty and inconsiderate connections generally attend with great disadvantages; and much of every man's good or ill fortune, depends upon the choice he makes of his friends.

A good-natured Spaniel overtook a surly Mastiff, as he was traveling upon the highroad. Tray, although an entire stranger to Tiger, very civilly accosted him; and if it would be no interruption, he said, he should be glad to bear him company on his way. Tiger, who happened, not be to be altogether in so growling a mood as usual, accepted the proposal; and they very amicably pursued their journey together. In the midst of their conversation, they arrived at the next village, where Tiger began to display his malignant disposition, by an unprovoked attack upon every dog he met. The villagers immediately sallied forth with great indignation to rescue their respective favorites; and falling upon our two friends, without distinction or mercy, poor Tray was most cruelly treated, for no other reason than being found in bad company.

FABLE 4.

THE PARTIAL JUDGE.

A farmer came to a neighboring lawyer, expressing great concern for an accident, which he said had just happened. "One of your oxen," continued he, "has been gored by an unlucky bull of mine, and I should be glad to know how I am to make you reparation." "Thou art a very honest fellow," replied the lawyer, "and wilt not think it unreasonable that I expect one of thy oxen in return." "It is no more than justice," quoth the farmer, "to be sure; but what did I say? – I mistake – it is *your* bull that has killed one of *my* oxen." "Indeed!" says the lawyer, "that alters the case: I must inquire into the affair; and if –" "And *if!*" said the farmer; "the business I find would have been concluded without an *if*, had you been as ready to do justice to others as to exact it from them."

FABLE 5.

THE CAT AND THE RAT.

A certain cat had made such unmerciful havoc among the vermin of her neighborhood that not a single rat or mouse venture to appear abroad. Puss was soon convinced that if affairs remained in their present state, she must ere long starve. After mature deliberation, therefore, she resolved to have recourse to stratagem. For this purpose, she suspended herself from a hook with her head downward, pretending to be dead. The rat and mice, as they peeped from their holes, observing her attitude, concluded she was hanging for a misdemeanor, and with great joy immediately sallied forth in quest of their prey. Puss, as soon as a sufficient number were collected together, quitting her hold, dropped into the midst of them; and very few had the fortune to make good their retreat. The artifice having succeeded so well, she was encouraged to try the event a second time. Accordingly, she whitened her coat all over rolling herself in a heap of flour, and in this disguise she lay concealed in the bottom of a meal tub. The stratagem was executed in general with the same effect as the former. But an old experienced rat, altogether as cunning as his adversary, was not so easily insnared. "I don't quite like," he said, "that white heap yonder. Something whispers me there is mischief concealed under it. "Tis true, it may be meal, but it may likewise be something I should not relish quite as well. There can be no harm at least in keeping at a proper distance; for caution, I am sure, is the parent of safety."

FABLE 6.

THE FOX AND THE BRAMBLE.

A fox, closely pursued by a pack of dogs, took shelter under the covert of a bramble. He rejoiced in an asylum, and for a while, was very happy; but soon found that if he attempted to stir, he was wounded by the thorns and prickles on every side. However, making a virtue of necessity, he forebode to complain, and comforted himself with reflecting that no bliss is perfect; that good and evil are mixed, and flow from the same fountain. The briers, indeed, said he, will tear my skin a little, but they keep off the dogs. For the sake of good, then let me bear the evil with patience; each bitter has its sweet; and these brambles, though they wound my flesh, preserve my life from danger.

FABLE 7.

THE BEAR AND THE TWO FRIENDS.

Two friends, setting out together upon a journey which led through a dangerous forest, mutually promised to assist each other, if they should happen to be assaulted. They had not proceeded far, before they perceived a bear making toward them in great rage.

There was no hope in flight; but one of them, being very active, sprang up into a tree; upon which the other, throwing himself flat on the ground, held his breath and pretended to be dead; remembering to have heard it asserted that this creature will not prey upon a dead carcass. The bear came up and after smelling of him some time, left him and went on. When he was fairly out of sight and hearing, the hero from the tree call out, – "Well, my friend, what said the bear." He seemed to whisper you very closely." "He did so," replied the other, "and gave me this good advice, never to associate with a wretch, who, in the hour of danger, will desert his friend."

Questions for Henry

"Henry, tell me the number of days in a year." "Three-hundred and sixty-five." "How many weeks in a year?" "Fifty-two." How many days in a week?" "Seven." "What are the called?" "Sabbath or Sunday, Monday, Tuesday, Wednesday, Thursday, Friday, Saturday." The Sabbath is a day of rest, and is called the Lord's Day, because God has commanded us to keep it holy. "On that day we are to omit labor and worldly employment, and devote the time to religious duties, and the gaining of religious knowledge.

"How many hours are there in a day and night?" "Twenty-four." "How many minutes in an hour?" "Sixty." "How many seconds in a minute?" "Sixty." Time is measured by clocks and watches; or by dials and glasses.

The light of the sun makes the day, and the shade of the earth makes the night. The earth revolves from west to east once in twenty-four hours. The sun is fixed or stationary; but the earth turns every part of its surface to the sun once in twenty-four hours. The day is for labor, and the night is for sleep and repose. Children should go to bed early in the evening, and all persons, who expect to thrive in the world, should rise early I the morning.

No. 148.

WORDS NEARLY, BUT NOT EXACLY, ALIKE IN PRONUNCIATION.

ac-**cept**, to take; ex-**cept**, to take out.

af-**fect**, to impress; ef-**fect**, what is produced.

ac-**cede**, to agree ex-**ceed**, to surpass.

pre-**scribe**, to direct; pro-**scribe**, to banish.

ac-cess, approach; **ex**-cess, superfluity.

al-**lu**-sion, hint reference; il-**lu**-sion, deception; e-**lu**-sion, evasion.

acts, deeds; **ax**, a tool for cutting

af-**fu**-sion, a pouring on; ef-**fu**-sion, a pouring out.

al-**lowed**, admitted, granted; a-**loud**, with a great voice.

er-rand, a message; **er**-rant, wandering.

ad-**di**-tion, something added; e-**di**-tion, publication.

bal-lad, a song; **bal**-let, a dance; **bal**-lot, a ball for voting, or a vote.

chron-i-cal, a long continuance; **chron**-i-cle, a history.

clothes, garments; **close**, conclusion.

con-sort, husband or wife; **con**-cert, harmony.

de-**scent**, a falling, a slope; dis-**sent**, a differing.

de-**cease**, death; dis-**ease**, sickness.

e-**lic**-it, to call forth; il-**lic**-it, unlawful.

im-**merge**, to plunge; e-**merge**, to come forth.

fat, fleshy; **vat**, a tub or cistern.

gest-ure, motion, **jest**-er, one who jests.

i-dle, not employed; **i**-dol, an image.

im-**pos**-tor, a deceiver; im-**post**-ure, deception.

naugh-ty, bad; **knot**-ty, full of knots.

in-**gen**-u-ous, frank; in-**ge**-ni-ous, skillful.

line, extension in length; **loin**, part of an animal.

loom, a frame for weaving; **loam**, a soft loose earth.

med-al, an ancient coin; **med**-dle, to interpose.

pint, half a quart; **point**, a sharp end.

rad-ish, a garden vegetable; **red**-dish, somewhat red.

ten-or, course continued; **ten**-ure, a holding.

talents, ability; **talons**, claws.

val-ley, low land; **val**-ue, worth.

WORDS SPELLED ALIKE, BUT PRONOUNCED DIFFERENTLY

Au-gust, the eighth month; au-**gust**, grand.

băss, a tree; a fish; **bāss**, lowest part in music.

con-**jure**, to entreat; **con**-jure, to use magic art.

des-ert, a wilderness; des-**sert**, fruit, etc., at dinner.

gal-lant, brave, gay (happy), gal-**lant**, a gay (happy) fellow.

ġill, the fourth part of a pint; **ḡill**, part of a fish.

hin-der, to stop; **hind**-er, further, behind.

in-va-lid, one not in health; in-**val**-id, not firm or binding.

low-er, (*ow* as in *cow*), to be dark; **lōw**-er, not so high.

lĭve, to be or dwell; **līve**, having life.

rēad, to utter printed words; **rĕad** [*red*], past tense of *read*.

rec-ol-lect, to call to mind; re-col-**lect**, to collect again.

re-**form**, to amend; **re**-form, to make anew.

rec-re-ate, to refresh; re-cre-**ate**, to create anew.

rout, defeat; **route**, a way or course.

slough, a place of mud; **slough** [*sluff*], a cast skin.

tär-ry, like tar; **tăr**-ry, to delay.

tēars, water from the eyes; **teârs**, [he] rends.

wĭnd, air in motion; **wīnd**, to turn of twist.

WORDS PRONOUNCED ALIKE, BUT SPELLED DIFFERENTLY.

ail, to be in trouble; **ale**, malt liquor. What *ails* the child? *Ale* is fermented liquor, made from malt.

heir, one who inherits; **air**, the atmosphere. The Prince of Wales is *heir* to the crown of England. We breathe *air*.

awl, an instrument; **all**, the whole. The *awl* is a tool used by shoemakers and harness-maker. *All* quadrupeds, that walk and do not leap, walk upon four.

al-tar, a place for offerings; **al**-ter, to change. The Jews burned sacrifices up-on an *altar* of stone. The moon *alters* its appearance every night.

ȧnt, a little insect; **äunt**, a sister to a parent. Your father's or your mother's sister is your *aunt*. The little *ants* make hillocks.

ark, a vessel; **arc**, part of a circle.

as-**cent**, steepness; **as**-**sent**, agreement.

au-ger, a tool; **au**-gur, one who fortells.

bail, surety, **bale**, a pack of goods.

ball, a sphere; **bawl**, to cry aloud. Boys love to play *ball*. Children *bawl* for trifles.

base, low, vile; **bass** or **base**, in music.

beer, a liquor; **bier**, a carriage for the dead. *Beer* may be made from malt and hops. They bore the body to the grave on a *bier*.

bin, a box; **been**, participle of *be*.

ber-ry, a little fruit; **bu**-ry, to inter. Black*berries* and rasp*berries* grow on briers. The farmer, when he plants seeds, *buries* them in the ground.

beat, to strike; **beet**, a root. Cruel horsemen *beat* their horses. Molasses may be made from *beets*.

blew, did blow; **blue**, a dark color The wind *blew*. The color of the sky is *blue*.

boar, a male swine; **bore**, to make a hole. A wild *boar* is a savage beast. Miners *bore* holes in rock, and burst them with powder.

bow, to bend the body; **bough**, a branch.

bell, to ring; **belle**, a fine lady. The great *bell* in Moscow, weighs two hun-dred and twenty tons. The *belles* and the *beaux* are fond of fine shows.

117

beau, a fine gentleman; **bōw**, to shoot with. A fine *beau* wears fine clothes. The *rainbow* is caused by the sun's shining upon the falling rain.

bread, a kind of food; **bred**, educated. Well-*bred* people do not always eat wheat *bread*.

bur-row, for rabbits; **bor**-ough, and incorporated town.

by, near at hand; **buy**, to purchase; **bye**, a dwelling. We judge of people's motives *by* their actions. We cannot *buy* a seat in heaven with our money.

be, to exist; **bee**, an insect.

beach, a sea-shore; **beech**, a tree. *Beech* wood makes a good fire. The waves beat on the *beach*.

boll, a pod of plants; **bowl**, an earthen vessel; **bole**, a kind of clay. The *boll* of plants is a seed vessel. Eat a *bowl* of bread and milk.

but, a conjunction; **butt**, two hogsheads. A *butt* contains two hogeheads; *but* a barrel, 31 ½ gallons.

brake, a weed; **break**, to part asunder. *Brakes* are useless weeds. We *break* flax and hemp in dressing.

Cain, a man's name; **cane**, a shrub or staff.

call, to cry out, or name; **caul**, a net enclosing the bowels. We *call* the membrane that covers the bowels a *caul*.

can-non, a large gun; **can**-on, a law of the church. Brass *cannon* are more costly than iron. Church laws are *canons*.

ces-sion, a grant; **ses**-sion, the sitting of a court. The courts of New York hold their *sessions* in the City Hall.   Since the *cession* of Florida, the United States have been bounded on the south by the Gulf of Mexico.

can-vas, course cloth; **can**-vass, to examine. Sails are made of *canvas*. Inspectors *canvass* votes.

ceil, to make a ceiling; **seal**, to fasten a letter; **seal**-ing, setting a seal; **ceil**-ing, of a room. *Seals* are caught both in the northern and the southern *seas*. We *seal* letters with wafers and *sealing wax*. Masons *ceil* the inner roof with lime mortar. A plastered *ceiling* looks better than a ceiling made of boards.

cens-er, an incense pan; **cen**-sor, a critic.

course, way, direction; **coarse**, not fine.

cote, a sheep-fold; **coat**, a garment.

core, the heart; **corps**, a body of soldiers.

cell, a hut; **sell**, to dispose of.

cen-tu-ry, a hundred years; **cen**-tau-ry, a plant.

chol-er, wrath; **col**-lar, for the neck.

cord, a small rope; **chord**, a line.

cite, to summon; **site**, situation; **sight**, the sense of seeing.

com-ple-ment, a full number; **com**-pli-ment, act of politeness.

cous-in, a relation; **coz**-en, to cheat.

cur-rant, a berry; **cur**-rent, a stream.

deer, a wild animal; **dear**, costly.

cask, a vessel for liquids; **casque**, a helmet.

ce-dar, a kind of wood; **ce**-der, one who cedes.

cede, to give up; **seed**, fruit, offspring.

cent the hundredth part of a dollar; **sent**, ordered away; **scent**, a smell.

cel-lar, the lowest room; **sell**-er one who sells. Farmers are *sellers* of apples and cider, which are put into *cellars*.

clime, a region; **climb**, to ascend.

coun-cil, an assembly; **coun**-sel, advice

sym-bol, a type; **cym**-bal, a musical instrument.

col-or, hue; **cul**-ler, one who selects.

dam, to stop water, **damn**, to condemn.

dew, falling vapors; **due**, owing.

die, to expire; **dye**, to color.

doe, a female deer; **dough**, bread not baked.

fane, a temple; **feign**, to disemble (fake).

dire, horrid; **dy**-er, on who colors.

dun, to urge for money; **dun**, a brown color, **done**, perform.

dram, a drink of spirit; **drachm**, a small weight.

e-**lis**-ion, the act of cutting off; e-**lys**-ian, blissful, joyful.

you, second person; **yew**, a tree; **ewe**, a female sheep.

fair, handsome; **fare**, customary duty.

feat, an exploit; **feet**, plural of *foot*.

freeze, to congeal; **frieze**, in a building.

hie, to haste; **high**, elevated lofty.

flea, an insect; **flee**, to run away.

flour, of rye or wheat; **flow**-er, a blossom.

forth, abroad; **fourth**, in number.

foul, filthy; **fowl**, a bird.

gilt, with gold; **guilt**, crime.

grate, iron bars; **great**, large.

grown, increased; **groan**, an expression of pain.

hail, to call, also frozen rain; **hale**, healthy.

hare, an animal; **hair**, the fur of an animal.

here, in this place; **hear**, to hearken.

hew, to cut; **hue**, color.

him, objective of *he*; **hymn**, a sacred song.

hire, wages; **high**-er, more high.

heel, he hinder part of the foot; **heal**, to cure.

haul, to drag; **hall**, a large room.

I, myself; **eye**, organ of sight.

isle (*īle*), an island; **aisle**, of a church.

in, within; **inn**, a tavern.

in-**dite**, to compose, in-**dict**, to prosecute.

kill, to slay; **kiln**, for burning bricks.

knap, a protuberance, **nap**, a short sleep.

knave, a rogue; **nave**, of a wheel.

knead, to work dough; **need**, necessity.

kneel, to bend the knee; **neal**, heat.

knew, did know; **new**, fresh, not old.

know, to understand; **no**, not.

knight, a title; **night**, darkness.

knot, a tie; not, **no**, denying.

lade, to fill, to dip; **laid**, placed.

lain, did lie; **lane**, a narrow street.

leek, a root; **leak**, to run out.

less-on, a reading; **les**-sen, to diminish.

li-ar, one who tells lies; **li**-er, one who lies in wait; **lyre**, a harp. A *liar* is not believed. The *lyre* is a musical instrument.

led, did lead; **lead**, a heavy metal.

lie, an untruth; **lye**, water drained through ashes.

lo, behold; **low**, humble; not high.

lac, a gum; **lack**, want.

lea, grass-land; **lee**, opposite wind.

leaf, of a plant; **lief**, willingness.

lone, solitary; **loan**, that is lent.

ore, learning; **low**-er, more low.

lock, a catch to a door; **loch**, a lake.

main, ocean; the chief; **mane**, of a horse. The Missouri is the *main* branch of the Mississippi. A horse's *mane* grows on his neck.

made, finished; **maid**, an unmarried woman. Galileo *made* the telescope. A charming *maid* or maiden.

male, the he kind; **mail**, armor, bag for letters. The *male* bird has a more beautiful plumage than the female. The *mail* is opened at the post office.

man-ner, mode of action; **man**-or, lands of a lord. Children should imitate the *manners* of polite people. The farms of the English nobility are called *manors*.

meet, to come together; **meat**, flesh, food; **mete**, measure. The Hudson and East rivers *meet* at the Battery. Salt will preserve *meat*.

mean, low, humble; **mien**, contenance.

mewl, to cry; **mule**, a beast.

mi-ner, one who works in a mine; **mi**-nor, less, or one under age.

moan, to grieve; **mow**, cut down.

moat, a ditch; **mote**, a speck. Forts are surrounded by a *moat*. *Mote* is an atom.

more, a greater portion; **mow**-er, one who mows. A brigade of soldiers is *more* than a regiment. *Mowers* mow grass.

mite, an insect; **might**, strength. A *mite* is an insect of little *might*.

met-al, gold silver, etc.; **met**-tle, briskness. Brass is a compound *metal*. A lively horse is a horse of *mettle*.

nit, egg of an insect; **knit**, to join with a needle.

nay, no; **neigh**, as a horse.

aught, any thing; **ought**, morally owed, should.

oar, a paddle; **ore**, of metal. Boats are rowed with *oars*. *Ores* are melted to separate the metal from the dross.

one, a single thing; **won**, did win. One dollar is *one* hundred cents. The most depraved gambler *won* the money.

oh, alas; **owe**, to be idebted.

our, belonging to us; **hour**, sixty minutes.

plum, a fruit; **plumb**, a lead and line. The builder uses the *plumb* and line to set his walls perpendicular. *Plums* grow on trees.

pale, without color; **pail**, a vessel.

pain, distress; **pane**, a square glass. *Panes* of glass are put into window fames. *Pains* are distressing.

pal-ate, part of the mouth; **pal**-let, painter's board; a bed. A person who has lost his *palate* cannot speak plain. The painter holds his *pallet* in his hand. The child sleeps on a *pallet*.

pleas, to plead; **please**, to give pleasure. Polite people *please* their companions. The courts of common *pleas* are held in the courthouses.

pole, a long stick; **poll**, the head.

peel, to pare of the rind; **peal**, sounds. On the Fourth of July, the bells ring a loud *peal*. The farmer *peels* the bark from trees for the tanner.

pair, a couple, pare, to cut off the rind, **pear**, a fruit. Shoes are sold by *pairs*. People *pare* apples to make pies. *Pears* are not so common as apples.

plain, even or level; **plane**, to make smooth. The carpenter planes boards with his *plane*. The essential principles of religion are written in *plain* language. Babylon stood upon an extended *plain*.

pray, to implore; **prey**, booty, plunder. The cat *preys* upon mice. We should *pray* for our enemies.

prin-ci-pal, chief; **prin**-ci-ple, rule of action. The Hudson is the *principal* river of New York. A man of good *principles* merits our esteem.

prof-it; advantage; **proph**-et a foreteller. There is no *profit* in profane swearing. The *prophet* Daniel was a prisoner in Babylon.

peace, quietude; **piece**, a part. Good people love to live in *peace*. Our largest *piece* of silver coin is a dollar.

pan-el, a square in a door; **pan**-nel, a kind of saddle.

raise, to lift; **raze**, to demolish.

rain, water falling from clouds; **reign**, to rule. God sends his *rain* on the just and the unjust. Horses are guided by the *reins* of the bridle. Queen Victoria *reigns* over Great Britain and Ireland.

rap, to strike; **wrap**, to fold together. The Laplander *wraps* himself in furs in the winter. When we wish to enter a house we *rap* at the door.

read, to pursue; **reed**, a plant. *Reeds* grow in swamps, and have hollow, jointed stems. We should *read* the Bible with seriousness.

red, a color; **read**, did read. We should often think upon what we have *read*. The hyacinth bears a beautiful large *red* flower.

reek, to emit steam; **wreak**, to revenge. Nero *wreaked* his malice upon the Christians. Brutus held up the dagger *reeking* with the blood of Lucretia.

rest, to take ease, **wrest**, to take by force. We *rest* on beds. The English *wrested* Gibraltar from the Spaniards.

rice, a sort of grain; **rise**, source, beginning. *Rice* grows in warm climates. The *rise* of the Missouri is in the Rocky Mountains.

rye, a sort of grain; **wry**, crooked. Paste is made of *rye* flour. Children make *wry* faces when they eat sour grapes.

ring, to sound, a circle; **wring**, to twist. Some ladies are fond of gold *rings*. The bell *rings* for church. Washerwomen *wring* clothes.

rite, ceremony; **right**, just. Baptism is a *rite* of the Christian church. It is not *right* to pilfer.

write, to make letters with a pen; **wright**, a workman. *Wheelwrights* make carts and wagons.

rode, did ride; **road**, the highway. Cumberland *road* leads from Baltimore to Wheeling. King David *rode* upon a mule.

rear, to raise; **rear**, the hind part.

rig-ger, one who rigs vessels; **rig**-or, severity. *Riggers* rig vessels; that is, fit the shrouds, stays, braces, etc., to the masts and yards. Hannibal crossed the Alps in the *rigor* of winter.

ruff, a neck-cloth; **rough**, not smooth.

rote, repetition of words; **wrote**, did write. Children often learn the alphabet by *rote* before they know the letters. Oliver Goldsmith *wrote* several good histories.

roe, a female deer; **row**, a rank. A *roe* deer has no horns. Corn is planted in *rows*. Oarsmen *row* boats with oars.

roar, to sound loudly; **row**-er, one who rows.

rab-bet, to cut, as the edge of a board, in a sloping manner; **rab**-bit, an animal. The joiner *rabbets* boards. *Rabbits* are lively animals.

sail, the canvas of a ship; **sale**, the act of selling. This house is for *sale*. We *sail* for Liverpool to-morrow.

sea, a large body of water; **see**, to behold. The river Danube runs into the Black *Sea*. Owls cannot *see* well when the sun shines.

sa-ver, one who saves, **sa**-vor, taste or odor.

seen, beheld; **scene**, part of a play; **seine**, a fish net. We have never *seen* a more dazzling object than the sun in summer. A thunderstorm is a sublime *scene*. Fishermen catch shad in *seines*. The city of Paris stands on the river *Seine*.

sen-ior (*sēn-yur*); **seign**-ior, a Turkish king. John Smith, *Senior*, is father to John Smith, Junior. The Sultan of Turkey is also called the Grand *Seignior*.

seam, where the edges join; **seem**, to appear. The sun *seems* to rise and set. Neat sewers (*sō*-erz) make handsome *seams* with their needles.

shear, to cut with shears; **sheer**, clear, unmixed. Sheep-shearers *shear* the wool from the sheep. When the wolf sees the sheep well guarded he *sheers* off.

sent, ordered away; **cent**, a small coin; **scent**, smell.

shore, sea coast; **shore**, a prop. Waves dash against the *shore*. When ship-builders build vessels they *shore* them up with props.

so, in such a manner; **sow**, to scatter seed. A sower *sows* his seeds.

sum, the whole; **some**, a part. We all have *some* knowledge. The *sum* of four and five is nine.

sun, a fountain of light; **son**, a male child. "A wise *son* makes a glad father." Without the *sun* all animals and vegetables would die.

stare, to gaze; **stair**, a step. The Jews were not permitted to have *stair*s to their altars. Do not let children *stare* at strangers.

steel, hard metal; **steal**, to take by theft.

suck-er, a young twig; **suc**-cor, help. *Succor* a man in distress. *Suckers* sprout from the root of an old stock.

slight, to despise, **sleight**, dexterity. Children should never *slight* their parents. Indians used to live in very *slight* buildings, called wigwams. Some have a good *sleight* at work.

sole, of the foot; **soul**, the spirit. The *sole* of a shoe is the bottom of it. The sun is the *sole* cause of day. Our *souls* are immortal.

slay, to kill; **sley**, a weaver's reed; **sleigh**, a carriage on runners. Mankind *slay* each other in cruel wars. A *sleigh* or sled runs on snow and ice.

sloe, a fruit; **slow**, not swift. A *sloe* is a black wild plum. The sloth is *slow* in moving.

stake, a post; **steak**, a slice of meat. Tents are fastened with *stakes*. Beef*steaks* are good food.

stile, steps over a fence; **style**, fashion, diction. *Stiles* are steps over fences. Goldsmith wrote in a clear plain *style*.

tacks, small nails; *tax*, a rate, tribute. Shoemakers drive *tacks* into the heels of shoes. People pay a heavy *tax*.

throw, to cast away; **throe**, plain of travail.

tare, an allowance in weight; **teār**, to rend. *Tares* grow among wheat. Grocers subtract the *tare* from the gross weight. Never *tear* your clothes.

tēar, water from the eyes; **tier**, a row. We shed *tears* of sorrow when we lose our friends. Ships often carry two *tiers* of guns.

team, of horses or oxen; **teem**, to produce. A *team* of horses will travel faster than a team of oxen. Farmers rejoice when their farms *teem* with fruits.

tide, flux of the sea, **tied**, fastened. The *tide* is caused by the attraction of the moon and sun. A black ribbon is *tied* on the left arm and worn as a badge of mourning.

their, belonging to them; **there**, in this place. Good scholars love *their* books. *There* are no tides in the Baltic Sea.

the, definite article; **thee**, objective case of *thou*.

too, likewise; **two**, twice once.

toe, extremity of the foot; **tow**, to drag. Men have a great *toe* on each foot. Horses *tow* the canal boats. *Tow* is hatcheled from flax.

vail, a covering; **vale**, a valley. Women wear *vails*. The valley of the Mississippi is the largest *vale* in the United States.

vial, a little bottle; **viol**, a fiddle. A *vial* of laudanum. A base-*viol* is a large fiddle, and a violin is a small one.

vane, to show which way the wind blows; **vein**, for the blood. The *vane* shows which way the wind blows. Arteries convey the blood from the heart and *veins*.

vice, sin; **vise**, a gripping instrument.

wait, to tarry; **weight**, heaviness. Time *waits* for no one. Butter is sold by *weight*.

wear, to carry, as clothes; **ware**, merchandise. Ladies wear sashes round the *waist*. Foolish children *waste* their time in idleness.

way, road course; **weigh**, to find the weight. We *weigh* gold and silver by Troy Weight. The *way* of a good man is plain.

week, seven days; **weak**, not strong. Sickness makes the body *weak*. Seven days constitute one *week*.

wood, timber; **would**, past time of *will*.

weather, state of the air; **wether**, a sheep. The *weather* is colder in America than in the same latitudes in Europe. Among the flock of sheep were twenty fat *wethers*.

Some Sentences Illustrating Homonyms

The planks of vessels are fastened with copper *bolts*. Millers separate the bran from the flour by large sieves called *bolts*.

The breech of a gun is its *butt* or club end. A ram *butts* with his head. We import b*utts* of spirits.

Clothiers smooth their clothes with *calendars*. Almanac makers publish new *calendars* every year.

Live fish are kept in the water, near our fish markets, in *caufs*. Consumptive people are afflicted by bad *coughs*.

Farmers are *sellers* of apples and cider, which are put into *cellars*.

Mead is a pleasant drink. Lying is a *mean* practice. We *mean* to study grammar.

Miners work in mines. *Minors* are not allowed to vote.

David *moaned* the loss of Absalom. When grass is *mown* and dried we call it hay.

Fishes are caught in a *net*. Clear profits are called *net* gain.

A bird *flew* over the house. The smoke ascends in the *flue*.

Gums *ooze* through the pores of wood. The tanner puts his hides into *ooze*.

The comma is the shortest *pause* in reading. Bears seize their prey with their *paws*.

The *peak* of Teueriffe is fifteen thousand feet high. The Jews had a *pique* or ill will against the Samaritans.

The British Parliament is a legislative assembly, consisting of the House of *Peers* and the House of Commons. Our vessels lie near the *piers* in our harbor.

The student *pores* over his books day after day. The Niagara River *pours* down a precipice of a hundred and fifty feet. We sweat through the *pores* of the skin.

Panel doors are more expensive than batten doors. The courts *impanel* jurors to judge causes in court.

The barber shaves his patrons with a *razor*. Farmers are *raisers* of grain.

The writer *signs* his name. Heavy clouds are *signs* of rain.

The lark *soars* into the sky. A boil is a *sore* swelling.

Saul *threw* his javelin at David. The Israelites went *through* the Red Sea.

The plumbline hangs *straight* toward the center of the earth. The *Straits* of Gibraltar separate Spain from Morocco.

Lions have long bushy *tails*. The *tale* of Robinson Crusoe is a celebrated romance.

Earthen *ware* is baked in furnaces. A Turk *wears* a turban instead of a hat.

Wheat is a *better* grain than rye. One who lays a wager is a *bettor*.

Carpenters bore holes with an *auger*. An *augur* foretells.

Bears live in the woods. An oak *bears* acorns. We *bear* evils. Trees *bare* of leaves.

Many things are possible which are not practical. That is possible which can be performed by any means; that is practicable which can be formed by the means, which are in our power.

Bank notes are redeemable in cash.

WORDS OF IRREGULAR ORTHOGRAPHY

any (ĕn-ny), many (mĕn-ny), demesne (de-meen), bat-eau (bat-ō), beau (bō), beaux (bōze), bu-reau (bū-ro), been (bĭn), bu-ry (bĕr-ry), bu-ri-al (bĕr-ĭ-al), bus-y (bĭz-zy), isle (īle), isl-and (ī-land), does (dŭz), says (sĕz), said (sĕd), lieu (lū), adieu (a-dū), ghost (gōst), corps (kōre), ache (āke), half (häf), calf (cäf), calve (käv), one (wūn), once (wŭnçe), done (dŭn), gone (gŏn), folks (fōks), ra-tio (rā-sho), va-lise (va-lēçe), o-cean (ō-shun), though (thō), broad (brawd), could (ko͝od), would (wo͝od), should (sho͝od), debt (dĕt), phlegm (flĕm), croup (kro͞op), tomb (to͞om), womb (wo͞om), wolf (wo͝of), yacht (yŏt), dough (dō), neigh (nā), sleigh (slā), weigh (wā), gauge (ḡāġe), bough (bou), slough (slou), doubt (dout), issue (ĭsh-shṳ), tis-sue (tĭsh-shṳ), busi-ness (bĭz-ness), bus-i-ly (bĭz-ĭ-ly), colonel (kûr-nel), haut-boy (hō-boy), masque (mȧsk), sou, sous (so͞o), gui-tar (ḡĭ-tär), pur-lieu (pûr-lu), su-gar (sho͝og-ar), vis-count (vī-kount), ap-ro-pos (ap-ro̤-pō), flam-beau (flăm-bo), right-eous (rī-chus), car-touch (kär-tooch), in-veigh (in-vā), sur-tout (sur-to͞oh), wom-an (wo͝om-an), wom-en (wĭm-en), bis-cuit (bĭs-kit), cir-cuit (sĭr-kit), sal-mon (săm-un), isth--mus (ĭs-mus), neigh-bor (nā-bur), piqu-ant (pĭk-ant), piqu-an-çy (pĭk-an-çy), ptis-an (tĭz-an), phthis-ic (tĭz-ik), sol-dier (sōl-jer), vict-uals (vĭt-tl̲s), ca-tarrh (ka-tär), bou-quet (boo-kā), bru-nette (brṳ-nĕt), ga-zette (ga-zĕt), in-debt-ed (in-dĕt-ed), lieu-ten-ant (lu-tĕn-ant), qua-drille (kwa-drĭl), pneu-mat-ics (nu-măt-iks), mort-gage (môr-ḡĕj), seign-ior (seen-yur), se-ragl-io (se-răl-yo), asth-ma (ăst-mȧ), beau-ty (bū-ty), beau-te-ous, (bū-te-us), bdell-ium (dĕl-yum), ca-noe (ka-no͞o), plaid (plăd), schism (sĭzm), feoff-ment (fĕf-ment), hal-cy-on (hăl-sĭ-on), mis-tle-toe (mĭz-zl-to), psal-mo-dy (săl-mo-dy̆), bal-sam-ic (băl-săm-ik).

IN THE FOLLOWING WORDS, l IS SILENT.

ba̤lk, ca̤lk, cha̤lk, sta̤lk, ta̤lk, wa̤lk.

THE FOLLOWING END WITH THE SOUND OF **f**.

cŏŭgh, clŏŭgh (a cleft), tŏŭgh, rŏŭgh, slŏŭgh (The cast-off skins of a serpent, etc.) e-**nŏŭgh**, cŏugh (cawf), trough (trawf), läugh (läf).

h AFTER **r** IS SILENT.

rheu̱m, rheu̱-**măt**-ic, **rheu**-ma-ti̱s̱m, rhȳme, **rhu̱**-barb, **rhĕt**-o-ric, **rhăp**-so-dy, rhī-**nŏç**-e-ros.

g IS SILENT BEFORE **n**.

de̱ign (dān), de̱igned, de̱igning; fe̱ign, fe̱igned, fe̱igning; re̱ign, re̱igned, re̱igning; **poign**-ant.

l BEFORE **m** IS SILENT IN THE FOLLOWING.

cälm, **cälm**-ly, **cälm**-ness, be-**cälm**, bälm, **bälm**-y, em-**bälm**, älms̱, **älms̱**-house, **älms̱**-ġĭv-ing, psälm, quälm, **quälm**-ish, **psälm**-ist, hōlm.

IN THE FOLLOWING, **geon** and **gion** ARE PRONOUNCED AS *jun*; **con**, AS *un;* **cheon**, AS *chun;* **geous** AND **gious**, as *jus.*

blŭd-ġeon, **dŭd**-ġeon, **gŭd**-ġeon, **stûr**-ġeon, **lē**-ġion, **rē**-ġion, con-**tā**-ġion, re-**lĭ**-ġion, **sûr**-ġeon, **dŭn**-ġeon, **pĭġ**-eon, **wĭd**-ġeon, **lŭn**-cheon, con-**tā**-ġioŭs, e-**grē**-ġioŭs, re-**lĭ**-ġioŭs, pro-**dĭ**-ġioŭs, **pŭn**-cheon, **trŭn**-cheon, **scŭtch**-eon, es-**cŭtch**-eon, cur-**mŭd**-ġeon, **gôr**-ġeoŭs, sac-ri-**lē**-ġioŭs.

IN THE FOLLOWING, **ou** AND **au** ARE PRONOUNCED AS *aw,* AND **gh** IS MUTE.

bought, brought, fought, sought, sought, thought, *w*rought, na̱ught, fra̱ught.

IN THE FOLLOWING, THE LETTERS **ue** AT THE END OF THE PRIMITIVE WORD ARE SILENT.

plāgue, vāgue, lēague, brōgue, rōgue, fa-**tīgue**, vōgue, tŏngue. mŏsque, in-**trīgue**, o-**pāque**, ū-**nïque**, pïque, har-**ăngue**, ăp-o-**lŏgue**, **căt**-a-lŏgue (or catalog), **dī**-a-lŏgue, **ĕc**-lŏgue.

No. 150. – 1,046 Words

1. *Regular verbs form the past time, and participle of the past, by taking,* **ed**, *and the participle of the present tense by taking* **ing**; *as,* called, calling, *from* call. *The letter* **p**. *stand for past tense;* **ppr**. *for participle of the present tense; and* **a**. *for agent.*

call, called, **call**-ing; burn, burned, **burn**-ing; plow, plowed, **plow**ing; plant, **plant**-ed, **plant**-ing; pray, prayed, **pray**-ing, cloy, cloyed, **cloy**-ing; jest, **jest**-ed, jesting; abound, **abound**-ed, **abound**-ing; al-**lay**, al-**layed**, al-**lay**-ing; al-**low**, al-**lowed**, al-**low**-ing; a-**void**, a-**void**-ed, a-**void**-ing; em-**ploy**, em-**ployed**, em-**ploy**-ing; pur-**loin**, pur-**loined**, pur-**loin**-ing; rep-re-**sent**, rep-re-**sent**-ed; rep-re-**sent**-ing; an-**noy**, an-**noy**-ed, an-**noy**-ing.

2. *Monosyllablic verbs ending in a single consonant after a single vowel, and other verbs ending in a single consonant after a single vowel and accented on the last syllable, double in the final consonant in the derivatives. Thus,* abet; **p**. abetted; **ppr**. abetting; **a**. abettor.

a-**bet**, a-**bet**-ted, a-**bet**-ting, a-**bet**-tor; fret, **fret**-ted, **fret**-ting, **fret**-ter; man, **man**-ned, **man**-ning; plan, **plan**-ned, **plan**-ning, **plan**-ner; wed, **wed**-ded, **wed**-ding; bar, **bar**-red, **bar**-ring, ex-**pel**, ex-**pel**-led; re-**bel**, re-**bel**-led, re-**bel**-ler; tre-**pan**, tre-**pan**-ned, tre-**pan**-ning, tre-**pan**-ner; ab-**hor**, ab-**hor**-red, ab-**hor**-rer; in-**cur**, in-**cur**-red, in-**cur**-ring.

3. *Verbs having a digraph, diphthong, or long vowel sound before the last consonant, do not double that consonant.*

seal, sealed, **seal**-ing, **seal**-er; heal, **heal**-ed, **heal**-ing; oil, oiled, oiling; hail, hailed, **hail**-ing; claim, claimed, **claim**-ing, **claim**-er; cool, cooled, **cool**-ing, **cool**-er; ap-**pear**, ap-**peared**, ap-**pear**-ing, ap-**pear**-er; re-**peat**, re-**peat**-ed, re-**peat**-ing, re-**peat**-er, re-**coil**, re-**coiled**, re-**coil**-ing, ve-**neer**, ve-**neered**, ve-**neer**-ing, ve-**neer**; a-**vail**, av-**ailed**, a-**vail**-ing, re-**strain**, re-**strained**, re-**strain**-ing, re-**strain**-er.

4. *Verbs ending in two consonants do not double the last.*

gild, gilded, **gild**-ing, **gild**-er; long, longed, **long**-ing, **long**-er; watch, watched, **watch**-ing, **watch**-er; dress, dressed, **dress**-ing, **dress**-er; paint, **paint**-ed, **paint**-ing, **paint**-er; charm, charmed, **charm**-ing, **charm**-er; re-**sist**, re-**sist**-ed, re-**sist**-ing, re-**sist**-er; con-**vert**, con-**vert**-ed, con-**vert**-ing; dis-**turb**, dis-**turbed**, dis-**turb**-ing, dis-**turb**-er.

5. *Verbs ending in a single consonant, preceded by a single vowel, the last consonant or syllable not being accented, ought not to double the last consonant in the derivatives.*

bi-as, **bi**-ased, **bi**-as-ing; **bev**-el, **bev**-eled, **bev**-el-ing; **can**-cel, **can**-celed, **can**-cel-ing; **ca**-rol, **ca**-roled, **ca**-rol-ing; **cav**-il, **cav**-il-ed; **cav**-il-ing; **chan**-nel, **chan**-neled, **chan**-nel-ing; **chis**-el, **chis**-eled, **chis**-el-ing; **lev**-el, **lev**-eled, **lev**-el-ing; **coun**-sel, **coun**-seled, **coun**-sel-ing; **cud**-gel, **cud**-geled, **cud**-gel-ing; **driv**-*el*, **driv**-*e*led, **dir**-vel-ing; **du**-el, **du**-eled, **du**-el-ing; **e**-qual, **e**-qualed, **e**-qual-ing; **gam**-bol, **gam**-boled, **gam**-bol-ing; **grav**-el,

grav-eled, **grav**-el-ing; **grov**-el, **grov**-eled, **grov**-el-ing; **par**-al-lel, **par**-al-leled; **par**-al-lel-ing; **jew**-el, **jew**-eled; **jew**-el-ing; **kern**-el; **kern**-eled; **kern**-el-ing; **la**-bel, **la**-beled, **la**-bel-ing; **lau**-rel, **lau**-reled, **lau**-rel-ing; **lev**-el, **lev**-eled, **lev**-el-ing; **li**-bel, **li**-beled, **li**-bel-ing; **mar**-shal, **mar**-shaled, **mar**-shal-ing; **par**-cel, **par**-cel-ed; **pen**-cil, **pen**-ciled, **pen**-cil-ing; **pom**-mel, **pom**-meled, **pom**-mel-ing; **quar**-rel, **quar**-reled, **quar**-rel-ing; **rev**-el, **rev**-eled, **rev**-el-ing; **ri**-val, **ri**-valed, **ri**-val-ing; **row**-el, **row**-eled, **row**-el-ing; s**hov**-*el*, **shov**-*e*led, **shov**-*e*l-ing; **shriv**-el, **shriv**-eled, **shriv**-el-ing, **tram**-mel, **tram**-meled, **tram**-mel-ing; **trav**-el, **trav**-eled, **trav**-el-ing; **tun**-nel, **tun**-neled, **tun**-nel-ing; **wor**-ship, **wor**-shipped, **wor**-ship-ing; **mod**-el, **mod**-eled; **mod**-el-ing; **wag**-on, **wag**-oned, **wag**-on-ing; **clos**-et, **clos**-et-ed, **clo**-set-ing; **riv**-et, **riv**-et-ed, **riv**-et-ing; **lim**-it, **lim**-it-ed, **lim**-it-ing; **ben**-e-fit, **ben**-e-fit-ed, **ben**-e-fit-ing; **prof**-it, **prof-**it-ed, **prof**-it-ing; **buf**-fet, **buf**-fet-ed, **buf**-fet-ing.

6. *The name of the agent, when the verb admits it, is formed in like manner, without doubling the last consonant,* as caviler, worshiper, duelist, libeler, traveler. *So also adjectives are formed from the verbs without doubling the last consonant, as* libelous, marvelous.

7. *When the verbs end in* **e** *after* ***d,*** *and* **t***, the final* **e** *in the past tense and participle of the perfect tense, unites with* **d** *and forms an additional syllable, but it is dropped before* ing. *Thus,* abate, abated, abating.

ab-di-cate, **ab**-di-ca-ted, **ab**-di-ca-ting; **ded**-i-cate, **ded**-i-ca-ted, **de**-di-ca-ting; **med**-i-tate, **med**-i-ta-ted, **med**-i-ta-ing; **im**-pre-cate, **im**-pre-ca-ted, **im**-pre-ca-ting; **vin**-di-cate, **vin**-di-ca-ted, **vin**-di-cat-ing; de-**grade**, de-**gra**-ded, de-**grad**-ing; **suf**-fo-cate, **suf**-fo-ca-ted, **suf**-fo-ca-ting; **ed**-u-cate, **ed**-u-ca-ted, **ed**-u-ca-ting; **in**-vade, **in**-va-ded, **in**-va-ding; **con**-cede, **con**-ce-ded, **con**-ce-ding; **cor**-rode, **cor**-ro-ded; **cor**-ro-ding; **de**-lude, **de**-lu-ded, **de**-lu-ding; **in**-trude, **in**-tru-ded, **in**-tru-ding; **ex**-plode, **ex**-plo-ded; **ex**-plo-ding; **de**-ride, **de**-ri-ded; **de**-ri-ding.

8. *In verbs ending in* **e** *after any other consonant than* **d** *and* **t** *past tense is formed by the addition of* **d***, and this letter with the final* **e** *may form a distinct syllable; but usually the* **e** *is not sounded. Thus* abridged, *is pronounced* abridjd; abased, abāste. *Before* ing, **e** *is dropped.*

a-**base**, a-**based**, a-**ba**-sing; a-**bridge**, a-**bridged**, a-**brid**-ging; con-**fine**, con-**fined**, con-**fi**-ning; com-**pose**, com-**posed**, com-**po**-sing; re-**fuse**, re-**fused**, re-**fu**-sing; pro-**nounce**, pro-**nounced**, pro-**noun**-cing; **man**-age, **man**-aged, **man**-a-ging; re-**joice**, re-**joiced**; re-**joi**-cing; **cat**-e-chise, **cat**-e-chised; **cat**-e-chi-sing; **com**-pro-mise, **com**-pro-mised, **com**-pro-mi-sing; **crit**-i-cise, **crit**-i-cised, **crit**-i-ci-sing; em-**bez**-zle, em-**bez**-zled, em-**bez**-zling; **dis**-o-blige, **dis**-o-bliged, **dis**-o-bli-ging, dis-**fig**-ure, dis-**fig**-ured, dis-**fi**-gur-ing; un-der-**val**-ue, un-der-**val**-ued, un-der-**val**-u-ing.

134

Note. Although **ed** *in the past tense and participle is thus blended with the last syllable of the verb, yet when a noun is formed by adding* ness *to such participles the* ed *becomes a distinct syllable. Thus* blesseded *may be pronounced in one syllable; but* bles-sed-ness, *must be in three.*

9. *Verbs ending in* ay, oy, ow, ew *and* ey, *have regular derivatives in* ed *and* ing.

ar-**ray**, ar-**rayed**, ar-**ray**-ing; al-**lay**, al-**layed**, al-**lay**-ing; pray, prayed, **pray**-ing; stay, stayed, **stay**-ing; de-**lay**, de-**layed**, de-**lay**-ing; **al**-loy, **al**-loyed, **al**-loy-ing; em-**ploy**, em-**ployed**, em-**ploy**-ing; de-**stroy**, de-**stroyed**, de-**stroy**-ing, an-**noy**, an-**noyed**, an-**noy**-ing; en-**dow**, en-**dowed**, en-**dow**-ing; re-**new**, re-**newed**, re-**new**-ing; con-**vey**, con-**veyed**, con-**vey**-ing; **fol**-low, **fol**-lowed, **fol**-low-ing; be-**stow,** be-**stowed**, be-**stow**-ing; con-**voy**, con-**voyed**, con-**voy**-ing; **fol**-low, **fol**-lowed, **fol**-low-ing; be-**stow**, be-**stowed**, be-**stow**-ing; **con**-voy, **con**-voyed, **con**-voy-ing.

But a few monosyllables, as pay, say, *and* lay, *change* y *into* **i**, *as* paid, said, laid.

10. *Verbs ending in* **y** *change* **y** *into* **i** *in the past tense and participle of the perfect, but retain it in the participle of the present tense.*

cry, cried, **cry**-ing; **de**-fy, **de**-fied, **de**-fy-ing; ed-i-fy, **ed**-i-fied; **ed**-i-fy-ing; dry, dried, **dry**-ing; **car**-ry, **car**-ried, **car**-ry-ing; **mar**-ry, **mar**-ried, **mar**-ry-ing.

11. *Verbs ending in* **y** *change this letter to* **i** *in the second and third persons, and in words denoting agent. Thus:*

Present Tense

Solemn Style:	I cry, thou criest, he criedst.	I try, thou triest, he trieth.
Familiar Style:	he cries, [crier (agent).]	he tries, [trier (agent).]

Past Tense

Solemn Style:	I cried, thou criedsd.	I tried, thou triedst.
Familiar Style:	he/we/ye/they cried.	he/we/ye/they tried.

12. *Verbs ending in* ie *change* ie *into* y *when the termination* ing *of the present participle is added, as* die, dying, lie, lying.

The past tense, and participle of the present, are regular.

died   lied   tried   hied   vied

FORMATION OF THE PLURAL NUMBER OF NOUNS

13. *The regular plural of nouns is formed by the addition of* **s** *to the singular, which letter unites with most consonants in the same syllable, but sounds like* **z** *after all the consonants except the aspirate* **f, p, q, t, k,** *or* **c** *with the sound of* **k.**

slab, slabs; lad, lads; chief, chiefs; bag, bags; back, backs; roll, rolls; ham, hams; chain, chains; crop, crops; tear, tears; straight, straights; post, posts; port, ports; sight, sights; sign, signs.

a. When the noun ends in **e**, *if* **s** will coalesce with the preceding consonant, *it does not form an additional syllable.*

bride, brides; blade, blades; simile, smiles; knave, knaves; date, dates; note, notes; bone, bones; cake, cakes; flame, flames.

b. If **s** *will not coalesce with the preceeding consonant, it unites with the* **e** *and forms an additional syllable.*

grace, **gra**-*ces; spice,* **spi**-*ces; maze,* **ma**-*zes; fleece,* **fleec**-*es; pledge,* **pledġ**-*es; staġe,* **staġ**-*es.*

14. *When nouns end in* **ch, sh, ss**, *and* **x**, *the plural is formed by the addition of* **es.**

church, churches; peach, peaches; bush, bushes; glass, glasses; dress, dresses; fox, foxes.

15. *Nouns end in* **y** *after a consonant, form the plural by the changing of* **y** *into* **i**, *and is addition of* **es**; *the termination* **ies** *being pronounced* **īze**, *in monosyllables, and* **ĭz** *in most other words.*

fly, flies; crȳ, cries; skï, skies, **cit**-y, **cit**-ies, **du**-ty, **du**-ties; **glo**-ry, **glo**-ries; **ru**-by, **ru**-bies, **la**-dy, **la**-dies; **fu**-ry, **fu**-ries; **ber**-ry, **ber**-ries; **mer**-cy, **mer**-cies; **va**-can-cy, **va**-can-cies.

16. *Nouns ending in* ay, ey, oy, ow, ew, *take* s *only to form the plural.*

day, days; way, ways; bay, bays; **de**-lay, **de**-lays; **val**-ley, **val**-lēys; **mon**-ey, **mon**-eys; at-**tor**-ney, at-**tor**-neys; **sur**-vey, **sur**-veys; boy, boys; bow, bows; clew clews.

17. *Nouns ending in a vowel take* s or es.

sea, seas; hoe, hoes; woe, woes; pie, pies.

18. *When the singular ends in* f, *the plural is usually formed by changing* f *into* v, *with* es.

life, lives; wife, wives; beef, beeves; loaf, loaves; leaf, leaves; shelf, shelves; wharf, wharves; calf, calves; half, halves; sheaf, shaves; their, thief, thieves.

Adjectives formed from nouns the addition of y.

bulk (noun), bulky (adjetive); flesh, fleshy; silk, silky; milk, milky; pith, pithy, rain, rainy; hill, hilly.

Some nouns when they take y, *lose* e *final.*

flake, flaky; plume, plumy; scale, scaly; smoke, smoky; stone, stony; bone, bony.

Adjectives formed from nouns by ly.

friend (noun), **friend**-ly (adjective); home, **home**-ly; love, **love**-ly; time, **time**-ly; man, **man**-ly; cost, **cost**-ly; earth, **earth**-ly; lord, **lord**-ly.

Nouns formed from adjectives in y, *by changing* y *into* i *and taking* ness.

hap-py (adjective), **hap**-pi-ness (noun); **loft**-y, **lof**-ti-ness; **la**-zy, **la**-zi-ness; **emp**-ty, **emp**-ti-ness; **drow**-sy, **drow**-si-ness; **diz**-zy, **diz**-zi-ness; **sha**-dy, **sha**-di-ness; **chil**-ly, **chil**-li-ness.

Adverbs formed from adjectives in y, *by changing* y *into* i, *and the addition of* ly.

craft-y (adjective), **craft**-i-ly (adverb); **luck**-y, **luck**-i-ly; **loft**-y, **loft**-i-ly; **gloom**-y, **gloom**-i-ly.

Adverbs formed from adjectives by the addition of ly.

fer-vent (adjective), **fer**-vent-ly (adverb); **pa**-tient, **pa**-tient-ly; **brill**-iant, **brill**-iant-ly; **op**-u-lent, **op**-u-lent-ly; **em**-in-ent, **em**-in-ent-ly; **per**-ma-nent, **per**-man-ent-ly.

Nouns formed from adjectives by adding ness.

au-da-cious (adjective), **au**-da-cious-ness (noun); ca-**pa**-cious, ca-**pa**-cious-ness; of-**fi**-cious, of-**fi**-cious-ness; li-**cen**-tious-ness; ra-**pa**-cious, ra-**pa**-cious-ness; in-**ġe**-ni-ous, in-**ġe**-ni-ous-ness.

Adjectives formed from nouns less, *adverbs by* ly, *and nouns by* ness.

bound	boundless	boundlessly	boundlessness
fear	fearless	fearlessly	fearlessness
hope	hopeless	hopelessly	hopelessness
blame	blameless	blamelessly	blamelessness
need	needless	needlessly	needlessness
faith	faithless	faithlessly	faithlessness

Adjectives formed from nouns by ful, *from which adverbs are formed by* ly, *and nouns in* ness.

art (noun), **art**-ful (adjective), **art**-ful-ly (adverb), **art**-ful-ness (noun); care, **care**-ful, **care**-ful-ly, **care**-ful-ness; pain, **pain**-ful, **pain**-ful-ly, **pain**-ful-ness; grace, **grace**-ful, **grace**-ful-ly, **grace**-fuly-ness; skill, **skill**-ful, **skill**-ful-ly, **skill**-ful-ness; peace, **peace**-ful, **peace**-ful-ly, **peace**-ful-ness.

The termination ist *added to words denots an* agent.

art, **art**-ist; form, **form**-a-list, **lo**-yal, **lo**-yal-ist; **or**-gan, **or**-gan-ist; **du**-el, **du**-el-ist; **hu**-mor, **hu**-mor-ist.

In some words, y *is changed to* i.

zo-**ol**-o-ġy, zo-**ol**-o-ġist; or-ni-**thol**-o-ġy, or-ni-**thol**-o-ġist.

139

The prefix ante *denotes* before.

date, **ante**-date; past, **ante**-past; cham-ber, **ante**-cham-ber; pe-nult, **ante**-pen-ult; di-lu-vian, **ante**-di-luv-ian; **nup**-tial, **ante-nup**-tial.

The prefix anti *usually denotes* opposition *or* against.

Christ, **anti**-christ; Christian, **anti**-christian; febrile, anti-febrile.

Be, *a prefix, generally denotes* opposition *or* against.

daub, be-daub; dew, be-dew; friend, be-friend; labor, be-labor; numb, be-numb; moan, be-moan; speak, be-speak; sprinkle, be-sprinkle

The prefix con, *or* co, *denotes* with *or* opposite; con *is changed into* col *before* l.

co-equal, co-exist, co-habit, con-form, co-eval, co-extend, con-firm, con-join

The prefix counter *denotes* against *or* opposition

balance, counter-balance; act, counter-act; evidence, counter-evidence; plea, counter-plea; work, counter-work; part coun-ter-part

The prefix de *denotes* down from; *sometimes it gives* a negative sense.

base, de-base; bar, de-bar; compose, de-compose; cry, de-cry' form, de-form; fame, de-fame; face, de-face; garnish, de-garnish

Dis *denotes* separation, department; *hence it gives words* a negative sense.

able, dis-able; agree, dis-agree; allow, dis-allow; belief, dis-belief; credit, dis-credit; esteem, dis-esteem; grace, dis-grace; honor. dis-honor.

Fore *denotes* before, *in time, sometimes in place.*

bode, fore-bode; father, fore-father; know, fore-know; noon, fore-noon; tell, fore-tell; taste, fore-taste; warn, fore-warn; run, fore-run

In, *which is sometimes changed into* il, im, *and* ir, *denotes* in, on, upon, *or against; it gives to adjectives* a negative sense, *as* in infirm; *sometimes it is* intensive; *sometimes it denotes* to make; *as* bank, imbank; brown, imbrown; bitter, imbitter.

In the following, it gives a negative sense.

material, im-material; moderate, im-moderate; mutable, im-mutable; pure, im-pure; active, in-active; applicable, in-applicable; articulate, inarticulate; attention, in-attention; cautious, in-cautious; defensible, in-defensible; discrete, in-discrete; distinct, in-distinct; religious, ir-religious; reverent, ir-reverent; revocable, ir-revocable

Non *is used as a prefix, giving to words a negative sense.*

appearance, non-appearance; compliance, non-compliance; conformist, non-conformist; resident, non-resident

Out, *as a prefix, denotes* beyond, longer than, *or* more than.

leap, out-leap; live, out-live; venom, out-venom; resident, non-resident over, *as a prefix, denotes* above, beyond, excess, too much.

balance, over-balance; bold, over-bold; burden, over-burden; charge, over-charge; drive, over-drive; feed over-feed; flow, over-flow; load, over-load; pay, over-pay

Trans, *a prefix, signifies* beyond, across *or* over

plant, trans-plant; Atlantic, trans-atlantic; form, trans-form

Pre, *as a prefix, denotes* before, *in* time *or* rank.

caution, pre-caution; determine, pre-determine; eminent, pre-eminent; mature, pre-mature; occupy, pre-occupy; suppose, pre-suppose; conceive, pre-conceive; concert, pre-concert; exist, pre-exist

Re, *a prefix, denotes* again *or* repetition.

assert, re-assert; assure, re-assure; bound, re-bound; dissolve re-dissolve; embark, re-embark; enter, reenter; assume, re-assume; capture, re-capture; collect, re-collect; commence, re-commence; conquer, re-conquer; examine, re-examine; export, re-export; pay, re-pay; people, re-people

Un, *a prefix, denotes* not, *and gives to words* a negative sense.

abashed, **un**-abashed; abated, **un**-abated; abolished, **un**-abolished; acceptable, **un**-acceptable; adjusted, **un**-adjusted; attainable, **un**-attainable; biased, **un**-biased; conscious, **un**-conscious; equaled, **un**-equaled; graceful, **un**-graceful; lawful, **un**-lawful; supported, **un**-supported

Super, supra, *and* sur, *denote* above, beyond, *or* excess.

abound, super-abound; eminent, super-eminent; mundane, supramundane, charge, sur-charge

He seldom lives frugally, who lives by chance, or without method. Without frugality, none can be rich; and with it, few would be poor. The most necessary part of learning is to unlearn our errors. Small parties make up in diligence what they want in numbers. Some talk of subjects which they do not understand; other praise virtue, who do not practice it. The path of duty is always the path of safety. Be very cautious in believing ill of your neighbor; but more cautious in reporting it.

OF NUMERALS

FIGURES	LETTERS	NAMES	NUMERAL ADJECTIVES
1	I	one	first
2	II	two	second
3	III	three	third
4	IV	four	fourth
5	V	five	fifth
6	VI	six	sixth
7	VII	seven	seventh
8	VIII	eight	eighth
9	IX	nine	ninth
10	X	ten	tenth
11	XI	eleven	eleventh
12	XII	twelve	twelfth
13	XIII	thirteen	thirteenth
14	XIV	fourteen	fourteeneth
15	XV	fifteen	fifteenth
16	XVI	sixteen	sixteeneth
17	XVII	seventeen	seventeenth
18	XVIII	eighteen	eighteenth
19	XIX	nineteen	nineteenth
20	XX	twenty	twentieth
30	XXX	thirty	thirtieth
40	XL	fourth	fortieth
50	L	fifty	fiftieth
60	LX	sixty	sixtieth
70	LXX	seventy	seventieth
80	LXXX	eighty	eightieth
90	XC	ninety	ninetieth
100	C	one hundred	one hundredth
200	CC	two hundred	two hundredth
300	CCC	three hundred	three hundredth
400	CCCC	four hundred	four hundredth
500	D	five hundred	five hundredth
600	DC	six hundred	six hundredth
700	DCC	seven hundred	seven hundredth
800	DCCC	eight hundred	eight hundredth
900	DCCCC	nine hundred	nine hundredth
1000	M	one thousand &c.	one thousandth
1829	MDCCCXXIX	one thousand eight hundred and twenty-nine	

½ one half.   1/3 one third   ¼ one fourth   1/5 one fifth   1/6 one sixth   1/7 one seventh
1-1   1-11   1-111   1-1111   1-11111   1-111111

1/8 one eight   1/9 one ninth   1/10 one tenth   2/5 two fifths   4/5 four fifths   9/10 nine tenths
1-1111111   1_11111111   1-111111111   11-111   1111-1   111111111-1

WORDS AND PHRASES FROM FOREIGN LANGUAGES, FREQUENTLY OCCURRING IN ENGLISH BOOKS, RENDERED INTO ENGLISH

L. *stands for Latin,* F. *for French,* S. *for Spanish.*

Ad captandum vulgus, L. to captivate the populace.

Ad finem, L. to the end.

Ad hominem, L. to the man.

Ad infinitum, L to endless extent.

Ad libitum, L. at pleasure.

Ad referendum, L. for further consideration.

Ad valorem, L. according to the value.

Alma mater, L. cherished mother.

A mensa et thoro, L. from bed and board.

Anglice, L. according to the English manner.

Avalanche, F. a snow-slip; a vast body of snow that slides down a mountainside.

auto da fé, S. act of faith; a sentence of the Inquisition for punishment of heresy.

Beau monde, F, the gay (happy) world.

Bona fide, L. in good faith.

Bon mot, F. a witty repartee.

Cap-à-pie, F. from head to foot.

Caput mortuum L. the dead head; thee worthless remains.

Carte blanche, F. blank paper; permission without restraint.

Chef d'oeuvre, F. a masterpiece.

Comme il faut, F as it should be.

Campos mentis. L. of sound mind.

Coup de main, F. sudden enterprise or effort.

Dernier ressort, *F*, of last resort.

Dieu et mon droit, F. God of my right.

Ennui, F. weariness, lassitude.

E pluribus unum, L. one out of, or composed of many [*The motto of the United States.*]

Ex, L out; as ex-minister, a minister out of office.

Excelsior, L. more elevated. [*The motto of the State of New York.*]

Ex officio, L. by virtue of office.

Ex parte, L. on one side only.

Ex post facto, L. after the deed is done.

Extempore, L. without premeditation.

Fac similie, L. a close imitation.

Fille de chamber, F. a chambermaind.

Fortier in re, L. with the firmness in acting.

Gens d'armes, F. armed police.

Habeas corpus, L. that you have the body [*A writ for delivering a person from prison.*]

Hic jacet, L. here lies.

Honi soit qi mal y pense, F. shame be to him that evils thinks.

Hotel dieu, F. a hospital

Impromptu, L. without previous study.

In statu quo, L. in the former state.

In toto, L. in the whole.

Ipse dixit, L. he said.

Ipso facto, L. the fact.

Je-d'eau, F. a waterspout.

Jeu d'esprit, F. a play of wit.

Lex talionis, L. the law of retaliation; as, an eye for an eye, etc.

Literatim, L. a substitute.

Locum tenens, L. the great charter.

Magna Charta, L. the great charter.

Maximum, L. the greatest.

Memento mori, L. be mindful of death.

Minimum, L. the smallest

Mirabile dictu, L. wonderful to tell

Multum in parvo, L. much in a small company.

Nem. con., or *nem dis,* L. no one dissenting; unanimously

Ne plus ultra, L. the utmost extent

Nolens volens, L. whether he will or not.

Nom de plume, F. a literary title.

Non compos mentis, L. not of a sound mind.

Par nobile fratrum, L. a noble pair of brothers

Pater patrioe, L. the father of his country.

Per annum, L. by the year.

Per diem, L. by the day.

Per cent, L. by the hundred.

Per contra. L. contrariwise.

Per se, L. by itself considered.

Prima facie, L. at the first view.

Primum mobile, L. first cause of motion.

146

Pro bono publico, L. for the public good.

Pro et. con, L. for and against.

Pro patria, L. for my country.

Pro tempore, L. for the time.

Pro re nata, L. as occasion requires; for a special emergency

Pugnis et calcibus, L. with fists and feet, with all the might.

Quantum, L. how much.

Quantum sufficit, L. a sufficient quantity.

Qui transtulit sustinet, L. he who has born them sustains them.

Quid nunc, L. a newsmonger.

Re infecta, L. the thing not done.

Sanctum Sanctorum, L. the Holy of Holies.

Sang froid, F. in cold blood, indifference.

Sans souci, F. free and easy; without care.

Secundum artem, L. according to art.

Sic transit Gloria mundi, L. thus passed away the glory of the world.

Sine die, L. without a delay specified.

Sine qua non, L. that without which a thing cannot be done.

Soi disant, F. self-styled.

Suaviter in modo, L. agreeable in manner.

Sub judice, L. under consideration.

Sub rosa, L. under the rose, or privately.

Summum bonum, L. the chief good.

Toties quoties, L. as often as.

Toto coelo, L. wholly, as far as possible.

Utile dulci, L. the useful with the agreeable.

Vade mecum, L (lit. *go with me*); a convenient companion; a handbook.

Veni, vidi, vici, L. I came, I saw, I conqured.

Versus, L. against.

Via, L. by the way of.

Vice versa, L. the terms being exchanged.

Vica voce, L. with the voice.

ABBREVIATIONS EXPLAINED.
(Old Style [APA 2009] abbreviations are used for States.)

Ans. Answer; *A. A. S.* Fellow of the American Academy; *A. B.* Bachelor of Arts; *Abp.* Archbishop. *Acct.* Account. *A. D.* Anno Domini, the year of our Lord; *Adm.* Admiral. *Admr.* Administrator; *Admx.* Administratrix. *Ala.* Alabama; *A. M.* Masters of arts; before noon; in the year of the world; *Apr.* April; *Ariz.* Arizona; *Ark.* Arkansas; *Atty.* Attorney; *Aug.* August; *Bart.* Baronet; *B. C.* Before Christ; *B. D.* Bachelor of Divinity; *Bbl.* Barrel; *bbs.* barrels. *Cal.* or *Calif.* California; *C. Centum,* a hundred; *Capt.* Captain. *Chap.* Chapter. *Col.* Colonel; *Co.* Company; *Com.* Commissioner, Commodore. *Cr.* Credit; *Cwt.* Hundred weight. *Conn.* or *Ct.* Connecticut; *C. S.* Keeper of the Seal; *Cl.* Clerk, Clergyman; *Co.* or *Colo.* Colorado; *Cong.* Congress. *Cons.* Constable; *Cts.* Cents; *D. C.* District of Columbia; *D. D.* Doctor of Divinity; *Dea.* Deacon; *Dec.* December; *Del.* Delaware; *Dept.* Deputy; *do.* Ditto, the same; *Dr.* Doctor, or Debtor; *D.V.* Deo volente, God willing; *E.* East; *Ed.* Editor. *E. & O. E.* Errors of omission accepted. *e. g.* for example. *Eng.* England, English; *Esp.* Esquire. *Etc.* et caetera, and so forth; *Ex.* Example; *Exec.* Executor; *Execx.* Executrix. *Feb.* February; *Fla.* Florida; *Fr.* France, French, Francis; *F. R. S.* Fellow of the Royal Society [Eng.]; *Gen.* General; *Geo.* George; *Ga.* or *Geo.* Georgia; *Gov.* Governor; *Hon.* Honorable. *Hund.* Hundred; *H. B. M.* His *or* Her Britannic Majesty; *Hhd.* Hogshead; *Idib.* In the same place; *Idaho.* Idaho; *i. e.* that is [id est]; *id.* the same; *Ill.* Illinois; *Ind.* Indiana; *Ind. Ter.* Indian territory; *Inst.* Instant; *Io.* or *Iowa.* Iowa; *Ir.* Ireland; *Jan.* January; *Jas.* James; *Jac.* Jacob; *Josh.* Joshua; *Jun.* or *Jr.* Junior; *K.* King; *Kan.* or *Kans.* Kansas; *Ky.* or *Ken.* Kentucky; *Kt.* Knight; *L.* or *Ld.* Lord or Lady; *La.* or *Lou.* Louisiana; *Lieut.* Lieutenant. *Lond.* London; *Lon.* Longitude; *Ldp.* Lordship; *Lat.* Lattitude; *LL.D.* Doctor of Laws; *lbs.* Pounds; *L S* Place of the seal; *M.* Marquis, Meridian; *Mass.* Massachusetts; *Matt.* Matthew; *Mch.* or *Mich.* Michigan; *Mch.* March; *M. D.* Doctor of Medicine; *Md.* Maryland. *Me.* Main; *Mich.* Michigan; *Mr.* Mister, Sir.; *Messrs.* Gentleman. Sirs.; *Minn.* Minnesota; *Miss.* Mississippi; *Mo.* Missouri. *Mont.* Montana; *MS.* Manuscript; *MSS.* Manuscripts; *Mrs.* Mistress; *N.* North; *N. B.* Take Notice; *N. C.* or *N. Car.* North Carolina; *Nebr.* Nebraska; *Nev.* Nevada; *N. Mex.* New Mexico; *N. H.* or *N. Hamp.* New Hampshire; *N. J.* New Jersey; *No.* Number; *Nov.* November; *N. S.* New Style; *N. Y.* New York; *O.* Ohio; *Obt.* Obedient; *Oct.* October; *Oreg.* or *Ore.* Oregon; *O. S.* Old Style; *Parl.* Parliament. *Pa.* or *Penn.* or *Penna.* Pennsylvania; *per.* by, as, per yard, by the yard; *Per cent.* By the hundred; *Pet.* Peter; *Phil.* Phillip; *P. M.* Post Master, afternoon; *P. O.* Post Office; *Ps.* Psalms; *Pres.* President; *Prof. Professor. Q.* Question, Queen; *q. d.* (*quasi dicat*), as if he should say; *q. l.* (*quantum libet*), as much as you please; *q. s.* (*quantum sufficit*), a sufficient quantity. *Regr.* Register. *Rep.* Representative. *Rev.* Reverend; *Rt. Hon.* Right Honorable; *R. I.* Rhode Island. *S.* South, Shilling; *S. C.* or *S. Car.* South Carolina; *St.* Saint; *Sect.* Section; *Sen. Senator, Senior. Sept.* September; *Serv.* **Servant.** *S. T. P.* Professor of Sacred Divinity. *S. T. D.* Doctor of Divinity; *ss.* to wit, namely; *Surg.* Surgeon; *Tenn.* Tennessee; *Ter.* Territory; *Tex.* Texas; *Theo.* Theophilus; *Thos.* Thomas; *Ult. the last, or the last of the month. U. S.* United States; *U. S. A.* United States of America; *V.* (*vide*), See; *Va.* Virginia; *viz.* to wit, namely; *Vt.* Vermont; *Wash.* Washington; *Wis.* or *Wisc.* Wisconsin; *Wt.* Weight; *Wm.* William; *W. Va* or *W. Vir.* West Virginia; *Wyo.* Wyoming; *Yd.* Yard; *&* (et) And; *&c* (= *etc.*) And so forth.

PUNCTUATION

The *comma* (,) indicates a short pause. The *semicolon* (;) indicates a pause somewhat longer than the comma; the *colon* (:) a still longer pause; and the *period* (.) indicates the longest pause. The period is placed at the close of a sentence.

The interrogation point (?) denotes that a question is asked, as, *What do you see?*

An exclamation point (!) denotes wonder, grief, or other emotion.

A parenthesis ( ) includes words not closely connected with other words in the sentence.

Brackets or hooks [ ] are sometimes used for nearly the same purpose as parenthesis, or to include some explanation.

A dash (–) denotes a sudden stop, or a change of subject, and requires a pause, but of no definite length.

A caret (∧) shows the omission of a word or letter, which is placed above the line, the
the
caret being put below, thus *give me book.*
∧

An apostrophe (') denotes the omission of a letter or letters, thus lov'd, tho't.

A quotation is indicated by these points " " placed at the beginning or ending of the passage.

The index (☞) points to a passage, which is to be particularly noticed.

The paragraph (¶) denotes the beginning of a new subject.

The star or asterisk (*), the dagger (†), and other marks (‡, §, ∥) and sometimes letters and figures, are used to refer the reader to notes in the margin.

The diaresis (¨) denotes that the vowel under it is not connected with the preceding vowel.

CAPITAL LETTERS

A CAPITAL letter should be used at the *beginning* of a sentence. It should begin all proper *names of persons, cities, towns, villages, seas, rivers, mountains, lakes, ships, &c.* It should begin *every line of poetry,* a *quotation,* and often an important word.

The name or appellation of *God, Jehovah, Christ, Messiah,* &c., should begin with a capital.

The pronoun *I,* and the interjection *O* are always in capitals.

No. 151. – 92 Words

THE LETTER q IS EQUIVALENT TO k. THE u FOLLOWING, AND NOT ITALICIZED, HAS THE SOUND OF w; ITALICIZED u IS SILENT.

ăq-ue-duct, ăq-uĭ-līne, an-tĭq-ui-ty, ĕq-ui-ty, ĕq-ui-ta-ble, ĕq-ui-ta-bly, in-ĭq-ui-ty, in-ĭq-ui-toŭs, lĭq-uid, lĭq-*u*or, lĭq-ue-fȳ, lĭq-ue-făc-tion, lĭq-ue-fī-a-ble, liq-ue-fȳ-ing, lĭq-uid-āte, lĭq-uid-ā-tion, ob-lĭq-ui-ty, u-bĭq-ui-ty, pĭq-*u*ant, rĕq-ui-sĭte, req-ui-sĭ-tion.

IN THE FOLLOWING WORDS t IS NOT SOUNDED.

chās-ten, hās-ten, glĭs-ten, fȧst-en, lĭst-en, moist-en, ŏft-en, sŏ-ft-en.

EI AND *IE* WITH THE SOUND OF *E* LONG.

The letters *ei* and *ie* occur in several words with the same sound, that is of long *e* but persons are often at a loss to recollect which of these letters stands first. I have therefore arranged the principal words of these classes into two distinct tables that pupils may commit them to memory, so that the order may be made a familiar as letters of the alphabet.

WORDS OF WHICH THE LETTER *e* STANDS BEFORE *i*.

çēil, çēiling, conçēit, conçēive, deçēit, deçēive, perçēive, dissēize, ēither, invēigle, lēisure, nēither, obēisançe, obēisant, reçēive, reçēipt, sēignior, sēine, sēize, sēizin, sēizūre.

achiēve, griēve, griēvançe, griēvoŭs, aggriēve, beliēf, beliēve, briēf, chiēf, fiēf, fiēnd, brigadiēr, breviēr, fiērçe, liēf, liēġe, liēn, miēn, niēçe, piēr, piērçe, priēst, reliēf, reliēve, repriēve bombardiēr, cannoniēr, reliēvo, retriēve, shiēld, shiēling, shriēk, siēġe, thiēf, thiēve, tiēr, tiērçe, wiēld, yiēld, finançiēr, cavaliēr, çhevaliēr.

No. 152 – WORDS DIFFICULT TO SPELL

(1) - 19 words

a-**bey**-ançe, a-**çĕrb**-i-ty, āche (*āk*), ac-quĭ-**ĕsçe**, **ā**-er-onạut, **ăġ**-ĭle, a*l*ms, ăm-a-**teụr**, ăm-e-thў̆st, ăn-a-**lȳze**, ăn-o-dȳne, **ăn**-s*w*er, a-**nŏn**-ў̆-moŭs, an-**tïque**, **ăq**-ue-duct, arch-**ān**-ġel, a-**skew**, ăv-oir-du-**poiṣ**, äў̆e, (*äĭ*).

(2) – 18 words.

ban-**dăn**-ȧ, bȧsque, (*bȧsk*), **bāss**-vī-ol, bā-**zäar**, **bēa**-c*o*n, beaux (*bōz*), **bĭs**-cuĭt (*-kĭt*), **bȯr**-ō*ugh*, **bọ**-ṣom, brụiṣe (*brooz*), **bọu**-doir (*-dwôr*), **bū**-reau (*-rō*), cạ*l*k (*kawk*), ca-**prïçe**, ca-**rouṣe**, ca-**tăs**-tro-phe, **cạu**-cus, **chā**-os (*kā-*).

(3) – 21 words

chärġe-a-ble, chĭ-**mē**-rȧ, **chĭv**-al-ry, *chўle* (*kīl*), chȳme (*kīm*), **çĭc**-a-trĭçe, clïque (*kleek*), **cō**-cōa (**kō**-*kō*), **cŏl**-lēague, col-**lō**-quĭ-al, cōm*b* (*kom*), **cŏm**-plai-ṣănçe, **cŏn**-duĭt (*dĭt*), con-**dīgn**, con-va-**lesçe**, con-**vẹy**, corps (*kōr*), **coun**-ter-feĭt, **cọu**-rĭ-er, **coûrt**-e-sy, **coûrt***e*-sy.

151

(4) – 17 words

coŭs-*i*n, cŏx-cōm*b*, crọup, cru̯i̯s̱e, crŭm*b*, crўpt, cu̱k-o͞o, cū-po-là, de-fĭ-cient, **dĕm**-a-gŏgue, **dī**-a-lŏgue, **dĭl**-i-ġençe, dis-**guī̱s̱e**, dĭ-**shĕv**-*e*l, **dŏm**-i-çĭle, **dou***g*h-ty, dràught (*draft*).

(5) - 19 words

dўs-en-tĕr-y, **dўs**-pĕp-sy, **ēa**-gle, ef-fer-**vĕs**çe, e-lec-**trĭ**-cian, **ĕl**-e-phant en-çy̱-clo-**pē**-di-à, en-**frăn**-chĭ̱s̱e, e-**quĕs**-tri-an, ĕr-y-sĭp-e-las, ĕs-pi-on-āġe, ex-**cru̱**-ci-āte, e̱x-**ha̱ust**, fa-**tĭgue**, fic-**tĭ**-tioŭs, fläunt, flo-**rĕs**-çençe, for-**băde**, **fŏr**-eign-er.

(6) – 20 words

frăn-chĭse, frĭc-as-**see**, **fûr**-lŏug*h*, **gāy**-e-ty, gāuġe, **ga**-zĕlle, *g*h**ast**-ly, *g*hōst *(***gōst***)*, *g*hou̱l (gool), ġĭ-**răffe**, *glā*-çiẽr, (-*seer*), gnärl*e*d, **gō**-pher, **gôr**-ġeoŭs (-*jus*), gọur-**mänd**, **grănd**-eūr, gro-**tĕsque**, guăr-an-**tee**, **guăr**-an-ty, **gŭd**-ġeon (-*jun*).

(7) – 19 words

guĭl-lo-tïne, **guĭn**-ea (*ḡĭn-e*), guĭ̱s̱e (*ḡīz*), **ġyp**-sy, heärth, **hĕif**-er, ***h*êir**-lo͞om (*âr-*), **hĕm**-i-sphēre, **hĕrb**-aġe, hī-e-ro-**glўph**-ic, hōax, hŏugh (*hŏk*), **how**-itz-er, **hŏs**-*t*ler, **hȳ**-a-çĭnth, hȳ-**ē**-nà, hȳ-**pĕr**-bo-là, **īce**-bĕrg, ĭch-**neū**-mon.

(8) – 18 words

ĭeh-thy-**ŏl**-o-ġy, ī-**çĭ**-cle, ī-**dȳl**, **ĭm**-be-çĭle, in-**dĭġ**-e-noŭs, in-**ġēn**-ioŭs (-*yus*), in-**trĭgu**-er, ī-o-**dĭde**, ī-**răs**-çi-ble, **jăs**-mĭne, **jĕop**-ard-y, **jăve**-lin, **joûr**-ney, **jūi**-çy, ka-**leī**-do-scōpe, kān-ga-**rōō**, *knĭck*-knack, **lăb**-ȳ-rinth.

(9) – 19 words

lar-ȳnx, **lĭc**-o-rĭçe, lieū-**tĕn**-ant, lĭ-**tĭġ**-ioŭs, **lōath**-sȯme, **lŭnch**-eon (-*un*), **lŭs**-cioŭs, lux-ū-ri-ançe, **lȳnx**, ma-**çhïne**, Ma-**dēi**-rȧ, ma-**ġi**-cian, mal-**fēa**-sançe, ma-**lĭ**-cioŭs, ma-**līgn**, **măn**-a-cle, man-**eū**-ver, **ma**-ny (*mĕn-ȳ*), **măr**-riaġe.

(10) – 19

mēa-sl*e*s, **mē**-di-ō-cre, **mēr**-can-tĭle, me-**rĭ**-no, mĕt-a-**môr**-phose, mī-**ăs**-mȧ, mĭ-**lĭ**-tiȧ, **mill**-ion-âire, **mĭs**-chĭef, **mĭs**-sion-a-ry, **moi**-e-ty, **mȯn**-eys, **mȯn**-eyed (*ĭd*), **mor*t***-ġaġed, **môr**-tĭse, mus-**täçhe**, **mŭs**-çle (-*sl*), mu-**sĭ**-cian, mos-**quï**-to (-*kē*-).

(11) – 19 words

năp*h*-thȧ, ne-**gō**-ti-āte, **neigh**-bor-hŏŏd, neū-**răl**-ġi-ȧ, nȳmph, o-**bēi**-sançe, of-**fĭ**-cioŭs, **ō**-rġe, om-**nĭ**-scient, **ō**-nȳx, op-**tĭ**-cian, **ôr**-phan, **pæ**-an, **păġ**-eant-ry, păn-e-**ġȳr**-ic, **păr**-a-lȳze, **păr**-ox-ȳsm, **pā**-tri-äreh, pe-**cūl**-iar.

(12) 18 words

pe-**lĭsse** (-*less*), **pē***o*-ple, pe-**rĭph**-e-ry (-*rĭf*-), per-**nĭ**-cioŭs, per-**suāde**, **phā**-e-tȯn, **phō**-to-graph, **phy̆**-s-ic, phy̆s̲-i-ŏg̣-no-my, phy̆-**s̲ïque**, pĭ-ăz̲-zȧ, pict-ūr-**ĕsque**, **pĭg̣**-eon, pȯm-aҫe, **pȯr**-phy̆-ry, **prāi**-rie, pre-**cō**-cioŭs, pro-**dĭg̣**-ioŭs, pro-**fĭ**-cien-ҫy,

(13) – 18 words

prŏph-e-ҫy, **pûr**-lieŭs̲, py̆r-o-**tĕch**-nics, quạr-**tĕtte** (-*ĕt*), quay (*kē*), **quī**-nīne, quiot, **răs̲p**-ber-ry, **rĕck**-*o*n, rec-on-**noi**-ter, re-**crụit**, *r*hap-so-dy, *r*heu̲-ma-tis̲m, r*hī*-**noç**-e-ros, *r*hu̲-bärb, rhȳme, **rō**-guish, rụ-tȧ-**bā**-gȧ.

(14) – 18 words

sā-ti-ate (-*shĭ-āt*), **scạl**-lop, scär-la-**tĭ**-nȧ, **sçĭm**-i-ter, **sçĭs̲**-s̲ors, scoûrg̣e, scur-**toire**, (-*twôr*), sçȳthe, **sĕn**-sū-al (-*shu̲-al*), shrewd, **sĭl**-*h*ọu-ĕtte (-*ĕt*), slūiçe, **sōl**-dier (-*jer*), **sọuve**-nïr, **spē**-ciēs̲, **sphē**-roid, sphĭn̲x, stăt-ū-**ĕtte** (-*ĕt*).

(15) 19 words

stē-re-o-tȳpe, **stȯm**-aeh, sū-per-**fĭ**-cial, **sûr**-feĭt, tăb-**leaux** (-*lōz*), tam-bọur-**ïne**, **tĕeh**-nic-al, tur-**quois̲** (-*koiz*), **tȳ**-phoid, ū-**nïque**, **văl**-iant, va-**lïse**, vex-**ā**-tioŭs, **vĭl**-lain-oŭs, **vĭ**-ti-āte (-*shĭ-āt*), wēird, *w*rĕs-*t*le, *w*retch-ed, yạcht (*yŏt*).

(16) – 17 words

băc-eha-**nā**-li-an, bru̱-**nĕtte** (*-nĕt*), çhăn-de-**liēr**, ca-**tärr***h* (*-tär*), co-**quĕtte** (*-kĕt*), cro-**que̱t** (*-kā*), dĭs-**tieh** (*-tĭk*), e-**clä***t* (*e-klä*), ĕl-ee-**mŏs**-y̆-na-ry, é-**lïte** (*ā-leet*), en-**nuï** (ŏng-**nwē**), et-i-**quette** (*-kĕt*), ḡhĕr-kin, ġy̆m-nā-s̱i-um, hĭc-cough (*-kup*), **hō**-sier-y (*hō-zher-*), ĭd-i-o-sy̆n-cra-sy.

(17) – 19 words

Ind-ian (*-yan*), **meer**-sçha̱um, **na̱u**-seoŭs *(-shus)*, phlegm (*flĕm*), *psȳ*-**ehŏl**-o-ġy, queue (*kū*), **rā**-ti-o (*-shĭ-o*), să-o-**nā**-ceoŭs, **āid**-de-camp (***ād***-*de-kŏng*), **bay**-o̱u (**bī**-oo), belles-**let**-tres, (*bel-**lĕt**-tr*), **bĭl**-let-do̱ux (***bĭl***-*le-doo*), blanc-***manage*** (*blo-mŏnj*), brag-ga-**dō**-ci-o (*brag-ga-**dō**-shĭ-o*), **buoy**-an-çy, (***bwooy̆***-*an-çy̆*), çham-**pāgne** (*sham-**pān***), **clăp**-bōard (***klăb***-*bōrd*), **ca̱out**-cho̱uc (**koo**-chook), cärte-**blänçhe** (kart-**blänsh**).

(18) – 20 words

cŏn-scieņçe (***kŏn***-*shens*), da-**guĕrre**-o-tȳpe (*da-**ḡĕr**-o-tīp*), **däh**-liȧ (**däl**-yȧ), dé-**brïs** (*dā-**brē***), di̱s-**çĕrn**-i-ble (*diz-**zĕrn**-i-bl*), en-**cōre** (*ŏn-**kōr***), măd-em-oi-**s̱ĕlle** (*măd-mwa̱-**zĕ**l*), mag-nē-si-ȧ (*mag-nē-zhi-a*), men-**ăg**-e-rie (*men-**ăzh**-e-ry̆*), mĭgn-on-**ĕtte** (*mĭn-yon-ĕt*), **na̱u**-se-āte (***naw***-*she-āt*), pen-i-**tĕn**-tia-ry̆ (*pĕn-i-**tĕn**-sha-ry*), pōrt-**măn**-teau (*pōrt-**măn**-tō*), **ren**-dez-vo̱us (***rĕn***-*de-voo*), **rĕs**-tau-rant (***rĕs***-*to-rant*), **rīght**-eoŭs (***rī***-*chus*), **ser**-ġeant (***sär***-*gent* or *sẽr-*), **sŭb**-tle-ty (**sŭt**-l-ty̆), vign-**ĕtte** (*vĭn-**yĕt***), **whort**-le-bĕr-ry (**hwûrt**-l-bĕr-ry̆).

Webster's Spelling Book Method for Teaching Reading and Spelling

Student Progress Chart

Student _____ Grade ____ School _____ Teacher _____

Table 1 Syllabary 1 CV: b c d f g	Table 2 Syllabary 2 CV: h j k l m n	Tables 3 Syllabary 3 CV: p r s t v w	Table 4 Syllabary 4 VC: b c d f g	Table 5 Syllabary 5 VC: j k l m n j p	Table 6 Syllabary 6 VC: r s t v x z	Table 7 Syllabary 7 CCV: bl cl fl gl pl sl	Table 8 Syllabary 8 CCV: br cr dr fr gr pr tr wr	Table 9 Syllabary 9 th ch sh ph	Table 10 Syllabary 10 qu sp s tsk sc sw
Table 11 Syllaabry 11 spl spr str shr scr scl	Table 12 Short Vowel CVC	Table 13 Short Vowel CVC	Table 14 Short Vowel CVC	Table 15 Short Vowel CVC	Table 16 Short Vowel CVC	Table 17 Long Vowel CVE	Table 18 Long Vowel CVE	Table 19 Long Vowel CVE	Table 20 Long Vowel CVE
Table 21 CVCC	Table 22 CVCC & CCVCC	Table 23 CVCC & CCVCC	Table 24 CVCT	Table 25 CVST	Table 26 CV Open Syllables 2-syll. Accent 1st	Table 27 CVCC Words	Table 28 CCVC	Table 29 CCVC & Sent.	Table 30 CVCC Words
Table 31 CCVCC Words	Table 32 2-Syl, Accent 2nd & Sent.2nd	Table 33 ee ee, oo	Table 34 ee, ōō	Table 35 ōō, ōō, & Sent.	Table 36 ck	Table 37 ck, lk, nk	Table 38 nk, rk, sk sh, ss, ft	Table 39 sk, rl, lm, rm, etc	Table 40 ff, dd, gg, ll, bb
Table 41 ll, nn, n, rr, sh	Table 42 VC Words & Sent.	Table 43 s for plural & Sent.	Table 44 2-Syl, Accent 1st	Table 45 dge, g = j	Table 46 se, ch, Sent.	Table 47 ose pse ice, ime, ere, & Sent. .	Table 48 oi, ou,	Table 49 ou, ow, ice, ise & Sent.	Table 50 ĕa, oa ai ue, etc.
Table 51 ye, ee, ai, oa, ea	Table 52 ĕa, ōa, āi, ŏw ōu & Sent.	Table 53 ĕa, ōs, āi,	Table 54 3-Syl, Accent 1st Closed-Syl, & Sent.	Table 55 VCe & Sent.	Table 56 2-Syl, Accent1st & Sent.	Table 57 ou, ow, ai, ea, oa, etc.	Table 58 ai, ea, oa, , etc.	Table 59 ĕa, ōa, ew, ōw, & Sent.	Table 60 au, aw, augh
Table 61 VCe & Sent.	Table 62 3-Syl, Accent 1st	Table 63 3-Syl, Accent 2nd	Table 64 2-Syl, Accent 1st & Sent.	Table 65 2-Syl, Accent 1st	Table 66 2-Syl, Accent 1st	Table 67 4-Syl, Accent 1st & Sent.	Table 68 3-Syl, Accent 2nd & Sent.	Table 69 ay, ey	Table 70 oy, aw
Table 71 wa, (a=ŏ), work, etc.	Table 72 ow, cy, ir, wa, etc. & Sent.	Table 73 2-Syl, Accented 1st & Sent.	Table 74 2-Syl, Accented 1st & Sent.	Table 75 3-Syl, Accented 2nd & Sent.	Table 76 3-Syl, Accented on 3rd	Table 77 2-Syl, Accented 1st, & Sent.	Table 78 3-Syl. Accented 1st	Table 79 2-Syl, Accented 2nd & Sent.	Table 80 2-Syl, Accented 1st &Sent.
Table 81 3-Syl, Accented 2nd & Sent.	Table 82 4-Syl, Accented 1st	Table 83 3-Syl, Accented 1st	Table 84 2-Syl, Accented 1st & Sent.	Table 85 3-Syl, Accented 1st & Sent.	Table 86 2-Syl, Accented 2nd & Sent.	Table 87 2-Syl, Accented 1st. &Sent.	Table 88 2-Syl, Accented 1st & Sent.	Table 89 2-Syl, Accented 2nd & Sent.	Table 90 5-Syl, Ac- cented 2nd & Sent.
Table 91 2-Syl, Accented 2nd & Sent.	Table 92 2-Syl, Accented 2nd & Sent.	Table 93 4-Syl. Accent 3rd Weak accent 1st & Sent.	Table 94 3-Syl. Accented 1st.	Table 95 2-Syl, Accented 2nd	Table 96 1-Syl, Aspirated th & Sent.	Table 97 2-Syl, Accented 1st	Table 98 2-Syl, Accented 1st ōw, & Sent.	Table 99 2-Syl, Accented 1st & Sent.	Table 100 4-Syl, Accented 2nd & Sent.
Table 101 4-Syl, Accented 2nd & Sent.	Table 102 5-syl, Accented 2nd & Sent.	Table 103 6-syl, Accented 4th	Table 104 3-Syl, Accented 1st	Table 105 5-Syl, Accented 3rd	Table 106 3-syl, Accented 2nd	Table 107 4-syl Accented 3rd & Sent.	Table 108 3-Syl, Accented 1st	Table 109 2-Syl, Accented 2nd & Sent.	Table 110 3-Syl, Accented 2nd & Sent.
Table 111 3-Syl, Accented 1st -ate short, & Sent.	Table 112 2-Syl, Accented 1st	Table 113 3-Syl, Accented 1st & Sent.	Table 114 a̤ a̤ll, aw, wha̤t (ŏ)	Table 115 2-Syl, Accented 1st & Sent.	Table 116 2-Syl, Accented 1st	Table 117 4-Syl, Accented 2nd A unmarked in ate.	Table 118 4-syl,Accented 2nd	Table 119 4-Syl, Accented 2nd -ate w/o long sound	Table 120 4-syl, Accented 2nd & Sent.
Table 121 7-Syl, Accented 5th 8-syl, Accented 6th & Sent.	Table 122 th has aspirated sound	Table 123 th has vocal sound adj in ous & Sent.	Table 124 3-Syl, Accented 2nd Adj. -ous & Sent.	Table 125 5-Syl, Accented 3rd & Sent	Table 126 Various 1-Syl. words, th, & Sent.	Table 127 wh – hw or w & Sent.	Table 128 x = gz Sent.	Table 129 tian & tion = chun icn – yen, etc.	Table 130 sier, zier, shion, sia; ion - zhun
Table 131 c before h has k sound	Table 132 g before e, i, and y has hard sound	Table 133 c = s & g = j ending prim or sec acct. syl.	Table 134 ci & ti = sh	Table 135 ci, ti = sh united with preceding syl.	Table 136 ci & ti = shi	Table 137 Misc. 3 Syl- Accent 2nd; 4-Syl Acc. 3rd 5- Syl, Accent 4th, etc.	Table 138 3-Syl, Accented 1st Ending in ize	Table 139 4-Syl & 5-syl. Accent on primitive	Table 140 Sounds of ng
Table 141 d, t, and u in capture, verdure & Sent.	Table 142 g & k before n always silent	Table 143 ch = sh	Table 144 ea = ĕ or e in term.	Table 145 Silent g in ign, hard g resumed	Table 146 e, i y mute before n	Table 147 Fables	Table 148 Words spelled or pronounced alike or nearly alike	Table 149 Word of irregular orthography	Table 150 Verbs, Nouns, Adj. Misc.
Table 151 q = k, t not sounded ci/ie	Table 152 Words difficult to spell								

Prepared by Donald L. Potter on 2/24/10. Table labeled on 2/8/11. Revised & expanded on 3/22/14.

Observations on the Key to Pronunciation

January 10, 2009

Since I use cedilla (ç) for the *soft* c, there is no need to code the *hard* c with a line through it. It is sufficient to write: c for *hard* k. The c with strikethrough looks a lot like *e* to my students. I used strikethrough (e) in the explanation but not in the Tables. The hard c of ch has the strikethrough, eh.

The line under s and x are not quite like Webster, which appears to be connected to the letter by a tiny line in the middle. I found the "combining up tack below," but for now the underline seems to be sufficient. It is very hard to see it clearly even in the good print of the 1908 edition. Combining print is much more difficult (requiring more work) than the simple underline - which works with any font.

The crossed **t** (t) of the **th** isn't quite the same since Webster's appears to be a line touching the top of the **t**.

I prefer Webster to the newer dictionaries because he did not use the schwa. The introduction of the schwa as a diacritical mark has done much to limit the effectiveness of the modern dictionary for the purposes of teaching the common conventions of English orthography.

I used **bold** to indicate accented syllables instead of Webster's accent marks because it is easier for children to understand. Experieince teaching the program has proven that the move from written accents to bold type was a good idea.

It was on January 10, 2008, after months of diligent searching, that I was finally able to locate all the diacritical marks used in the 1908 edition of *Webster's Elementary Spelling Book.* Thanks to Dr. Eugene Roth Jr. for assistance in helping me find all the diacritical marks.

Thanks also to Mrs. Elizabeth Brown for using this book in her tutoring and providing valuable feedback. Her informative website is www.thephonicspage.org. Mrs. Brown's success using this this book with her tutoring students was one of the main reasons that I went ahead with the publication.

Special thanks to reading teacher, researcher, and reading historian Miss Geraldine Rodgers whose brilliant essay, "Why Webster's Way was the Right Way," motivated me to explore the power of *Webster's Spelling Book Method* for teaching reading from the "sounds of the letters" instead of from the "meaning of the words." You can read her essay on my website.

Note from Internet Publisher: Donald L. Potter

November 10, 2008

This book is an adaptation of the 1908 edition of Noah Webster's *Elementary Spelling Book* to the needs of twenty-first century students. It is quite similar to the 1829 edition, which first introduced modern diacritcal marks in place of the numerals (superscripts) used in previous editions to assist in pronouncing words.

Previously I had typed and published the 1824 *American Spelling Book*. I taught the 1824 edition in my classroom with great success. I have seen students improve their reading levels by several grades in a very short period of time with Webster. It is a little known fact that the current grade-level system of teaching reading can have a retarding effect on student's advancement in reading. Many students who are performing on grade level in reading are often reading far below their personal potential. I experimented years with teaching polysyllables to second-grade bilingual students and regular English speaking first-grade students. The results completely changed my opinion of the capabilities of young students if they were systematically taught how to read polysyllables.

Grade levels are determined by tests like the *Fries Readability Formula*, the *Flesch-Kincaid Formula,* or the *Dale-Kincaid Formula.* With the *Fries Formula*, the average number of syllables and sentences in a 100 words passage are used to determine reading level. It was obvious that restricting students to small words and short sentences can have a severe retarding effect on their advancement in grade level ability. When I taught the first graders to read polysyllables, they experienced dramatic improvement on standard grade level reading assessments. Several were able to pass the *1987 Riverside Informal Reading Inventory* 5th and 6th grade levels. The *Accelerated Reader Program*, for example, strictly controls reading levels. The same is true of most grade level curriculum materials.

Students in Noah Webster's day did not experience this unfortunate retarding effect because they learned to read polysyllables at an early age with spelling books. In Webster's day, **Spelling Books were used to teach *reading* and spelling.** Their reading books consisted of material of interest to children but not restricted to small words or short sentences. The *Bible* in the KJV, *Pilgrim's Progress,* and the *Metrical Version of the Psalms* (*Psalter*) were often their first reading materials. Notice that Noah Webster's reading lessons are decodable. They are perhaps the first decodable text for promoting reading without guessing.

Special thanks to Dillon DeArmond, one of my 6th grade tutoring students in 2008, who was the first student of mine to complete *Webster's Spelling Book Method for Teaching Reading and Spelling*. His editorial assistance has been invaluable. His progress with Webster was excellent. He went on to become an Advanced Academic Placement student in junior high and high school.

Kathy González, a homeshool mother in Australia, rendered great service with the proofreading.

Notice these definitions from Webster's 1828 Dictionary: "**Spelling Book**: A book for teaching children to spell and read. **Spell**: to tell or name the letters of a word, with proper division of syllables, for the purpose of learning the pronunciation, children learn to read by first *spelling* the word." On page 26 of the 1783 *Grammatical Institutes of the English Language*, Part I, Webster wrote, "Spelling is the foundation of reading and the greatest ornament of writing."

For those who might question the wisdom of teaching kids to read some words beyond their level of comprehension, let me suggest a consideration of the following quote from the "Preface" to the 1908 *Elementary Spelling Book*: "The reading lessons are adapted, as far as possible, to the capacities of children, and to their gradual progress in knowledge. The lessons will serve to substitute variety for dull monotony of spelling, show the practical use of words in significant sentences, and thus enable the learner to better understand them. The consideration of diversifying the studies of the pupil has also had its influence in the arrangement of the lessons for spelling. It is useful to teach children the signification of words, as soon as they can comprehend, but the understanding can hardly keep pace with the memory, and the minds of children may well be employed in learning to spell and pronounce words whose signification is not within the reach of their capacities; for what they do not clearly comprehend at first, they will understand as their capacities are enlarged."

It is important to note that the division of syllables is not based strictly on roots, prefix and suffixes, that is etymology. Webster's 1908 *Elementary Spelling Book* clearly states, "In Syllabication it has been thought best not to give the etymological division of the Quarto Dictionary, but to retain the old mode of Dr. Webster as best calculated to teach *young* scholars the true pronunciation of words." Previous experience with a polysyllable reading program that I developed eight years ago lead me to recognize the wisdom of Webster's original method of dividing syllables according to pronunciation, similar to the respelling in our modern dictionaries.

In the 1822 edition of his *American Spelling Book*, Webster informs us, "In nine-tenths of the words in our language, a correct pronunciation is better taught by a natural division of the syllables and a direction for placing the accent, than by a minute and endless repetition of characters." For this reason, I have curtailed the use of diacritical marks as much as possible, especially the breve in closed syllables.

I always have the children orally spell some of the words we have read to help fix the spelling in their minds. Students can practice looking the words up in a dictionary.

It is important to keep in mind that the spelling book in Webster's day was considered a method of **teaching reading** and spelling - not just spelling, as in our day.

One of the chief advantages of Webster's method is the way the words are grouped according to **accent**. This **crucial aspect of word identification** is largely overlooked in modern reading and spelling methods. It is especially important for second language learners.

I recommend that students practice both oral and written spelling. All written spelling should be done in cursive, as it was done in Webster's day. Manuscript was not introduced into American schools until 1922, with the results that handwriting, spelling, and composition have deteriorated considerably since Webster's day.

Unknown words can be explained by definition or use in illustrative sentences. Example: "*Demeanor* is how you act. You have a nice *demeanor*. You *act* nice."

Revised on 11/13/2020.

FLESCH-KINCAID GRADE LEVELS

FOR WEBSTER'S 1908 ELEMENTARY SPELLING BOOK

Table	Grade Equivalent	Table	Grade Equivalent	Table	Grade Equivalent
16	0.4	74	5.3	110	9.9
25	0.7	75	9.3	111	10.6
26	4.0	77	3.8	112	6.3
32	5.1	79	7.0	113	10.1
35	0.7	80	3.8	114	7.3
43	1.4	81	8.0	116	8.2
44	4.8	82	6.8	117	10.5
46	1.3	85	8.1	120	10.3
47	1.3	87	4.0	121	12.9
49	1.3	88	5.8	123	8.3
53	2.4	89	6.3	124	7.1
54	8.9	90	9.5	125	10.7
55	3.4	92	5.8	126	5.3
56	4.4	93	7.5	127	5.5
59	1.2	96	3.7	128	9.1
61	1.6	98	4.9	131	9.1
64	7.5	99	6.3	137	12.0
66	6.4	100	10.0	142	7.1
67	8.8	101	7.7		
68	7.6	102	11.7		
72	2.5	107	7.7		
73	5.2	109	4.5		

TABLE 147

The Dog: 3.4; The Stage: 5.0; The Squirrel: 6.4: The Boy who Stole the Apple: 3.1; The Country Maid and Her Pail: 10.2; The Two Dogs: 10.7. The Partial Judge: 6.6; The Fox in the Bramble: 8.9; The Bear and the True Friends: 6.9; Questions for Henry: 4.2.

Only the sentences were examined for grade equivalent. The tables of individual words were not used in this study. This study was done using the 2003 Microsoft Word.

The Truth about Reading and the Spelling Approach

Excerpt from The Spelling Progress Bulletin: Winter 1968

by Leo G. Davis

WHOLE WORD APPROACH: Unquestionably the "w-w" (whole-word) experiment has turned out to be the most deplorable blunder in academic history. It not only produced countless youngsters who can't read, but also saddled us with a crew of teachers, *few of whom have any practical knowledge of the fundamentals of alphabetical orthography.* Expecting a 5-yr-old to develop a lasting mental picture of a whole word is basically identical to the "turky-track" approach to literacy that has been a millstone around the Oriental's neck for eons. But worse yet, under current practices the child is expected to "figure out" words to which he has never been exposed, and without any knowledge of what phonics we do have. Idiotic! With that kind of thinking (?) going into our school programs *it's a wonder that any child ever learns to read*! As a natural result of the "look-GUESS" fiasco, current researchers are looking for "guessing" aids (clues) by which children may guess strange words. **They haven't done enough research to discover that there were no guessing aids prior to the w-w debacle, because children were taught to SPELL the words before trying to read them**.

SPELLING APPROACH: Prior to the w-w fiasco there were no "reading" failures per se, because all up-coming, new words were listed as SPELLING exercises ahead of the narratives introducing them, and vocabularies of other texts were controlled to minimize the chances of children encountering strange words, until they had learned to use the dictionary, after which there was no instruction in reading (decoding). In the old-fashioned spelling class children were taught meticulous pronunciation, spelling, encoding, meaning, word recognition, self-expression (in defining words), **all in one course**. The initial "attack" on words was made in the SPELLING class, rather than in literature. Although we frequently forgot exactly how to spell a given word, we seldom failed to recognize it where it was already spelled. Thus there were **NO "reading" failures**, *just SPELLING failures, due to the idiotic inconsistencies of traditional orthography*. Current researchers seem to look upon spelling as the result of reading, rather than as the traditional approach there-to. They seem to expect children to "catch" spelling thru exposure, like they do the measles

See Ronald P. Carver's *Causes of High and Low Reading Achievement* (2000) for a modern defense of spelling as a method of improving reading achievement.

For more information on the **Spelling Book Method for Teaching Reading and Spelling,** see my *Spelling Book Resource Page* on my website: www.donpotter.net.

Made in the USA
Las Vegas, NV
30 October 2023

79977174R00092